WHY BANKS FAIL

UNRELENTING BANK RUNS,
THE CONUNDRUM OF CENTRAL BANKING &
SOUTH AFRICA'S PLACE IN THE GLOBAL ORDER

DAVID BUCKHAM

WITH ROBYN WILKINSON
& CHRISTIAAN STRAEULI

PRAISE FOR *THE END OF MONEY* AND *THE AGE OF MENACE*

"A fascinating and enjoyable read, even though it is at times shocking
to trace the roots of the collective loss of trust in banking."
– MICHAEL JORDAAN, BUSINESS LEADER & VENTURE CAPITALIST

"We are living in interesting times. Following the global financial
crisis, trust in the financial system has waned, spawning political
movements that have birthed Trump and Brexit, and delivered
shots across the bow of the established financial system in the
form of cryptocurrencies. And *The End of Money* is an
indispensable guide to this new world."
– MICHAEL AVERY, *BUSINESSTECH*

"*The End of Money* is absolutely fascinating – worth a read if you want
to contextualise the world of banking and finance over the last century."
– MAYA FISHER-FRENCH, AUTHOR OF *MAYA ON MONEY*

"A truly gripping – and at times terrifying – read... *The End of Money*
is lucid and thorough, and should be essential reading for anyone
interested in financial markets, from novice investor to professional."
– GIULIETTA TALEVI, *FINANCIAL MAIL*

"David Buckham, Robyn Wilkinson and Christiaan Straeuli brilliantly
capture history and recent developments of the modern political
economy, global financial systems and banking (particularly investment
banking) – our new Cold War."
– GIVEN MKHARI, ENTREPRENEUR

"21st-century capitalism and the democracies that enabled it are
self-destructing. This book is a sobering – and impeccably researched
– warning of what is likely to come next."
– BRUCE WHITFIELD

"A rollicking read on peak capitalism gone rogue."
– SIMON BROWN

ABOUT THE AUTHORS

David Buckham is the founder and CEO of Monocle Solutions, a global management consulting firm specialising in banking and insurance. He has diverse experience within the banking and financial markets space, having guided regulatory implementations in banks around the world for two decades. He has worked in Iceland, Denmark, Luxembourg, Australia, Singapore, Hong Kong, Malaysia, the UK and South Africa.

Robyn Wilkinson and **Christiaan Straeuli** are professional writers within the financial services industry. All three authors live in Johannesburg and hold master's degrees in English literature. Their first book, *The End of Money*, was published in 2021 and is a national bestseller. Their second book, *The Age of Menace*, was published internationally as *Unequal* in 2023.

Published in South Africa by Mercury
an imprint of Burnet Media

Burnet Media is the publisher of Mercury and Two Dogs books
www.burnetmedia.co.za
PO Box 53557, Kenilworth, 7745, South Africa

Published 2023
1 3 5 7 9 8 6 4 2

Publication © 2023 Burnet Media
Text © 2023 David Buckham,
Christiaan Straeuli, Robyn Wilkinson

Cover design: Aimee Robinson

All rights reserved. No part of this publication may be reproduced, stored in a retrieval system or transmitted, in any form or by any means, electronic, mechanical, photocopying, recording or otherwise, without the prior written permission of the copyright owners.

Distributed by Jacana Media
www.jacana.co.za

Printed and bound by Tandym Print
www.tandym.co.za

ISBN 9781990956638

Set in Adobe Garamond Pro 11.5pt

Also available as an ebook

To Pieter, Willie and Jaco,
who were there from the beginning

CONTENTS

PREFACE	**8**
INTRODUCTION	**12**
PART I	**18**
Silicon Valley Bank	**19**
The Medicis: Bankers of the Renaissance	**27**
The Frequency of Bank Failures	**35**
PART II	**44**
A Short History of Money: 1	**45**
John Law and the Banque Générale	**52**
The Fundamentals of Banking	**60**
A Short History of Money: 2	**70**
PART III	**76**
Market Conduct	**77**
Credit Suisse	**91**
The South African A2 Banking Crisis	**104**
The South African Greylisting	**118**

PART IV	**127**
Bad Actors and the Problem of Hubris	**128**
The Creation of the Federal Reserve	**136**
Cryptocurrencies and the Proliferation of Variety	**150**
Doomsday Stress-testing	**162**
PART V	**174**
The Power of the Dollar	**175**
BRICS Ambitions, De-dollarisation and South Africa's Place in the Global Order	**183**
CONCLUSION	**190**
ADDENDUM	**204**
NOTES	**211**
BIBLIOGRAPHY	**229**
ACKNOWLEDGEMENTS	**232**
INDEX	**233**

PREFACE

Monday, 13 March 2023.

As a banking crisis unfurls across the United States, a blacked-out SUV speeds from the lush suburb of Menlo Park to San Francisco International Airport. In the back seat sit 55-year-old Gregory Becker and his wife Marilyn Bautista – and they're fleeing the storm. For over a decade, Becker served as CEO of Silicon Valley Bank (SVB), now the epicentre of the financial tempest. Three days ago, on Friday the 10th, SVB collapsed dramatically, with $209 billion in assets, making it the largest bank failure in the world since the 2007/08 Global Financial Crisis, and the second-largest in US history. And now, as thousands of panicked depositors attempt to recover their funds from the failed bank, Becker and his wife are headed for more tranquil climes. In Terminal 3 of the airport, they board United Airlines flight 1749, and sit back for a First Class ride to the tropical island of Maui, Hawaii. There, in a gated community in Lahaina on the west of the

PREFACE

island, they settle into their $3.1-million beach villa, while back at SVB headquarters, more than 2,000 miles away, Becker's erstwhile deputies are left to face the intense scrutiny of depositors, investors, regulators and the public.

Four days before escaping to Hawaii, on 9 March, as the bank was in the process of collapsing, Becker urged investors and depositors to remain calm. "We have been long-term supporters of you," he said in a video call. "The last thing we need you to do is panic." Becker's appeal for calm came after a surprise announcement revealed that SVB had incurred a significant loss following the emergency sale of its most easily tradeable investments to raise liquidity levels. The announcement sparked a run on the bank, and within a day customers had withdrawn one quarter of SVB's total deposits. The share price tanked.

Nine days before SVB announced its dire financial position, triggering the share price collapse, Becker had sold more than 12,000 of his shares in the bank, equating to some $3.6 million. The bank's Chief Financial Officer, Daniel Beck, had sold $575,000 worth of shares on the same day. Less than two weeks later, on Friday 10 March, examiners from the Federal Deposit Insurance Corporation arrived at SVB's offices in Santa Clara, California, and a few hours after their inspection of the financials, it was announced that the bank would be taken into receivership. Just three days later, Becker, with $3.6 million of additional cash in his account, was enjoying the balmy Hawaiian weather in his shorts and flip-flops. In the meantime, most of SVB's customers' deposits were frozen. Many of the bank's clients were large payroll-related companies, such as Accounting Connections, HR management specialist Rippling, and Patriot Software, and with their funds trapped inside the collapsing bank, thousands of ordinary people found their salaries going unpaid. Patriot Software, for example, had over $100 million in customer payroll funds sitting in its SVB account when the bank was taken into curatorship; its customers, now unable to pay their employees, included thousands of small retail businesses, from boutique fashion stores to family-run bed-and-breakfasts.

It seems unthinkable that, in 2023, such a significant and hugely disruptive banking failure could transpire in an economy as large and sophisticated as California's – the fifth-largest economy in the world, if it were its own country. That such a pronounced failure of leadership and risk management could occur following the Global Financial Crisis similarly defies belief, especially given the thousands of pages of intrusive regulation imposed on the business of banking, and the enormous levels of government, fiscal and monetary support provided in the years since.

And yet it did.

In the space of just seven weeks, between 10 March and 1 May, three banks failed in the United States, and Credit Suisse, one of the world's megabanks, folded in Europe in a sudden-death event. How, after all that was learnt from the Crisis a decade and a half earlier, could banking still be so prone to failure? And in a world that has become increasingly ideologically divided – fractured by a previously unthinkable conflict in Europe, relentless and increasing trade wars, and the rise of populist autocratic leaders – what implications does this have for our future economic security?

We live in a time characterised by a growing disregard for democracy, an unimagined rise in human rights violations and a perpetual barrage of bureaucratic mistruths. It is at such a time that citizens within liberal democracies can lose trust in their institutions

PREFACE

and in money itself; that the siren calls of cryptocurrency find their acolytes, totalitarian regimes sidestep G7 sanctions with relative ease, and a greater proportion of the world's population fall within countries that are turning away from the world's reserve currency, the US dollar. If the global foundation of economic exchange is continually prone to self-harm, then the Orwellian possibilities of a truly divided world – what is now known as multipolarity – become ever more real.

In a world increasingly at odds with itself, the question is: why does banking as an industry repeatedly find itself at the edge of a precipice, and what can be done about it?

INTRODUCTION

INTRODUCTION

When I graduated from university in the 1990s, investment banking was the most desirable and exciting career choice on offer. Many of my friends had entered that field, and it seemed particularly alluring, current and of the moment. It had a certain gravitas in a world that felt borderless, free and filled with potential; the Berlin Wall had come down, communism had failed, and South Africa had finally unshackled itself from apartheid to be embraced by the international community. This was a time of optimism, and we were young and educated. But having studied neither business administration nor accounting, I struggled to find a job. It was ultimately through a variety of software enterprise sales jobs that I found a path to working in banking and, having majored in mathematics, I was eventually able to secure work as an equity trader at a small investment bank in Cape Town.

Within a year of my entry into my chosen career, the optimism with which I viewed the industry was soured somewhat by the failure of Saambou, one of the largest banks in South Africa. The collapse of the 60-year-old bank, in 2002, triggered the subsequent failure of others, including the bank where I was working, PSG Investment Bank. In what came to be known as the A2 Banking Crisis, 22 South African banks ultimately failed, including other prominent names such as FirstCorp Merchant Bank and Board of Executors.

At the time, it struck me as particularly unusual that such a large proportion of our banks had collapsed so suddenly. To my mind, this could not have been a purely random event. I was happy to move on, however, as I wanted to relocate to Johannesburg to start a business consulting to banks on the issue of risk management, an element of the industry I found fascinating. It was at that point that I started Monocle Solutions. Six years later, we had worked hard to build client relationships, but rather than breaking into the South African market, we had found it easier at that stage to work with banks in foreign lands – in Iceland, Denmark, Singapore, Malaysia, Hong Kong, Luxembourg and the UK. By the time the 2007/08 Global Financial Crisis hit, approximately three-quarters of all our business came from banks incorporated outside of South Africa.

The Crisis was, of course, unprecedented, and for Monocle the irony that most of our clientele was global at the time was compounded by the relative ease with which South African banks survived the upheaval. Our first client to default was a Hong Kong bank that held a raft of Lehman "Minibonds", an instrument devised by Lehman Brothers to circumvent regulations that restricted investment banks from being funded by individual depositors. Lehman had sold a significant number of these Minibonds through local banks to pensioners in Hong Kong and, as a result of the bank being forced to absorb these losses, it was unable to pay us, as well as many other service providers. Then another major client – a century-old Danish bank – failed in a sudden-death moment, when it was hit by rumours of substantial losses in its mortgage-backed security portfolio and was unable to replenish a three-month money market repo agreement. Next, I received a call from a client in Iceland, one of the country's three largest privatised banks: it had also collapsed through a sudden liquidity shortfall, along with its peer banks in a failure of faith in the Icelandic banking system and in the Icelandic króna. The entire Icelandic banking system had failed, virtually overnight. Shortly thereafter, another doomed client, a specialist UK bank, failed almost instantaneously when word got out that its leveraged finance portfolio, consisting mainly of high street London retail businesses, had incurred significant losses.

INTRODUCTION

Within months, four major clients of ours, dispersed around the world, had defaulted or failed. Having experienced the A2 Banking Crisis as a young equities trader, and then having been at the coalface during the Global Financial Crisis, it was becoming clear to me that banking as a commercial practice must be inherently and significantly riskier than is generally perceived.

In 2010, I decided to undertake a research project with several master's students and Monocle employees to calculate the number of bank failures that had resulted from the Crisis. Our starting point was *The Banker* magazine's authoritative list of the "Top 1,000 World Banks" for 2007, prior to the Crisis. What had happened to those banks on the list in the three years that followed? By reviewing their financial statements, we could work out the number of banks that technically failed within that sample set. Since banks are often not allowed to fail outright, but are rather bailed out by their respective central banks, and thus effectively by their country's taxpayers, an important step in the analysis was to use a broad definition of failure; one that went beyond insolvency, and included limitless central bank support in the form of free liquidity and significant government equity bailouts. According to our research, of those top 1,000 banks, 106 had failed or were bailed out over the three-year period from 2007 onwards – a staggering 10.6% of the largest banks in the world. Once again, this fact bore witness to the undeniable risk that seemed to be deeply ingrained into the DNA of the international banking system.

In the wake of the Crisis, it was argued that with stricter regulation in banking, failures would be prevented in the future. But, since then, there have been numerous and continuous collapses of banks across the globe. In South Africa, these include the failure of African Bank and VBS, and the deregistration of Mercantile Bank. In America, the high-profile collapses of Silicon Valley Bank, First Republic and Signature Bank in 2023 were preceded by multiple bank failures across the country in the decade before. In Europe, the alarm bells sounded particularly loudly with the 2023 collapse of Credit Suisse, a 167-year-old "systemically important financial institution", ostensibly considered too big to fail. The increasing vulnerability of other systemically important European banks is deeply troubling.

Laws such as the Dodd-Frank Wall Street Reform and Consumer Protection Act (2010) in the US, as well as the entire raft of Basel regulations, have not prevented the tide of global bank failures. In fact, it has only been the unbounded and continuous bailouts and interventions by regulators – not the regulations themselves – that have prevented a domino effect of failures across the entire banking system. And it is precisely these interventions that have served to steadily undermine the idea of banking as a free-market enterprise. As this book will argue, many of the regulations that have been put in place to make banking safer have inadvertently made it more dangerous. In addition, with the introduction of market conduct regulations since the 9/11 terrorist attacks on the US, banks have been co-opted into becoming extensions of the state in the international fight against terrorism and crime, which further compromises their position as free-market agents while simultaneously making them more vital than ever to society.

In essence, a country's banking system is the brain that is meant to direct capital and liquidity as efficiently as possible to the body economic, ideally to continually improve the fundamental socioeconomic conditions of society. This has always been the underlying reason for my fascination with banking. But at its

INTRODUCTION

heart lies a paradox. Although banking has attempted to maintain the illusion of stability and staid austerity, it is by its very nature inherently risky. If there is any value in the notion of the free market, and if there is any validity to the concept of capitalism, then banking must be recognised as an innately risk-prone organ that will regularly fail, often idiosyncratically but sometimes systemically.

While there are always third-party causes and externalities that influence these events, the fundamental reason why banks fail is because their business model requires them to replenish liquidity frequently, if not daily – and this is very difficult to do, especially when trust in social institutions is lost. Over the past thirty years, there has been a steady erosion of trust in the institutions that uphold liberal democracies. This book aims to shed light on how this trust has been eroded, and offer suggestions on what can be done to ensure the future stability of the international banking system, and South Africa's place in it.

PART I

"The fundamental problem with banks is what it's always
been: they're in the business of banking, and banking,
whether plain vanilla or incredibly sophisticated,
is inherently risky."
– James Surowiecki, American journalist

SILICON VALLEY BANK

Prior to the dramatic failure of Silicon Valley Bank and his undignified exit, Gregory Becker had been involved with the bank for thirty years, standing at its helm for more than a decade. Becker took the reins in 2011 as CEO of SVB Financial Group (SVBFG), the umbrella company that housed the venture capital division, SVB Capital; the investment bank, SVB Securities; and the commercial bank, SVB. Before its collapse, the SVB group had traded on the tech-dominated Nasdaq stock exchange and appeared on the S&P 500 as one of the 500 largest publicly listed companies in the US from March 2018 onwards.

Originally incorporated in 1983 as Silicon Valley Bancshares, SVB was conceptualised over a poker game attended by former Wells Fargo executive Bill Biggerstaff and Stanford University professor Robert Medearis. Based in the technology capital of the US, if not the world, it would be a bank that focused on lending to early-stage tech start-ups – an idea that quickly gained traction. In the years that followed, SVBFG established itself as a financial partner for the ambitious tech start-ups and high-growth companies that inhabited Silicon Valley, branding itself as a bank that understood the unique needs of the burgeoning technology sector. Tapping into, embracing and amplifying the entrepreneurial spirit that defined the region, it went public in 1988.

Having survived the fallout of the dotcom bubble that burst in 2000, SVBFG rebounded quickly and began to expand its reach beyond Silicon Valley. SVB grew its balance sheet from under $5 billion in the early 2000s to $57 billion by 2018. The group pursued an aggressive growth strategy, funding high-risk ventures in volatile sectors, often without extensive due diligence. As a result of this rapid expansion, SVBFG would number 164 entities as subsidiaries by December 2022. These included dozens of strategic investment funds across the globe, most of which were incorporated in tax-friendly jurisdictions such as Delaware and the Cayman Islands, as well as other entities in the United Kingdom, Canada, Israel, India and China.

Most notably from 2018, SVB's asset base grew at an accelerating pace. As had been the case two decades before, tech optimism was rampant during the late 2010s, with investors eager to invest in any start-up they believed might be the next tech unicorn – a privately owned, high-growth company that reaches a billion-dollar valuation. This exuberance was fuelled by extremely loose monetary policy, with the Federal Reserve holding interest rates near zero for the years immediately following the Global Financial Crisis, and pumping trillions of dollars of liquidity into the market through several rounds of quantitative easing, both before and during the Covid-19 pandemic. This period of loose monetary policy and tech optimism also coincided with a rollback of banking regulations under the Trump administration that would directly affect SVB's fortunes.

Following the carnage of the Financial Crisis, the Obama presidency signed into law in 2010 the Dodd-Frank Wall Street Reform and Consumer Protection Act, a complex and broad-ranging set of regulations, commonly known as Dodd-Frank. Alongside many other regulations affecting the financial system, Dodd-Frank required all US banks with balance sheets larger than $50 billion to undergo an annual stress test by the Federal Reserve. In addition, it required these banks to hold greater amounts of capital of higher quality to absorb trading and loan losses in adverse conditions, maintain high levels of liquidity to meet short-term obligations in the event of an economic downturn, and draft a "living will" to plan for a quick and orderly dissolution in the case of bank failure.

In the years to follow, the argument arose that these new regulations were needlessly stifling the ability of banks to grow, and so should be rolled back. As CEO of SVBFG, Gregory Becker was one of those who actively lobbied for this in Congress, arguing that the regulations were "unnecessarily" burdening SVB. Despite warnings from various quarters, the Economic Growth, Regulatory Relief, and Consumer Protection Act was passed on 24 May 2018: henceforth, the threshold for mandatory stress-testing on an annual basis would apply only to banks with assets exceeding $250 billion. Before the passing of the Act, the nonpartisan Congressional Budget Office noted that the rollback would "increase the likelihood that a large financial firm with assets of between $100 billion and $250 billion would fail".

Meanwhile, SVB's balance sheet exploded in size. Directly benefiting from the unprecedented money supply and stimulus cheques unleashed in response to the Covid-19 pandemic, by the

Federal Reserve and the US government respectively, SVB tripled its deposits from $70 billion to more than $200 billion in the two years from 2020 to 2022. This tidal wave of money created an environment in which investors became frenzied, pushing stock markets to all-time highs on an almost weekly basis. Specifically, it exacerbated the already frothy atmosphere enveloping West Coast tech firms, driving the market capitalisations and price-to-earnings ratios of companies such as Apple, Amazon, Microsoft and Tesla to previously unthinkable levels. At SVB, the deposits poured in. On the face of it, this was a boon, and by 2023 SVB had become the sixteenth-largest bank in the US – but it now found itself in a dilemma. Having received so much money so quickly in the form of deposits, it found that it was unable to create loans and advances nearly fast enough to match its influx of liabilities.

To earn some modicum of return on these deposits, SVB invested heavily in long-term Treasury bonds at a time when interest rates across the yield curve were being held at all-time lows. Between 2020 and 2022, the bank grew its bond portfolio almost five-fold, from $27 billion to $127 billion. Although US government bonds are traditionally considered one of the safest asset classes, this would ironically prove to be a costly mistake when the Federal Reserve was eventually forced to pivot from the extremely loose monetary policy it had pursued since the Financial Crisis. In March 2022, the Fed began a series of aggressive rate hikes to combat the wave of inflation that had started to overwhelm the US. Prior to 2022, the Fed had maintained a position that initial signs of inflation were "transitory" in nature, and by now the blame had been shifted to an energy price surge following the Russian invasion of Ukraine – but the underlying cause was a fifteen-year-long oversupply of money. Now, as a result of

SILICON VALLEY BANK

these dramatic interest rate increases, government bonds, the value of which are inversely related to interest rates, lost significant value over a short period. This in turn directly affected the value of SVB's bond portfolio, which held a greater proportion of assets in government bonds than virtually any other bank in the US.

On Wednesday 8 March 2023, the bank announced that it had sold $21 billion of its most liquid investments, including government bonds, to raise its liquidity levels. Following the emergency sale, the bank suffered a $1.8 billion loss due to a deterioration of its assets, specifically its long-term US Treasuries. To offset the loss, SVB declared that it would need to raise $2 billion of capital to shore up its balance sheet, a surprise announcement that ignited the panic to follow. Because of SVB's concentrated depositor base, largely comprised of tech companies and venture capital firms, the average size of each customer's deposits was larger than those of a typical commercial bank. In fact, almost 90% of SVB's depositors held more than $250,000 with the bank, the threshold up to which the Federal Deposit Insurance Corporation (FDIC) insures deposits. In an age of social media contagion and instantaneous electronic withdrawals, it was the perfect environment for a bank run. The day after the investment sales announcement – 9 March, the same day that Gregory Becker urged investors and depositors to remain calm – SVB's share price plummeted, dropping by 60% in a single day, from $267 to $106. By this time, depositors – including, as an example, Peter Thiel's influential Founders Fund venture capital firm – were already frantically withdrawing their funds from the bank.

As each customer withdrew their deposits, the already frenzied and fearful atmosphere surrounding SVB was amplified. Between the time of the announcement on 8 March and the end of the next day, the 9th, depositors had withdrawn $42 billion, equivalent to over 20% of the bank's total deposits, with more withdrawals expected to follow. The next morning, in an attempt to protect depositors and to minimise a systemic fallout from the imminent collapse of the bank, the FDIC announced that the bank had inadequate liquidity to continue operating, and that it would be taken into receivership.

In the interim, despite the efforts of the FDIC, the failure of SVB set off a wave of fear that swept across the US, affecting mid-sized banks throughout the nation. Two days after SVB's collapse, on 12 March – a Sunday – New York-based Signature Bank was shuttered by state banking officials following a run on the bank. And fifty days after that, California-based First Republic Bank was effectively closed and sold to JPMorgan Chase & Co. Over the course of a month and a half, the failure of these three banks – SVB, Signature Bank and First Republic Bank – marked the most severe US banking crisis since the Global Financial Crisis. The combined assets of the three banks equated to $532 billion – a sum that is significantly larger than the $309 billion worth of total assets held by Washington Mutual when it collapsed in September 2008, and which remains the largest-ever commercial bank failure in the US to date.

It is tempting to blame Gregory Becker for the collapse of SVB. Certainly, there was a failure of leadership in the upper echelons of the bank, and the optics of his departure, two weeks after selling $3.6 million worth of his shares, raise moral questions. In the aftermath, government agencies were highly critical of the bank's risk management practices. "Silicon Valley Bank (SVB) failed because of a textbook case of mismanagement by the bank," noted a report by the Federal Reserve Board of Governors on 28 April 2023. "Its senior leadership failed to manage basic interest rate and liquidity risk."

Although true to an extent, such a statement greatly oversimplifies the reasons that the banking system in March 2023 seemed as vulnerable to failure as it was in 2008. In fact, the fundamental drivers were excess liquidity and misguided regulations. The Federal Reserve's policy of ongoing quantitative easing, combined with the US government's Covid-19 stimulus spending, led to an oversupply of deposits from SVB customers – so much so that the bank literally did not know what to do with the money it was receiving. It could not match the incoming deposits with outgoing loans, so it over-invested in government bonds in an attempt to earn some scintilla of return within the confines of an apparently safe asset class – but it did so in an environment within which a number of economists predicted a rapid rise in interest rates, and therefore associated bond market losses. With no effective stress-testing since the relaxation of asset limits in 2018, SVB was left to pursue this catastrophic path without adequate external oversight.

The failure of SVB is steeped in irony. In 2008 and its aftermath, banks failed because they held high-risk assets with extremely high levels of leverage; fifteen years later, banks were failing because they held low-risk assets with extremely low levels of leverage. It can thus be said that, while the Global Financial Crisis occurred because of too much credit and not enough money, the US banking crisis of 2023 occurred because of too little credit and too much money.

As a recurring theme throughout history, regulatory authorities and financial commentators have, instead of addressing the fundamental causes, found it more convenient to blame bad actors for the implosion of financial institutions and the continued fragility of the financial system. In the decade and a half between the Global Financial Crisis and the collapse of SVB, extraordinarily loose monetary policy and uncoordinated regulations have undermined efforts to put right a global financial system that came to a grinding halt in 2008. Rather than formulating a coherent set of policies and regulations to strengthen and stabilise the financial system, the Fed and other banking regulators have scored numerous own goals that have continued to erode the public's trust in banking and have greatly undermined the idea that banks should operate as free-market entities. Under such conditions, the collapse of banks like Silicon Valley Bank, Signature Bank and First Republic Bank was sadly predictable – and there will be more to come in future.

THE MEDICIS:
BANKERS OF THE RENAISSANCE

In 1975, Paolo dal Poggetto, the museum director at Florence's Cappelle Medicee, was searching for possible alternative exit routes that could be used by the droves of visitors who arrived daily to marvel at the carefully preserved architecture and art of the Basilica di San Lorenzo church complex. The Cappelle Medicee, or Medici Chapels, are housed within the complex. As he surveyed the buildings, Poggetto noticed in one of the rooms what looked to be the handle of a trapdoor hidden beneath an old wardrobe. Moving the wardrobe aside to investigate, he opened the door and descended steep steps, expecting to find a small storage space below. As his eyes adjusted to the dim light of the room, just visible beneath the thick layer of dust covering the walls was a series of drawings that were immediately familiar to him. Sketched in chalk and charcoal were images that closely resembled the frescoes of the Sistine Chapel and the outlines of some of the most famous Renaissance sculptures in the world – the works of Michelangelo.

27

Poggetto's discovery ignited a wave of excitement among art scholars, who confirmed that the drawings were undoubtedly the work of the Grandmaster himself. Michelangelo had been a close friend of the Medicis, a powerful banking family who had maintained significant authority in Florence by virtue of their wealth, and who were known for their patronage of the arts, having commissioned some of the most famous works of Filippo Brunelleschi, Donatello, Fra Angelico, Luca della Robbia and Botticelli.

In 1520, the Medicis appointed Michelangelo to design the Medici Chapels as a family mausoleum, but their friendship was brought to an abrupt end seven years later, when the family was forced out of Florence and into exile by a popular uprising. This revolt followed several attempted uprisings in the century before, brought on by fears that the Medicis had amassed too much power over the most important trade and cultural hub of Europe. With Florence having rejected a monarchy and been established as a republic in the year 1115, there were also fears that the Medicis were subverting the democratic aspirations of the city through their plutocratic rule. Although he had been close to the family, and benefited significantly from their patronage, Michelangelo supported the 1527 revolt, but it too would prove unsuccessful in the end. When the Medicis returned to Florence three years later, the artist went into hiding, fearing retribution. Three months after their restoration to power, the Medicis issued a formal pardon, enabling Michelangelo to return to complete the building of the Cappelle Medicee. For centuries, historians could only speculate about where he had hidden during those three months. Poggetto's discovery suggested that he had remained right under the Medicis' noses, in the small room below the very chapels he had designed.

THE MEDICIS: BANKERS OF THE RENAISSANCE

Wool merchants from northern Tuscany, the Medicis first established themselves in Florence during the 12th century in the early years of the republic. They soon became known as the owners of one of the largest and most profitable trading companies in the city, financing factories to produce silk and wool cloth for export, and eventually using their excess profits to enter the money-lending business. In 1397 they opened their own bank in the city. Under the leadership of Giovanni di Bicci de' Medici, the bank grew rapidly, and under his son Cosimo it became the largest in Florence. Cosimo also extended the Medici empire by opening bank branches across Italy, as well as in Geneva, Bruges and London.

By this time, the merging of trading and financial activities was becoming commonplace, as large trading companies – particularly in the Italian city-states – began to offer banking services to other merchants. This gave rise to the term "merchant banks", which were institutions that found ready employ in co-ordinating financial transactions between different geographical regions. Up until then, foreign trade had been somewhat restricted by the coinage that formed the primary means of payment for goods. Merchants trading in foreign cities faced a logistical problem in executing trades, having to transport large quantities of gold and silver coins across significant distances, usually by horse and cart, and then having to pay fees to moneylenders to exchange their coins into the currency of the destination city – altogether an impractical, unsafe and costly exercise. The emergence of large trading companies with branches and agents in widely dispersed commercial centres provided an innovative solution.

Using their branch structure, these companies were able to offer remittance services to merchants that ultimately negated the need for coinage. A Florentine merchant travelling to London, for example,

29

could deposit funds in his local currency (in gold florins or silver grosso and pennies) at a merchant bank in his home city, and then withdraw those funds at the London branch in the currency required to purchase goods there (in silver coins denominated in pounds, shillings and pennies). This process was facilitated using a bill of exchange. A precursor to paper money, this was a letter issued by a bank branch to a depositor on receipt of his funds which, in simplified terms, instructed a second bank branch to issue funds to the depositor, or to an agent appointed by the depositor, upon presentation of the document. To confirm the transaction, a similar document would be sent separately, using the bank's courier network, from the first branch to the second. The merchant could thus travel with a single document, rather than a cart full of coins, to conduct his business.

To ensure the bank made a profit on these transactions, a charge was usually built into the bill of exchange, either as administration fees or a commission, or otherwise incorporated into the particulars of the exchange rates involved. This was central to the functioning of merchant banks, enabling them to circumvent the papal ban on usury, which stemmed from the Christian belief that it was a sin to charge interest on a monetary loan. Noting that an exchange transaction was not technically the same as a loan, merchant bankers argued that their business was related to the commutation of monies or the buying and selling of foreign currency, and not to the extension of credit. If they were not issuing loans, they rationalised, then they were not charging interest and therefore not committing usury.

Over time, bills of exchange came to be used beyond just trading activities. Most notably – and somewhat ironically – the Catholic Church employed them to remit funds collected through taxes to the papal court. They were also used by governments that needed to

THE MEDICIS: BANKERS OF THE RENAISSANCE

pay their armies and allies, and crusaders, pilgrims and scholars who needed to access funds while travelling. Their popularity increased in no small part owing to the fact that merchant bankers had played a pivotal role in building credibility in the early banking system, having gone to great lengths to ensure their activities could not be mistaken for usury. Moneylenders and pawnbrokers, who were regarded as usurers, were ostracised by respectable society and spurned by the Church, which refused them the sacraments or a Christian burial. Shakespeare famously captured the combination of trading and financial activities that were commonplace at this time, and the negative societal perception of moneylenders, in *The Merchant of Venice*, first performed in London at the turn of the 17th century. Later, on its publication in 1866, the great Dostoevsky novel *Crime and Punishment* demonstrated the longevity of this perception, when the protagonist, Raskolnikov, justifies the murder of a moneylender as a utilitarian act that will ultimately benefit society by eliminating someone who he believes has profited off the misery of others. In sharp contrast, banking families of the 15th century, such as the Medicis, were at that time well-respected and trusted both by the Catholic Church and by the communities they served. That institutionalised trust would, however, be tested in time.

Although only one of the many banking houses that formed part of Europe's early banking system, the Medici bank was the most successful of its time. It is also credited with popularising early forms of financial innovations such as the holding company, fractional reserve banking, and the extensive use of double-entry accounting. It was upon these innovations that the medieval financial system began to grow more sophisticated, and as rules pertaining to usury were relaxed, merchant banks also began to extend their loan and deposit-taking activities, becoming the early forerunners to modern commercial banks. In the grander scope of history, however, the Medici bank played only a relatively short-lived role.

Following Cosimo's death in 1464, and the transition of authority over the Medici bank to his son Piero, the bank entered a period of decline. Internal weaknesses were amplified under the weight of challenging trading conditions as a result of the Byzantine-Ottoman War of 1453, which had ended in the Turks' capture of Constantinople, a major commercial centre for Genoan and Venetian merchants. Loans to sovereigns to fund the war, a contraction in international trade due to the conflict, and the long-lasting effects of the Black Death on Europe's population produced an economic depression in the second half of the 15th century that exerted a significant effect on the Florentine banking system.

To manage the effects of a deteriorating economic environment, Piero retrenched workers, closed some of the Medici bank branches, and ordered his branch managers to call in loans – though fearing social discontent and political upheaval, many failed to do so. These measures only temporarily staved off disaster. In 1478, the decline of the House of Medici began to accelerate, following a failed assassination attempt on Piero's sons by the Pazzi, a rival banking family believed to have been supported by Pope Sixtus IV. Although the younger of the two was killed, the elder son, Lorenzo, survived and in exacting his revenge, many of the Pazzi and their supporters were killed, and the remainder expelled from Florence. Inflamed by this response, the pope ordered that Lorenzo, his supporters and all members of the current and preceding Medici administration be excommunicated from Florence, placing the city under interdict, and forbidding the clergy from performing all holy services and rites to the subjects of Florence until the Medici left.

Supporting the pope, leaders from other regions of Italy began to make incursions on the city, but Lorenzo fought back, and ultimately succeeded in negotiating the end of the war. Having defended the city's independence, Lorenzo won the support and favour of the Florentine people, though the Medici business had suffered greatly by this point. Needing to raise funds to pay for mercenaries to protect Florence, which had no army, Lorenzo had borrowed heavily from his family's wealth and embezzled public funds to float the bank, while also raising taxes for the Florentines. The result was a significant credit crunch that ultimately led to the collapse of the bank. In 1494, the bank failed, and the Medicis were expelled from Florence, with all their property, business investments and real estate sequestrated and put into receivership. Although they returned in 1512 and remained a core feature of Florence's political and cultural landscape, continuing to fund the works of artists such as Michelangelo for a further two centuries, the Medicis were never able to reinstate the bank.

The Medici bank was one of many that was defunct by the end of the 15th century. In 1399, there were more than seventy banking houses in Florence operating internationally, but by 1460 this figure had more than halved, and by 1516 there were only eight banks left. A similar trend was evident in other major financial centres, such as Bruges and Venice. The history of banking at that time is, as such, one that demonstrates the inherent and unavoidable risks that have resided within the business of banking from its earliest beginnings.

The downfall of the Medici bank, in particular, is also a pertinent example of the inevitability of failure once public trust is lost.

Today, many of the causes that saw the precipitous decline in banking over the course of a century in medieval Florence are echoed in the banking crises of the 21st century, including the 2007/08 Global Financial Crisis and the banking crisis of 2023: the overextension of credit, adverse trading conditions and widespread political instability, not to mention challenging economic conditions precipitated by a pandemic and a major European war. As the Medici bank and many others failed before, the likes of Silicon Valley Bank and Credit Suisse still fail today. In fact, it is not too much of a stretch to imagine a similar consolidation in the contemporary US banking system – a system that is currently made up of more than 4,500 individual banks – as occurred in Florence half a millennium ago.

THE FREQUENCY OF BANK FAILURES

For almost as long as banks have existed, there have been bank failures. In medieval times, the demise of a bank was most commonly brought about by the overextension of credit to sovereigns for the funding of wars. Early examples include the collapse of the Florentine banks owned by the Bardi, Peruzzi and Acciaioli families after they had loaned vast amounts to King Edward III of England in the mid-14th century, to pay for his involvement in the Hundred Years' War. In these instances, the banks faced an impossible situation: failure to provide the credit would have led to the revoking of their royal licences to export wool, the most valuable commodity to the economies of the Italian city-states at the time. Mired in a war that showed no signs of ending, Edward repudiated his debts in 1343, defaulting on the thousands of gold and silver florins owed to the foreign bankers. With no recourse available to extract what was owed by a monarchy, some of the wealthiest families in medieval Europe were ruined, and an economic depression was triggered. A new generation of Florentine bankers, including the Medicis, soon replaced them, though loans to sovereigns would continue to be a risk for these institutions.

In the following centuries, bank runs came to be the most common reason for a bank's collapse. This was the case with Sweden's Stockholms Banco in 1656 and France's Banque Royale in 1720, with these crises of public confidence related to failed attempts to introduce paper money into the European financial system. In the 18th century, the problem of contagion – the domino effect of multiple bank failures, after a single bank experiences a bank run – became increasingly evident. During the commercial paper crisis of 1763, which began in Amsterdam before spreading to Germany and Scandinavia, more than a hundred banks are estimated to have failed, while during the British credit crisis of 1772-1773, bank failures in London triggered a domino effect that was felt in Amsterdam, Hamburg, St Petersburg, Genoa, Stockholm and Paris. Across the Atlantic, the New York Panic of 1792 marked the first stock market crash in America, soon followed by the Panic of 1796, which spread across the US and into interconnected UK markets.

During the 19th century there was a marked increase in bank failures, as the financial industry grew larger and more complex, in tandem with the rapid economic expansion that accompanied the Industrial Revolution in the developed world. Between 1810 and 1890, the UK experienced at least seven national-level banking crises, each characterised by significant reductions in capital arising from panics, and bank runs on several institutions in multiple locations. Although stability was restored relatively quickly in these cases, thanks to the Bank of England's role as the lender of last resort, each of these events had a negative effect on economic growth in the year immediately following it.

THE FREQUENCY OF BANK FAILURES

Perhaps the most notable individual bank failure of this time was that of Overend, Gurney and Company, a London-based bill broker and discount house, which was brought to the brink of collapse in 1866 due to a combination of risky investments and market disruptions that triggered mass defaults by its clients. The bank was then unable to secure short-term funding from the Bank of England, which refused to rescue it amid fears that its role as the lender of last resort was encouraging moral hazard; that is to say, injudicious risk-taking by agents or institutions who believe they are protected from potential negative consequences. This triggered a panic that ultimately resulted in the bank's failure and the collapse of roughly 200 other banks and companies associated with it. More than 140 years later, history would repeat itself during the 2007/08 Global Financial Crisis, when Lehman Brothers was similarly left to fail. The impact on highly interconnected global financial markets was so severe this time, however, that to allow further failures as an act of moral punishment would have made the already significant economic disruption far worse.

Bank failures were also common in the US during the Gilded Age, with rapid industrialisation driving significant economic development and, with it, increased financial speculation. Between 1863 and 1901, six banking panics occurred in the financial capital of New York, while regional panics took hold in the states of Illinois, Minnesota and Wisconsin in 1896, in Pennsylvania and Maryland in 1903, and in Chicago in 1905. The most significant panics of the era occurred in 1873 and 1893, affecting banks countrywide. The former stemmed from an overinvestment in the railway system, which grew so rapidly that new projects soon outstripped demand for carriage capacity, with large railway companies subsequently defaulting on their loan payments. The latter was the result of a substantial decrease in the US Treasury's gold reserves, which almost halved from $190 million in 1890 to $100 million three years later. With the US on the gold standard at the time, the fall in reserves ignited a fear that the Treasury could suspend the convertibility of banknotes to gold, prompting runs on banks throughout the country. During the panic, nearly 600 banks either temporarily suspended operations or failed outright, and the economy was pushed into a recession that lasted until mid-1897. In this period of American history, the Panic of 1893 is superseded in terms of severity only by the Panic of 1907. Incited by frenzied runs on banks and trust companies, this crisis was so disruptive that it became the trigger event for the creation of the Federal Reserve, prompting a country that had long resisted the centralisation of bank powers to concede that it could not continue to operate without the stabilisation of a central bank system.

The US experienced its most severe financial crisis during the harsh years of the Great Depression, when more banks failed than at any other time in its history. Even prior to this, the country experienced an average of more than 600 bank failures a year from 1921 to 1929, though these were generally small regional banks, and the damage largely contained. This already high rate of failure greatly accelerated between 1930 and 1933, when more than 9,000 banks of varying sizes closed across the country – roughly a third of all US banks in operation. During this period, depositors collectively lost more than $1.3 billion, equivalent to more than $27 billion in 2023. This collapse followed a decade of euphoric spending by the government and consumers alike during the Roaring Twenties, a period characterised by large-scale industrialisation, excessive lending and wild speculation driven by a seemingly unstoppable

THE FREQUENCY OF BANK FAILURES

stock market bull run, not unlike the heady markets and rife crypto speculation of the Covid-19 pandemic years just past. Owing to the highly integrated nature of the banking system at the time, the failure of Bank of Tennessee in 1930 caused a chain reaction of failures across the country, with customers of unrelated banks panicking and initiating unfounded runs on their local banks. Poor monetary policy decisions and a delayed reaction by the Fed prevented it from effectively calming the panic. The result was the country's longest, deepest and most widespread economic recession, the effects of which radiated around the world. Between 1934 and 1940, an average of fifty banks a year continued to fail in the US.

Then came a period of unusual financial stability. Between 1940 and 1970, there were close to zero bank failures in the US, as the once-volatile industry become one of solid and even staid dependability. It was a time in which the average banker's ambitions were modest and sustainable, as exemplified in the 3-6-3 rule: bankers paid 3% on deposits, earned 6% on loans, and were on the golf course by 3pm. It was an approach that engendered trust in the banking industry, and there is no little irony that this reputation appears to have lasted so long after the era ended.

The US entered another period of significant economic instability in the 1970s, brought on by the combined effects of the failure of the Bretton Woods System and the US's departure from the gold standard, in what is now called the Nixon Shock. From 1971, there was a dramatic increase in annual bank failures. This volatility was further compounded by the sudden increase in the price of oil imported to the West from the Middle East, which almost quadrupled between 1973 and 1974 during the OPEC oil crisis. Cumulatively, these events created the perfect environment for a stock market crash between 1973 and 1974, the effects of which were felt across the world. In the UK, in particular, they placed additional pressure on an already strained banking system. As a result of a significant decrease in housing prices, together with a steady rise in interest rates, smaller lenders found themselves on the verge of bankruptcy. The Bank of England subsequently bailed out some thirty banks, and intervened to assist thirty more.

In the US, this period of instability continued into the next decade, which saw the mass failure of Savings and Loan institutions, also known as "thrifts". Since the 19th century, these institutions had been instrumental in expanding the market in residential mortgages, and by 1980 they held roughly half of all outstanding home mortgages. Unlike commercial banks, however, the thrifts faced minimal regulations, and were therefore subject to widespread administrative abuse and did not adequately manage interest rate risk. When interest rates began to climb, they had to replace deposits with increasingly expensive fresh deposits while stuck with fixed-rate long-term loans on the asset side of their balance sheets. As a result, they began to fail on a massive scale. Between 1980 and 1995, more than 2,900 banks and thrifts, with collective assets of more than $2.2 trillion, collapsed across the US.

During the 20th century, bank failures were a truly international phenomenon. The Shōwa Financial Crisis of 1927 resulted in the failure of 265 banks across the Empire of Japan, brought on by the combined effects of an economic slowdown and the great Kantō earthquake of 1923. Towards the end of the century, Japan also endured a nationwide banking crisis, following a period in the 1980s that was marked by expansionary fiscal and monetary policies and rapidly rising asset prices, supported by the extension of bank credit on an unprecedented scale. Economic growth began to slow at the start of the 1990s, when the stock market and real estate bubbles burst, beginning Japan's "Lost Decade". Struggling under the weight of a high proportion of non-performing loans, some of the country's largest financial institutions collapsed in 1997, triggering runs on banks throughout the country. This situation was exacerbated by the ripples of the 1997 Asian financial crisis, which began with the collapse of the Thai baht and spread across most of East and Southeast Asia.

The 1990s were an economically tumultuous time for many countries, characterised by a radical increase in the sophistication of financial instruments and investment opportunities, combined with a lack of regulatory oversight in the banking industry. Perhaps the most infamous global example occurred in 1995, when "rogue trader" Nick Leeson single-handedly brought about the collapse of London-based Barings Bank, the second-oldest bank in existence, from its office in Singapore. Spain's biggest bank, Banco Español de Crédito, collapsed in 1994, the result of widespread fraud by members of its board, while Malaysia's prominent MBf Finance Berhad experienced several runs between 1997 and 1999. Malaysia's central bank ultimately took control of the bank. In the US, ever more complex and opaque derivative trading also led to the collapse or near-collapse of several investment firms and hedge funds, including Bankers Trust and Long-Term Capital Management. Additional nationwide banking crises occurred in Norway, Finland and Sweden, in Peru, Venezuela, Ecuador and Argentina, across Asia, and in Russia.

In the 21st century, the profound risk inherent in the business of banking has been no less pronounced. In 2001, Argentina's banking system was effectively paralysed when mass runs on banks prompted the government to restrict access to cash. The following year, the South African A2 Banking Crisis unfolded, with the failure of Saambou bank triggering the collapse or deregistration of another 21 banks. In 2003, Myanmar experienced a national-level banking crisis, during which a run on Asia Wealth Bank quickly spread to all private banks in the country. From 2001 to 2023, the US alone experienced more than 500 bank failures, the bulk of them related to the Global Financial Crisis. Some of the most recognisable names included in this wave of failures were Bear Stearns, Merrill Lynch, Countrywide Financial, Lehman Brothers, Wachovia and Washington Mutual. The latter, with a balance sheet of $309 billion at the time, remains the largest single bank failure in US history.

The effects of the Crisis were not confined to the US, but were felt worldwide, with an estimated 11% of the world's top 1,000 banks failing outright or being completely bailed out by their respective governments during or in the immediate aftermath of the Crisis. Notable individual bank failures that subsequently occurred from 2009 onwards took place in the Netherlands, Sweden, China, Bulgaria, Canada, Italy and the UK.

Prior to 2023, the three largest failures in the US after Washington Mutual had included IndyMac Bank in 2008, Colonial Bank in 2009 and First Republic Bank-Dallas in 1988. These have now been superseded by the collapse of Silicon Valley Bank, Signature Bank and First Republic Bank, which collectively held some $532 billion in assets at the time of their failure in the first half of 2023. Alongside these failures came the collapse of Credit Suisse, which was bought out by rival bank UBS under direction of the Swiss authorities, after it was brought to the brink of collapse by numerous scandals and substantial deposit withdrawals.

THE FREQUENCY OF BANK FAILURES

Over the centuries, there has been a sustained – and seemingly unavoidable – high frequency of bank failures around the world. Assessing the numbers through the long lens of history, two conclusions become apparent.

The first is that central banks and governments must make regular decisions on whether or not to let an individual bank fail, given the potential contagion effect and subsequent long-term detrimental economic impact that could result. There is usually an inevitability about this choice, however, with concerns about the broader economy almost always outweighing the concerns of moral hazard incurred when using taxpayers' money to save a supposedly independent financial institution. Over time, this pattern in regulating the financial system has relentlessly eroded public trust in the institution of banking.

The second is that the entire edifice of banking is simply much riskier than we are generally led to believe. It was only in the conception of banking promulgated during the post-World War II period of US global domination and an artificially weakened dollar, maintained through the Bretton Woods System, that banking as a system of global exchange came to be viewed as relatively stable. Since the 1970s, banking has reverted to its natural state and continued to demonstrate its innate precariousness.

See Addendum for a select list of bank failures across history.

PART II

"Getting the financial system to work well is critical to the success of an economy. To understand why, think of the financial system as the brain of the economy: that is, it acts as a co-ordinating mechanism that allocates capital, the lifeblood of economic activity, to its most productive uses by businesses and households. If capital goes to the wrong uses or does not flow at all, the economy will operate inefficiently, and ultimately economic growth will be low."
– Frederic S Mishkin, member of the Federal Reserve Board of Governors, 2006-2008

"The modern banking system manufactures money out of nothing. The process is perhaps the most astounding piece of sleight of hand that was ever invented."
– Sir Josiah Stamp, director of the Bank of England, 1928-1941

A SHORT HISTORY OF MONEY: 1

To understand the existential importance of banking in modern society, it is necessary to consider the true meaning embedded in the concept of money. Fundamentally, money must have three characteristics: it must operate as a unit of account, a means of exchange and a store of value.

All of these were present in cowrie shells, one of the oldest recognised forms of money, first used sometime around 1200BC. Found along the Pacific and Indian Ocean coastlines, these shells were valued among the indigenous populations of Asia, Africa and Oceania, worn ornamentally as jewellery or sewn into clothing, or used as talismans to ward off evil. Small, hardy and generally of a uniform size, they became a medium of exchange that eventually circulated throughout the world, with traders using them to enter markets to purchase goods and, at the height of the slave trade, people. Cowrie shells were still accepted as a form of payment in some parts of the world, especially in West Africa, into the 20th century.

In pre-industrial times, most commerce was conducted using a bartering system, where goods of intrinsic value – such as livestock, grain and textiles – were exchanged between two parties, who decided for themselves what constituted a fair trade. Alongside this, in some instances, there emerged an object that was collectively agreed to hold value, such as the cowrie, which provided a more standardised unit for conducting trade. Coins made from gold, silver and copper, which were moulded into units of uniform size and weight, were used from as early as the 6th century BC in regions such as Greece, Persia and China. Each coin had three currency values: the intrinsic value of the metal from which it had been coined, the legal value that was attributed to it by the issuing authority of the coin, and the market value. Although the three values were generally similar, the legal value tended to be the highest, as built into it was a fee levied by the minting authority for producing the coin. It is precisely when these values diverge from one another in the aggregate perception of society that market disruption occurs. This was demonstrated in the recent example of Bitcoin, where the connection between the intrinsic value of the coin and the market value ascribed to it has not been clear. The volatility in the market value of a single coin – which skyrocketed from just under $5,500 in March 2020 to a peak of almost $65,000 in December 2021, before dropping again substantially – is directly linked to the collective uncertainty regarding the coin's intrinsic value and its usefulness as a currency.

The use of coins as a medium of exchange did not become commonplace in Europe until the 12th century AD, and "payments in kind" – payments in whatever goods or services traders agreed to – therefore remained the dominant means of conducting exchanges for many centuries. This was largely because there was

A SHORT HISTORY OF MONEY: 1

limited need for coins during this time, as most transactions were conducted among members of the same community. On the supply side, minting of coins was also constrained by the availability of precious metals, as coins did not represent a unit of fixed monetary value, but instead derived their value directly from their weight in gold or, more commonly then, silver. A silver penny in Europe constituted the smallest and most widely used denomination, and was derived by splitting a pound unit of weight of silver into 240 pennies. For accounting purposes, twelve pennies were regarded as constituting one shilling, and twenty shillings constituted a pound. Once individual nobles began minting coins themselves, of varying proportions of silver, this monetary system became disorganised over time, with different currencies of increasingly varying value being in circulation simultaneously. Once again, one can observe a parallel phenomenon in the crypto market where, as of writing, there exist more than 20,000 different cryptocurrencies.

The 13th century saw the establishment of some degree of currency standardisation, based on a return to full silver coins, as well as the introduction of gold coins. First minted in Venice in 1203, silver coins known as grossi were equivalent to 24 local pennies. They were subsequently coined throughout the Italian city-states, with the grosso's silver content fixed across jurisdictions as equivalent to the sum of the silver contained in the pennies that equated to its standardised value. In Florence, one grosso might equate to ten pennies, for example, while in Rome, one grosso might be worth thirty pennies, depending on the silver content of the pennies in question. Soon grossi were being used throughout Europe, supporting the expansion of foreign trade in the region. Gold coins followed; the florin was minted in Florence, the genovino in Genoa, the ducat in

Venice and the French florin in France. These coins were generally reserved for large trade transactions, while grossi and pennies were more commonly used for everyday payments. Coinage at this time thus operated on three distinct systems: one based on pennies, one on grossi, and one on gold coins.

This historical trend demonstrates the societal need for standardisation and some form of centralisation of the underlying value of money that emerges over time, particularly in a world that supports global trade. A modern example is the creation of the euro as a common currency across twenty European countries.

The use of bills of exchange from the 13th century, made popular by the Medici bank and other merchant banks, marked an important evolutionary step in the medieval monetary system. A subsequent step was the introduction of paper money in European banking. Paper money had been used in some parts of the world, most notably China, since as early as the 7th century, but it was not until the 17th century that it became widely used in Europe. Sweden's Stockholms Banco – the predecessor to Sweden's central bank, Riksens Ständers Bank – is credited as being the first European bank to issue banknotes, following its establishment in 1657. Although overseen by a single general manager, Johan Palmstruch, the bank was initially conceptualised as two separate entities: an exchange bank, which took deposits that could later be withdrawn by the depositor for a fee; and a loans bank, which provided loans that were financed by the bank owners and secured against property. Palmstruch soon saw the advantages of combining the two businesses, however, as doing so would mean that the money deposited by account holders could be used to finance loans, rather than relying on the bank owners to provide capital. This was the first real example of what we conceive of as a modern-day bank, which uses

A SHORT HISTORY OF MONEY: 1

deposits to fund lending. But given that deposits are typically made for a shorter period than loans are extended, the inherent risk embedded in this idea soon became apparent. In our modern vernacular, we call this the problem of maturity intermediation – and this is the conundrum that resides, to this day, within the heart of banking.

The issue of short-term supply in the maturity intermediation problem, as Sweden experienced it, manifested in a shortage of copper, which resulted in the debasement of the country's copper coins in 1660. Like most European countries at this time, Sweden did not operate with a single currency but relied on two separate monetary systems, one based on silver and one on copper. When the copper content of the copper coin was reduced, its value as a currency was simultaneously eroded. Upon learning of the debasement, depositors attempted to withdraw the old copper coins they had deposited with Stockholms Banco, which contained a higher proportion of copper than the new coins, and which were therefore worth more. But as the bank had used these coins to extend loans, it did not have them physically available. To solve this problem, Palmstruch began to issue deposit certificates to the bank's customers that matched the value of the copper coins they had each deposited, and which gave the owner the right to withdraw the deposited amount in new coins. These notes were freely transferable, backed only by a promise that the bank would make future payment in metal.

The banknotes quickly became popular as they negated the need to carry coins to conduct transactions. To meet growing demand, Stockholms Banco began to increase the volume at which it was printing banknotes. Simultaneously, it began to issue banknotes as credit notes that could be used to make purchases and payments. With the number of loans the bank could provide no longer limited to the actual number of coins it held in deposits, lending rose sharply. But this brief period of rapid growth was followed by an inevitable fall. By 1663, the banknotes were losing value owing to the sheer volume in circulation, and when customers tried to withdraw their money, converting their banknotes to coins, the bank was unable to honour their requests, as it held insufficient metal reserves. A bank run ensued, resulting in the collapse of Stockholms Banco the following year. The Swedish government was forced to intervene and exchange the notes for coins, and in 1668 Palmstruch was sentenced to death for his mismanagement of the bank. This punishment was later converted to a prison sentence.

A more successful introduction of banknotes was achieved in 1695 by the Bank of England. To raise funds during the Nine Years' War, the bank began issuing handwritten running-cash notes to the public in exchange for deposits in gold and silver coins, with the promise to pay the bearer the value of the note on demand. Gradually, the bank transitioned to issuing fixed denomination notes; by 1745, notes ranging in standard value from £20 to £1,000 were being issued. Initially, a banknote functioned simply as a promise that the bank would redeem the note for its value in gold or silver coins upon its presentation by the bearer. From 1833 onwards, the notes became more widely circulated after a series of laws were passed in the UK allowing banknotes to be used as legal tender during peacetime, a change that was welcomed by the public, who enjoyed the ease of using banknotes in transactions and who trusted that the bank would settle the notes in coin when required.

Alongside these laws came others that defined a system of issuance in which only the Bank of England, as the central bank, was authorised to issue banknotes, and therefore control money supply.

A SHORT HISTORY OF MONEY: 1

This model was soon replicated throughout Europe. Critically, the Bank of England was restricted in its issuance, in that it could only issue new banknotes if they were 100% backed by silver and gold, and this practice subsequently became a global norm with the introduction of the gold standard from 1871. A central bank system in the US would, however, only emerge with the creation of the Federal Reserve in 1913.

Reflecting on this history, it is clear that money functions most effectively when it is backed by something of perceived value, when it is not oversupplied, and when it is issued by a centralised and trusted authority. It fails when trust is eroded, when too much is printed, or when, most pressingly for our times, the central authority is substantially doubted. All these elements were at play in the astonishing case of John Law and the Banque Royale in France more than 300 years ago.

JOHN LAW AND THE BANQUE GÉNÉRALE

In early August of 1715, King Louis XIV of France set off for a hunting trip on the grounds of Marly, a secluded royal estate seven kilometres north-west of Versailles. Following the expedition, he began to experience acute discomfort in his leg, and without the presence of a clear injury, his physician diagnosed him with sciatica, a common form of nerve pain. Several days later, however, black spots began to form on his leg – the telltale sign of a gangrene infection. Less than a month later, King Louis the Great, the Sun King, was dead, succumbing to the infection four days before his 77th birthday. Having assumed the crown at the age of four, Louis was, and remains, the longest-reigning monarch in history. In 1715, his sudden death not only left a political vacuum in France, but also thrust the country into financial turmoil.

Louis's great-grandson, Louis XV, was next in line to be king but, at five years old, the boy was many years away from holding power. Until then, the late king's nephew, Philippe II of Orléans, also

JOHN LAW AND THE BANQUE GÉNÉRALE

known as the Duke of Orléans, would step in as regent, holding the crown until Louis XV came of age. Once in power, however, Philippe II annulled the king's will, and with it the sway of the Regency Council that had been installed to diminish Philippe II's influence, thereby securing his position of authority. The new ruler now faced the dire economic conditions he had inherited from Louis XIV. The late king was known not only for his insatiable appetite – when his autopsy was performed, it was discovered that his stomach was double the size of the average man's – but also his spending habits. Several wars, including the War of Devolution, the Dutch War, the War of the Reunions, the Nine Years' War and the War of the Spanish Succession, had severely indebted France during his reign. The costly construction and upkeep of the palace of Versailles also depleted the country's finances to the point that Philippe II was faced with three billion livres worth of debt – equivalent to more than $30 billion today – during a time when France's silver and gold coin currency was subject to tumultuous fluctuations. To aid in the recovery of France's finances, Philippe II turned to an old acquaintance he had met at the gambling tables in Paris many years earlier: John Law.

John Law was born in Edinburgh in 1671, to a goldsmith father, a profession that earned both wealth and prestige, and a mother who was a descendant of the house of Argyll, a Scottish ducal family. By the age of twenty, six years after his father's death, Law had moved to London, where he spent his time socialising, gambling and expanding his knowledge of banking and commerce. As a gambler, Law made sizeable sums of money at times but also racked up substantial debts, which his doting mother paid off. In 1694, his fortunes took a dramatic swing, when his flirtation with the future Countess of Orkney landed him in a duel with her husband. In April that year, he killed the man and was sentenced to death because, though still common, duels had by then been outlawed. Law's only recourse was to orchestrate a jailbreak and flee the country. While he was on the run, he travelled extensively throughout Europe, and it was during this time that, having gained exposure to multiple financial systems in the region, he began to develop the monetary policies he would become known for. In particular, he formulated his ideas for the creation of the first fully fledged fiat currency in Europe. In Paris, he made a fortuitous acquaintance with the Duke of Orléans, who took an interest in his theories.

Years after his escape to Europe, after the death of Louis XIV, Law was summoned by the duke to appear before France's Council of Finance. The country's finances were in desperate need of resuscitation, and the economist presented a bold plan for a public reserve bank that would have the capability to collect taxes, boost investment, create commercial monopolies and control money supply. But the sheer ambition and scale of the plan spooked the council; Law's initial plan was rejected in October 1715, and he was subsequently forced to scale back his project and re-engineer his plans to form a private bank that had the authority to issue banknotes. This plan was approved, its appeal bolstered by the fact that Law offered to set up the bank at his own expense and to put his properties up as collateral for any losses incurred. On 2 May 1716, Law obtained a charter from the council to establish the Banque Générale.

To raise capital for the new bank, Law made a public offering of 12,000 shares, each priced at 5,000 livres. Investors were able to purchase these shares in cash or government bonds, called billets d'état. To start, Law purchased a quarter of the total shares. The bank then began issuing banknotes for the first time in France's

JOHN LAW AND THE BANQUE GÉNÉRALE

history, which were essentially a claim to silver and gold coins of a set value and weight that could be redeemed at a later date. The bank held specie – money in the form of coins – in reserve equivalent to approximately 50% of the value of the paper money in circulation. Banknotes were also issued in exchange for deposits made with the bank. The paper found favour with the people of France, for its convenience and because it allowed coin to be exchanged at a fixed, predetermined value, stabilising the haphazard fluctuations that the country's currency had been exposed to during the reign of Louis XIV. As a result of the desirability of paper money, the new currency soon traded at a premium.

The bank did exceptionally well in its first year, cementing Philippe II's confidence in Law's theories. The regent then allowed Law to begin implementing the remainder of his monetary plans and policies. The bank began to branch out from Paris into the provincial regions, which were instructed to complete transactions in banknotes instead of coin currency. A little more than two years after its establishment, the Banque Générale was nationalised when the crown bought out all its stockholders and renamed the institution the Banque Royale. Around the same time, in December 1718, a royal announcement suspended the convertibility of paper into gold and silver, creating a fiat monetary system. The paper money that the bank circulated was guaranteed by the crown, though Law remained in charge of the institution. This was the first time that the French public was asked to trust a central authority purely at its word.

Prior to this, in 1717, Law had initiated a second project to support his financial plans for France, which centred on the creation of the Compagnie de la Louisiane ou d'Occident – the Company of Louisiana and the West – in August of 1717. More popularly referred to as the "Mississippi Company", Law's new creation was given an exclusive 25-year lease to develop and populate French colonies dispersed along the vast Mississippi River in what would later become the United States. Through competitive bidding in late 1718, the Mississippi Company purchased all rights pertaining to tobacco production and distribution in the region, establishing a tobacco monopoly. In the first half of 1719, through various purchases and acquisitions of competing trading companies, it came to monopolise all French trading and commerce outside of Europe. By the end of that year, Law had purchased France's tax collection rights for 52 million livres, and had taken control of France's royal mints, as well as the rights to produce new coins. Law had also merged the Banque Royale and the Mississippi Company into one financial entity referred to as "The System".

It is almost beyond the realms of comprehension that a system unilaterally controlled by one man, and so vast and interconnected as to hold such significant sway over a country like France, could have existed two-and-a-half centuries before the futuristic dystopian visions articulated in the novels of George Orwell or Philip K Dick. In a little more than three years, Law had essentially gained control of France's entire monetary system, its colonial endeavours and its trading interests outside of Europe, and he had accumulated so much wealth that he was richer than the king of France. Some have claimed that, in relative terms, he was the wealthiest man who ever lived.

To fund the extensive infrastructure required to develop the French colonies, Law sold shares in the Mississippi Company to investors, who were easily convinced that their fortunes would be secured by the prosperous tobacco plantations in the colonies. Their interest was further piqued by the fact that shares could be purchased, in cash or

JOHN LAW AND THE BANQUE GÉNÉRALE

in government bonds, by making only a 10% initial payment. The acceptance of government bonds was pivotal to Law's plans to trade France's government debt for equity in the Mississippi Company. Shares were first sold at 500 livres, but the price jumped to 10,000 livres within a matter of months, owing to frenzied speculation based on the expectation that immense profits were to be made. A similar dynamic would repeat itself nearly three centuries later during the dotcom bubble in the late 1990s, when eager investors, expecting to reap great profits, poured untold sums of money into new tech start-ups that had no proven track record of success.

The Mississippi Company's share price spiked again when rumours circulated that natural silver and gold deposits had been discovered in the French colonies, and by January of 1720 a 40% dividend from the company pushed the share price up to 18,000 livres – 36 times their value when they were first sold. As the share price increased, more money was required to purchase them and, in turn, needed to be printed. Before the Banque Générale was nationalised, money supply had stood at 40 million livres. By January 1720, it had increased to one billion livres, and inflation had risen to a monthly rate of 23%. As an overlooked historical lesson, the 25-fold increase in money supply in France presaged the actions of the US Federal Reserve in the 21st century, when it increased its balance sheet from $800 billion in 2005 to $9 trillion in 2022 in a misguided attempt to paper over the Global Financial Crisis. In doing so, it brought with it wildly fluctuating markets, long-embedded inflation and public distrust in the system.

At around the same time, Law converted to Catholicism, making him eligible to be appointed the Controller General and Superintendent General of Finance. It was also at this time that the first documented use of the word "millionaire" was recorded. Everyone who invested, from aristocrats to footmen, saw their shares in the Banque Royale increase dramatically. Of course, this prosperity would prove to be unsustainable.

In early 1720, when the share price hit its peak, some investors looking to cash in on their investments began to sell their shares in the Mississippi Company. These investors specifically wanted gold and silver instead of the cash upon which Law had built France's entire monetary system. To stem the flow of gold leaving the bank's reserves, Law capped all payments in gold to 100 livres. As a result of the sales, the share price dipped, forcing Law to make numerous attempts to prop up the price once again. On 5 March, the share price of the Mississippi Company was pegged at 9,000 livres, essentially turning the company's equity into a monetary standard. By that time, the amount of money in circulation in France had doubled again to two billion livres.

Knowing that both banknotes and Mississippi Company shares were overpriced, Law desperately tried to reverse course. On 21 May, he initiated a royal decree that attempted to lower their prices. Yet, owing to the decree, people quickly lost confidence in the company and began to comprehend that the plentiful wealth of France's colonies along the Mississippi River had been greatly exaggerated. Fears of bankruptcy started spreading. Ironically, attempts made by the leaders of financial institutions to quell panic are very often the catalysts that actually trigger crises, as was the case more recently with Credit Suisse when Saudi National Bank announced that it would not provide the Swiss bank with any more capital. Similarly, Law's decree did little to dissuade doubts, and despite attempts to close the bank for periods to limit the number of withdrawals, people

JOHN LAW AND THE BANQUE GÉNÉRALE

continued to demand their funds. On 17 July 1720, this reached a pinnacle when the bank restricted transactions to ten-franc notes owing to dwindling reserves. Once this became public knowledge, huge crowds inundated the bank, and in the surging throng three people were crushed to death. By this time, Law had fled to the Palais Royal and found sanctuary with Philippe II. The mob of people followed Law, however, and surrounded the gates, bringing with them the bodies of those who had been trampled. A royal decree was released shortly thereafter announcing the end of Law's System – a system that had introduced fiat money, backed by nothing more than an institutional promise, and produced one of the first major national bank runs in history, in which a country's citizens entirely lost faith in their central bank.

By September 1720, the share price of the Mississippi Company had dropped to 2,000 livres, and by the time Law fled France, in December, it had slumped to half of that. France subsequently instituted a return to gold and silver coins, nullifying Law's paper money. After fleeing France, Law spent his final years gambling in Venice. He died of pneumonia, in poverty, in 1729, having been the wealthiest man in the world just nine years before.

THE FUNDAMENTALS OF BANKING

Banks can be thought of as the brain of the body economic, performing two functions that enable this body to operate effectively. At a basic level, banking keeps the body running through the provision of critical services that all participants in the economic system require, facilitating the storage and exchange of value to support savings and the purchase of everything from groceries to Boeing 787 Dreamliners. At a more sophisticated level, banking also performs an executive function, deciding on the most efficient allocation of oxygen and nutrients, in the form of funding and capital, which is delivered through the bloodstream to the attendant industries that form the organs and limbs of the body economic. Banking as a commercial pursuit is fundamental to overall health, yet, by its very nature, it is a riskier business than almost any other. This is because it depends on leverage – that is, on borrowing to fund the creation of assets – and because its primary preoccupation, money, is predominantly intangible, and based on the elusive concept of public trust.

THE FUNDAMENTALS OF BANKING

Banking is classically explained in terms of the double-entry bookkeeping system and the balance sheet, in which assets are recorded on one side, and liabilities and equity on the other. In any other business, assets are generally comprised of the physical property that a company owns and uses in its business; for example, its premises, equipment and stock. For a bank, however, assets are mostly constituted by the loans that are extended to its customers. These loans may be made to individuals, corporate entities, governments or government entities. Loans may be secured or unsecured, and may be extended for various time periods.

On the other side of the balance sheet – the funding side – banks borrow heavily from a range of depositors, as well as from other banks. They do this to a much greater extent than any other industry. A useful way to think about the deposit base of a bank is to conceptualise it as a pyramid. At the lowest level of the pyramid are the most voluminous number of depositors with the smallest value of deposits, comprised primarily of individuals who wish to save a portion of their income in fixed deposits or notice deposits. These are the individuals who would form a line outside a bank to withdraw their money if there was a crisis of confidence, creating a bank run that can lead to bank failure, as was the case with Northern Rock during the Global Financial Crisis.

One step up on the pyramid are deposits made by or on behalf of small- and medium-sized businesses. There are fewer of them, but the size of their deposits is larger. Another step up the pyramid are deposits made by large corporate entities, which may wish to store excess cash in expectation of paying a dividend or bonuses to their employees, for example, or simply to keep funds safe and available for strategic purposes. These deposits are larger in value than those found in the pyramid layer below, and depositors in this layer are generally seeking to obtain the highest yield possible without taking market risk. Most countries' central banks will not insure deposits of this size.

Up through this pyramid of deposits, there is an increasing paucity of participants and an increasing level of sophistication in deposits, which is reflected in the interest rate a bank will offer – generally, banks attempt to reward customers more for leaving their money in deposits for longer periods of time. In broad terms, however, deposits are, on aggregate, held for a shorter time than loans are typically extended for, leading to the problem of maturity intermediation. Managing the mismatch between these tenors is the primary focus of banks, which borrow from depositors in the short term, knowing that they must continuously replenish those deposits to offset the money they have lent out for longer periods of time.

In addition to deposits from individuals and businesses, the funding side of a bank's balance sheet is buttressed by money obtained in the interbank market, where one institution can acquire additional short-term funding by borrowing from another. These transactions are performed through over-the-counter (non-exchange-traded) financial instruments known as repurchase agreements, or repos. In exchange for cash, the borrowing bank provides assets, typically commercial paper or government paper, to the lending bank to be used as collateral in the agreement. This is treated as a temporary exchange, with the borrower committing to repurchase its securities from the lender on a specified date at a specified price, with an interest payment added to compensate for the lender's risk. To understand how critical this source of funding is for banks, one need only look to the Global Financial Crisis, when this process of negotiating repos came to a grinding halt. In short, the market of

THE FUNDAMENTALS OF BANKING

very sophisticated traders whose job it was to constantly replenish the liability side of their banks' balance sheet stopped loaning to each other, in an act of fear never previously experienced, which led to a total seizure of the global banking system. While the Crisis was initiated by a build-up of overextended credit in the mortgage market, it was the liquidity crisis created in the interbank market that caused banks to fail in moments of instantaneous capitulation, when they could not replenish their funding, and literally ran out of money.

With loans constituting a bank's assets, and deposits and repos constituting its liabilities, the final element of the bank's balance sheet to be considered is capital. All businesses must have capital to fund the equity portion of their ventures, and to demonstrate faith by their owners in their own businesses. All industrial enterprises make continuous use of capital, which is the money that is provided by investors or obtained by reinvesting retained earnings into the business, to build industrial plants, buy equipment or otherwise take advantage of opportunities that will yield returns. In banking, at its most basic level, capital is money or easily tradeable financial instruments – such as cash, bonds and equity – that is set aside to absorb losses resulting from a bank's operations and from its lending. These losses may, for example, stem from the failure of customers to repay their loans, from operating losses such as those associated with system downtimes or cyberattacks, or from taking unfavourable positions in the market. Capital cannot be used directly to make loans to customers, but must be held in reserve according to the size and risk of the loans made, and it therefore creates a drag effect on profits.

In theory, banks should hold enough capital to absorb losses, so that customers' deposits remain safely guarded. At the same time, they would wish to hold as little capital as possible so as to maximise their returns. The ratio of a bank's assets to equity, or more broadly capital, which can include loss-absorbing financial instruments that are not pure equity or retained earnings, is generally known as its leverage ratio. In theory, the higher this ratio, the more at risk of failure the bank is. Today, most banks maintain a leverage ratio of risk-weighted assets to capital of roughly 8 to 1. During the Global Financial Crisis, most investment banks had leverage ratios much higher than this, relying heavily on overnight funding to keep themselves afloat. When the interbank market froze, cutting off the primary source by which these institutions topped up the funding side of their balance sheets daily, this degree of leverage proved fatal.

The collective position held by central banks and policymakers at the time was that there could exist nothing worse for society than a total seizure of global banking systems – a seemingly inevitable outcome if other financial institutions were allowed to fail in the same way that Lehman Brothers had. To address the imminent mass collapse of these financial institutions, the Federal Reserve decided to create liquidity by buying any nature of fungible assets that an individual bank held on its balance sheet. At first, this included government bonds and corporate bonds. Eventually, the Fed bought mortgage-backed securities, some of which were ultimately near-worthless in value as a result of the instant repricing that took place in the teeth of the crisis. This process, through which a central bank purchases securities from the market to increase money supply, is known as quantitative easing. To access these funds, investment banks – which at the time of the Crisis were not regulated in the way commercial banks were – were forced to become bank holdings companies, bringing them under the ambit of banking regulators.

THE FUNDAMENTALS OF BANKING

In essence, the only way to unlock the interbank market during the Crisis was for the Fed to print so much money, and inject it into the banking system, that there would be no need to worry about liquidity. The end figure was enormous. Between the start of 2008 and late 2014, as the Fed continued to purchase assets from banks in exchange for cash, its balance sheet ballooned from a relatively stable $800 billion to $4.5 trillion. The Fed's asset-purchasing programme then accelerated radically during the Covid-19 pandemic, its balance sheet eventually reaching a gargantuan $9 trillion by March 2022.

Simultaneously, authorities in Europe and other countries that ascribed to the broadly accepted Basel Accords reacted with a raft of new regulations promulgated through the Basel Committee on Banking Supervision (BCBS), the multilateral body responsible for determining international standards for banking best practice. In 2010, the BCBS introduced the third iteration of the Basel Accords, with a particular focus on increasing minimum capital standards and liquidity risk thresholds for banks in a bid to prevent an event of the scale and severity of the Global Financial Crisis from ever occurring again. In theory, the more capital banks hold, the less they are leveraged and the safer they are, and it was for this reason that the new regulations focused on raising the CET1 ratio – the ratio between Common Equity Tier 1 capital, the highest quality of capital, and total risk-weighted assets. Risk-weighting assets refers to the practice of scaling different asset types according to their riskiness, with riskier assets attracting a higher capital requirement. After the Crisis, central bankers around the world significantly increased the quantity and quality of capital that had to be held against risk-weighted assets on a bank's balance sheet. This seemed logical and appropriate at the time. There are, however, two fundamental flaws to this approach.

First, at a systemic level, a banking sector that requires all banks to hold more capital is less attractive from an overall investment perspective, as increased capital means lower returns on equity, and therefore lower returns to shareholders. Ironically, then, the notion of increasing the capital requirement for banks to absorb losses, while sensible in theory, led to a massive worldwide requirement for greater investment in the banking industry after the Crisis at precisely the same time that society's trust in banks had been shattered. The perception that banks were extremely risky investments led to an erosion of the banking investment base, making it increasingly difficult for banks to attract new capital, and requiring them to retain dividends or to hold a rights issue that diluted existing investors.

From a geopolitical perspective, this problem of attracting investment has led to a marked change in the nature of investors, with potentially dangerous implications for the sanctity of banking within a liberal democratic free-market system. Take the example of Credit Suisse, which found itself on the brink of collapse towards the end of 2022, following a string of scandals that prompted the withdrawal of some $119 billion in funds by depositors during the fourth quarter of that year. Hopes of shoring up its capital base were significantly damaged in March 2023 when Saudi National Bank (SNB), Credit Suisse's largest shareholder, publicly refused to increase its investment. When asked by a Bloomberg reporter if SNB would consider increasing its share in Credit Suisse, Chairman Ammar Al Khudairy answered, "absolutely not", stating vaguely that there were "many reasons" for this decision. Immediately following the interview, Credit Suisse's share price dropped by 24%. Although the Swiss central bank subsequently offered a $54 billion liquidity backstop, this failed to mitigate the crisis of confidence in Credit

THE FUNDAMENTALS OF BANKING

Suisse, which was ultimately taken over by its rival UBS. This example raises important questions about the extent to which the fundamental system of exchange in liberal democracies has become dependent on the whims of representatives from non-liberal democracies, a risk that has not yet been properly baked into the pricing of bank stocks. It seems undeniable that this risk will increasingly make it more difficult to prevent a move towards geopolitical multipolarity, and so encourage the undermining of US dollar dominance, and the likelihood of a world in which there may not necessarily exist a single set of shared values.

Second, the danger of raising the CET1 ratio is even more pronounced on an individual-bank level, where regulators may have inadvertently increased the likelihood of failure. Should a disruptive market event occur, the capital requirement within an individual bank will be breached earlier than it would have been pre-Crisis, despite the bank in fact holding more capital, because the CET1 ratio will drop below its regulatory minimum much sooner. The end result: a substantial increase in the chance of technical failure. Once the bank is considered to be approaching technical failure – because it no longer meets the required CET1 ratio – peer banks will avoid rolling over funding, regarding the entity as being too risky to lend to. Before the capital buffer is ever called upon to absorb any potential credit losses, the bank will therefore be out of business owing to a short-term liability shortfall. Today, it is rare for a bank to fail because it has burnt through its capital buffer; rather, declining capital ratios are simply a precursor to a liquidity squeeze that can result in a bank's immediate failure.

As part of Basel III, legislation was also introduced that compelled banks to hold liquid assets which could be converted into cash that were equivalent to what was conceived of as one month of stressed cash outflows. This is known as the liquidity coverage ratio, with the one-year version called the net stable funding ratio. These ratios essentially force banks to hold sufficient liquidity of sufficient term so that they will no longer, in theory, suffer from a liquidity crisis. Although intended to safeguard the banking system and society at large, the cumulative and international effect of this plethora of regulations is that the ability of banks to leverage themselves and to expand their asset base has been significantly constrained.

Of even greater concern is the reality that, despite the extreme levels of money printing by the Fed and despite the introduction of numerous regulations intended to reduce risk in the banking system, we are still witnessing bank runs a decade and a half after the Global Financial Crisis. As we've seen, these include some of the largest bankruptcies in history.

After the facts in the case of Silicon Valley Bank were exposed, it was striking to realise that the bank's failure in March 2023 was ironically caused by too much liquidity, rather than too little – the result of a prolonged period of loose monetary policy. It was because the bank received such an excessive amount of money in deposits over such a short period of time that it decided to invest so heavily in long-term Treasury bonds to balance its liabilities, ultimately leading to its downfall.

This case in particular, and bank failures in general, demonstrate the fundamental truth that monetary policy and banking regulation alone cannot address the inherent underlying vulnerability of banking, which is that it depends on trust. SVB failed because at its moment

THE FUNDAMENTALS OF BANKING

of greatest need, its CEO pleaded with its customers and investors to keep faith and trust the bank, and in so doing exacerbated the rush of withdrawals. Trust is eroded most acutely when it is actively called for – this is one of the conundrums of banking.

To continue to replenish the stores of deposits that make up the liability side of the balance sheet, banks rely on the trust that society has placed in them as individual institutions and collectively as a global system. People need to believe that money holds value, and that the institutions that are entrusted with managing it are secure. Without trust, we invite chaos in the place of order, destabilising the very foundations upon which money, the banking system and society itself is built. And troublingly, in a world of shifting sands and multiple value centres, trust has become increasingly difficult to earn and maintain.

A SHORT HISTORY OF MONEY: 2

By 1900, almost all developed nations were on the gold standard, which established a monetary system in which countries effectively agreed to define their currencies in terms of a fixed weight of gold. In this system, if the US gold price was set at $200 an ounce, for example, a one-dollar note would entitle the holder to 1/200th of an ounce of gold held by the government. Because the government of each country was obliged to hold enough gold to pay out the denominated amount promised by the exchange of notes, the number of notes that could be printed at any given time was constrained, bringing much needed structure to a rapidly growing global financial system.

The amount of gold that governments held in reserve was highly dependent on global trade, as trade imbalances between nations were settled in gold at this time. This ensured price stability and, according to the "price-specie flow mechanism" theory proposed by Scottish philosopher and economist David Hume, it also ensured self-correction in the global monetary system. According to this theory,

A SHORT HISTORY OF MONEY: 2

a strong exporting economy running a balance of trade surplus would receive an inflow of gold, which in turn would increase the amount of money that could be printed and put into circulation. This would theoretically lead to a rise in domestic price levels and a decrease in international competitiveness, slowing exports and, over time, bringing down the balance of trade surplus and, therefore, the amount of money being printed, preventing inflation. The reverse would be true for countries running a balance of trade deficit.

This theory was put under enormous pressure just fourteen years into the 20th century, with the outbreak of global war. In times of economic hardship, when expansionary monetary policies were required, governments found the gold standard to be too restrictive, and with the onset of World War I, it was consequently suspended in the US and Europe. Although attempts would be made to return to the gold standard in the window of peace between the two World Wars, support for the gold standard waned globally in the aftermath of the original conflict, as many countries struggled to rebuild their economies and manage high unemployment levels. In the US particularly, a return to the gold standard was severely curtailed by the economic shocks of the Great Depression. Panicked by the instability of the dollar when the stock market crashed in 1929, Americans clung to gold for safety, exchanging their dollars for bullion, rather than leaving their money in the banks that were failing all around them. It was becoming increasingly evident that, while in times of peace the gold standard had been beneficial, in times of crisis it simply disintegrated. In 1933, in response to the run on gold, the US government not only suspended the convertibility of dollars to gold, but also demanded that all citizens return their bullion and coins to the state in exchange for dollars. This stimulated the flow of paper money through the economy once again and shored up America's gold reserves, which proved critical at the end of World War II, when the desire for a new monetary regime that would ensure greater international economic stability led to a return to gold, albeit in a modified sense.

Introducing an international monetary system based on fixed exchange rates, the Bretton Woods System was developed at the United Nations' Monetary and Financial Conference in 1944, under the leadership of British economist John Maynard Keynes and the chief international economist of the US Treasury, Harry Dexter White. At the time, the US was not only the most dominant country in the world both politically and economically, but it also held three-quarters of the world's gold supply, owing mainly to persistent balance of trade surpluses. It was thus decided that the US dollar would be pegged to the price of gold – set at $35 per ounce – and that other currencies would be pegged to the US dollar. A fixed exchange rate was then maintained by central banks around the world between their currencies and the dollar, effectively replacing the gold standard with a dollar standard. Currencies pegged to the dollar therefore still had a fixed value in terms of gold, and countries could exchange their dollars for gold should any doubts about the reserve currency's value arise.

For 25 years, this system ensured stability in the global economy, promoting international trade, supporting Europe's recovery from two World Wars, and contributing to significant economic growth in the US. This growth was supported by the Federal Reserve's monetary policies, under which interest rates were kept low, making money cheap, lending plentiful and short-term economic growth almost inevitable. Difficulties arose in the 1960s, however, when a period of heightened inflation began, with the interest rate climbing from

A SHORT HISTORY OF MONEY: 2

below 2% mid-decade to 6% by 1970, and ballooning to almost 15% by 1980. Fearing a rapid devaluation of the dollar, which was widely considered to be overvalued by this time, foreign investors retreated, while industrial production declined, the stock market cooled off, and unemployment began to steadily rise as the US entered a period of stagflation – the simultaneous rise of inflation and slowdown of the economy. Stagflation was a phenomenon that would embed itself for a decade, broken only by the drastic increases in interest rates that were implemented by the Fed under the leadership of Paul Volcker.

In the early 1970s, the US's position as the world's dominant exporter of goods also began to shift. As a result of the combined effects of the manufacturing boom produced by the Industrial Revolution and the development of America's transnational railway system, the US had experienced persistent balance of trade surpluses for a century, from 1870 to 1970. Starting in 1970, however, the economy began to orientate itself away from manufacturing goods towards the global provision of services, particularly financial services, which had grown significantly more sophisticated and sought-after by this time. As credit-based consumption grew within the US, imports of goods increased, particularly from Europe and Japan, and the US began to run balance of trade deficits. With the dollar operating as the world's reserve currency, foreign countries were also more willing to export products to the US, exchanging them for dollars and dollar-based securities, and holding these assets for longer periods.

With the US radically increasing its military spending and foreign aid during the Vietnam War in the late 1960s and early '70s, the net outcome was that fewer dollars were flowing into the country, and more were flowing out at this time. US dollar reserves held by other countries began to exceed the gold reserves held by the US, placing it in a precarious position should other nations decide to exchange their dollars for gold. With rising inflation causing a devaluation of the dollar, France announced its intention to do exactly this in 1971, with French president Georges Pompidou ordering a warship into New York harbour to retrieve his country's gold and deliver it to the Banque de France in Paris. Belgium, the Netherlands, the UK and Germany soon indicated that they would follow suit.

Faced with a growing balance of trade deficit and an impending run on gold, President Richard Nixon addressed his country on the evening of 15 August 1971, describing a new set of economic policies that would form the basis for what became known as the Nixon Shock. "We must create more and better jobs; we must stop the rise in the cost of living; we must protect the dollar from the attacks of international money speculators," he stated. Nixon proceeded to outline a plan to implement tax cuts and a ninety-day freeze on prices and wages – an unprecedented move in times of geopolitical peace. Most significantly, he declared the US's intention to suspend the dollar's convertibility to gold and to levy a 10% tariff on all dutiable imports until a new international monetary system could be agreed upon. This, it was believed, would push the US's trading partners to adjust the value of their currencies upward and their trade barriers downward, driving demand for US exports.

Nixon's policies were welcomed at home, helping to secure him a second presidential term, but they were met with general suspicion abroad, with many countries viewing the announcement of the decoupling of the dollar from gold as an act of American unilateralism. Nonetheless, in December 1971, the Smithsonian Agreement was reached between the Group of Ten (G10) industrialised countries, through which a modified system of fixed exchange rates was

A SHORT HISTORY OF MONEY: 2

established, based on the now devalued dollar. This was abandoned within fifteen months, however, as US inflation continued to drive down the value of the dollar, further compounded by the economic shock of the OPEC oil crisis. In March 1973, the six members of the European Community – the Netherlands, Belgium, Sweden, France, Germany and Italy – tied their currencies together and jointly floated the European Currency Unit (ECU) against the dollar. This move effectively signalled the end of the Bretton Woods System, as governments opted instead for a system of floating exchange rates, beginning the era of fiat currency that still exists today.

As pioneered by John Law in France in the early 18th century, fiat currency refers to money not backed by any tangible commodity such as gold or silver, which is issued by national governments and used as legal tender. It derives its value based solely on a promise made by the issuing central bank that it will be recognised and protected as a unit of value. No longer tied to any physical commodity with a limited supply, the rise of fiat currency has enabled the printing of money in a reasonably flexible manner to meet the needs of growing populations and to respond to economic changes, based on the idea of gradually increasing liquidity in the market when required. The emergence of fiat currency signalled a critical transition from a monetary system backed by commodities that were universally recognised as stores of value, to a monetary system that essentially relies only on trust – the trust held by citizens that their governments and central banks will guard the value of their currency, and not allow it to be inflated away by excessive money printing in the hopes of achieving immediate relief from financial crises at the expense of long-term stability.

PART III

"The main task of those who believe in the basic principles of capitalism must frequently be to defend this system against the capitalists."
– Friedrich Hayek, *The Intellectuals and Socialism* (1949)

"An Act to deter and punish terrorist acts in the United States and around the world, to enhance law enforcement investigatory tools, and for other purposes."
– US Patriot Act 2001

MARKET CONDUCT

"Today we take an essential step in defeating terrorism, while protecting the constitutional rights of all Americans," stated President George W Bush on 26 October 2001.

Addressing a conference room filled with representatives of the American Congress and the press 44 days after the September 11th terrorist attacks, the president was announcing the introduction of a law called the Uniting and Strengthening America by Providing Appropriate Tools Required to Intercept and Obstruct Terrorism Act. Today it is better known as the US Patriot Act. Having been passed with overwhelming support in Congress with a vote of 357-66, the law was adopted without amendment by Senate with a vote of 98-1. Senator Russell Feingold of Wisconsin was the only person to oppose it, raising concerns about the sweeping expansion of surveillance capabilities that the new law would afford US government agencies. "With my signature, this law will give intelligence and law enforcement officials important new tools to fight a present danger," said President Bush. "The changes, effective today, will help counter a threat like no other our nation has ever faced. We've seen the enemy and the murder of thousands of innocent, unsuspecting people. They recognise no barrier of morality. They have no conscience. The terrorists cannot be reasoned with."

Six weeks earlier, the world had watched in horror as two hijacked airliners – one a United Airlines flight, the other American Airlines – had crashed into the Twin Towers of the World Trade Center in New York. Within two hours, both the North and South towers had collapsed. Meanwhile, a third plane had crashed into the Pentagon, and a fourth into a field in Pennsylvania. Nearly 3,000 people were killed on the day, and a further 6,000 injured. In mere moments, the entire population of the world's most powerful country was reduced to a state of panic, fear and confusion, seemingly without warning. Wishing to assure the American people of their safety, and to project an image of dominance on the world stage, US policymakers responded hastily with a lengthy new piece of legislation intended to arm law enforcement agencies with new tools to detect and prevent terrorism for the explicit purpose of "preserving life and liberty", while also increasing the legal penalties for committing and supporting terrorist activities. The Patriot Act sanctioned the use of video surveillance and wiretapping on anyone suspected of terrorist activities, allowed for searches of these individuals and their property to be conducted without warrants, and expanded the capabilities of law officials to detain suspects. In addition, it enabled officials to access the personal information, including banking records, of a suspect without their knowledge or consent, and with little judicial review.

The unprecedented expansion of state surveillance capabilities became a point of much controversy, with many observers coming

MARKET CONDUCT

to echo Senator Feingold's concerns about the degree to which the new Act compromised civil liberties and individual rights to privacy. These fears were given credence twelve years later in the infamous data leak orchestrated by Edward Snowden, a contractor with the National Security Agency. The leak revealed that the US government had not been limiting its surveillance activities to individuals suspected of terrorist activities, but had been spying indiscriminately on the entire population. In 2015, certain provisions of the Act were amended, and it was renamed the US Freedom Act, though the degree to which US law enforcement agencies continue to use their surveillance powers remains contentious. Despite these abuses, when used for its stated intent, the Patriot Act has played an important role in reining in terrorism and slowing down organised crime, most notably through its applications in banking, where it triggered the development of a raft of new market conduct laws. These laws emerged from the realisation that a highly effective way to prevent terrorism and criminality is to make the financial intermediation process that supports these activities more transparent.

In 2004, the US National Commission on Terrorist Attacks upon the United States, better known as the 9/11 Commission, released a report detailing how in the years leading up to the attacks, several studies conducted by government commissions and private think-tanks had indicated the growing threat of terrorism in the US, and urged government intelligence agencies to strengthen their detection and prevention of terrorist activities. A critical area of concern for the commission was how the financing of the 9/11 attacks had gone largely unnoticed, despite the fact that the hijackers had used their real names to open US bank accounts, into which funds were transferred from facilitators in Germany and the United Arab Emirates, as well as from Khalid Sheikh Mohammed, "the principal architect of the 9/11 attacks". In total, it is estimated the attacks cost Al-Qaeda roughly $500,000, with $300,000 of this passing directly through the hijackers' bank accounts, to pay for flight training and living expenses in the US.

"Neither the hijackers nor their financial facilitators were experts in the use of the international financial system," the commission explicitly states in its report. "They created a paper trail linking them to each other and their facilitators. Still, they were easily adept enough to blend into the vast international financial system without doing anything to reveal themselves as criminals, let alone terrorists bent on mass murder."

At that time, banks were not required to monitor and report on suspicious transactions in a manner that would have connected the financial activities of the hijackers to other intelligence that had been gathered by US law enforcement agencies such as the CIA and FBI. If they had, it may not have gone unnoticed that in the days before the 9/11 attacks, trading in derivatives on both American Airlines and United Airlines stock had been unusually erratic, with the put-to-call ratio for the former reaching 6:1 and for the latter 25:1. A put option is a contract giving the buyer the right, but not the obligation, to sell a specified amount of an underlying security at a predetermined price, known as the strike price, within a specified timeframe. In theory, a put-to-call ratio should be about 1:1. The unusually high ratios seen in the airlines have led many researchers to postulate that the purchase of put options in the airlines' stocks may have been consistent with informed investors having prior knowledge of the attack, and

MARKET CONDUCT

having traded their positions in advance of it. Achieving a definitive conclusion on the issue was, however, complicated significantly by the fact that these transactions were often performed through shell companies based in offshore domiciles, which ensured that those who benefited from them were hidden behind an opaque screen that protected their anonymity and concealed their involvement in the financing of terrorism.

In the wake of 9/11, it thus began to dawn on policymakers that if stricter market conduct regulations were in place, the financial system could become a powerful extension of the state security apparatus, performing a pivotal function in monitoring illegal and terrorist activities. This realisation ushered in a new era of banking, in which the responsibilities of financial institutions have been significantly extended through, for example, anti-money laundering and combating the financing of terrorism regulations. Through these regulations, banks have been made responsible for investigating the origins of the funds that are transferred through their systems, and for flagging suspicious transactions, providing critical information to intelligence agencies in support of larger state efforts to detect and prevent criminal and terrorist activities.

Simultaneously, since 2010, the banking system has also played an increasingly important role in the global effort to prevent tax evasion and avoidance through the introduction of the Foreign Account Tax Compliance Act in the US, and the promulgation of intra-governmental Automatic Exchange of Information agreements throughout the world. The introduction of these laws followed startling admissions made in 2007 by Bradley Birkenfeld, a US-born banker working in Geneva at UBS, the largest bank in Switzerland. Birkenfeld provided US authorities with a detailed account of how he and his colleagues had been encouraged by their employer to routinely assist wealthy American clients by hiding their financial assets in opaque offshore trusts in tax havens such as Panama, Luxembourg, Singapore, Guernsey and various countries in the Caribbean. He described how false documentation was created to facilitate this process, generating millions of dollars in fees every year for the bank. "By concealing US clients' ownership and control in the assets held offshore, [UBS] managers and bankers... defrauded the IRS [Internal Revenue Service] and evaded US income tax," read Birkenfeld's official court statement. In 2008, suspecting that as many as 52,000 US-based clients were using UBS accounts to hide nearly $20 billion in assets, the US Department of Justice (DOJ) charged UBS with conspiring to defraud US authorities by impeding the activities of the IRS between 2001 and 2008. The following year, UBS settled the case by admitting to criminal wrongdoing in selling offshore banking services that enabled tax evasion, and agreeing to pay a $780 million fine. A year later, in 2010, Birkenfeld was convicted of conspiracy to defraud the US, and sentenced to forty months in a federal penitentiary – and two-and-a-half years after that, within weeks of his early release from jail, it was announced he would receive a $104 million reward from the IRS's Whistleblower Office for his contribution to uncovering the tax sandal. It was the largest whistleblower reward issued to any individual at the time. Meanwhile, after much contestation, UBS also agreed to hand over the details of some of its American clients with undisclosed Swiss bank accounts – an unprecedented concession for a Swiss bank with a long and proud history of protecting client confidentiality.

MARKET CONDUCT

Since the 1700s, Switzerland's fierce protection of banking secrecy had afforded it a certain gravitas among its wealthy European customers, who wished to keep their financial activities hidden. By the turn of the 20th century, this was a service that Swiss banks actively marketed to international customers. In an advertisement distributed in France in 1910, shortly after France increased its inheritance tax rates, for example, Swiss banks openly publicised that the regulatory environment in Switzerland "enables us to manage with the utmost discretion securities entrusted to our care by customers from abroad". The percentage change of the collective assets held by Swiss banks compared to French banks in subsequent years illustrates just how attractive this offer was: in 1913, the collective assets held by Swiss banks amounted to just 26% of those held by French banks, but by 1929, this number had increased to 73%. More broadly, in the wake of World War I, Swiss banks became an increasingly desirable option for high-net-worth individuals who wished to hide their financial assets from government investigations in their home countries, or who simply wanted to move their investments into a country with more economic stability.

In 1934, this centuries-long commitment to bank secrecy was codified with the passage of the Swiss Federal Act on Banks and Savings Banks, which made it a criminal offence for a Swiss bank to disclose any information on its clients without their consent or an accepted criminal complaint. The Act, at its core, created the concept of banker-client privilege, which, much like attorney-client privilege, assured bank clients of complete confidentiality. Most importantly, as far as the US was concerned, it also prohibited Swiss financial institutions from taking instruction from a foreign government seeking information on its citizens, and made it a crime for an individual to divulge business-related information to a foreign government. Popular accounts suggest that the law was initially passed with the honourable purpose of protecting the banking assets of those being persecuted by the Nazis, as it had followed Germany's passing of a law in 1933 – the same year Adolf Hitler was appointed chancellor of Germany – requiring all citizens of the Nazi regime to declare their foreign assets. More critical explanations postulate that the Act was always intended to attract foreign capital, legitimising bank secrecy to mould Switzerland's image as the most competitive wealth management centre in the world. Whatever the reasoning, the propensity for the Act to be used for more iniquitous purposes soon became apparent – before the end of World War II, Swiss banks were routinely hiding the financial assets of Nazis themselves, funnelling looted Jewish money through their accounts to supporters all over the world, and extending credit to the Axis powers.

Combined with Switzerland's political neutrality, social stability, sound economic policy, low levels of inflation and strong currency, bank secrecy laws made the country a highly desirable haven in the decades that followed for those wishing to hide assets, launder money or avoid taxes. In the latter case, Swiss banks became a particularly attractive option to individuals from the US, which requires all citizens, even those living abroad, to pay taxes on their income, wherever it may be derived. In 1970, taking the view that bank secrecy ultimately facilitates criminality, the US passed the Bank Secrecy Act, under which US financial institutions could be compelled to provide client information to local law enforcement authorities during criminal investigations. Under Swiss law, however, neither the Swiss nor the US government could access individuals' financial information directly from Swiss banks. This meant that they had to rely on citizens to

MARKET CONDUCT

accurately report their own tax-related information, spawning many opportunities to hide money in Swiss bank accounts. Although several treaties and agreements relating to the exchange of tax information in criminal cases were reached between the US and Switzerland in the period from 1973 to 2009, differing definitions of what constituted tax fraud rendered the agreements practically ineffectual. By 2008, it was estimated that $2.2 trillion, or roughly one-third of all global cross-border assets at the time, was safely concealed in Swiss banks.

In the process of reaching its settlement agreement with the Department of Justice in 2009, UBS initially refused to divulge the details of its American clients. After much negotiation, it agreed to provide the names of only 250 individuals who had committed tax fraud according to the narrow Swiss Criminal Code definition, which related to "affirmative acts of fraud or deception". The Swiss government forbade the bank from disclosing any other information but, under relentless pressure from US authorities, it ultimately capitulated, agreeing to allow UBS to provide the names of 4,450 American account holders that were suspected by the IRS of evading taxes. This would signal the beginning of the end for absolute Swiss bank secrecy.

The UBS scandal followed five months after details had emerged of how thousands of wealthy European and American customers had made use of Liechtenstein-based bank LGT to similarly evade billions of dollars in taxes, prompting further investigations by Germany, the UK and the US. As a result of the close succession of the two scandals, and the prolonged period of negotiation that followed the US's requests for account-holder information from UBS, the US launched a full-scale investigation in 2008, which concluded that the country was losing an estimated $100 billion in tax revenue per year due to offshore tax evasion. The US responded with the introduction of the Foreign Account Tax Compliance Act (FATCA), promulgated under President Barack Obama in 2010 as part of the Hiring Incentives to Restore Employment Act. Under FATCA, all American citizens, whether they live in the US or abroad, are required to file annual reports on any foreign account holdings they have and pay any taxes due on them, as are all US businesses that invest, operate or otherwise earn taxable income overseas. According to the Act, these revenues would be used to pay for incentives that were offered to businesses to increase their employment rates in the aftermath of the Global Financial Crisis.

Most importantly, under FATCA, it became a requirement for foreign financial institutions – including banks, wealth management firms, trust companies and insurers – to conduct a due diligence and verification process to identify the residency status of their clients. They are also required to register with the IRS and send periodic reports containing the identities of US citizens who hold accounts with them in these foreign locations, as well as details on the dividends, interest and other income that are credited to those accounts. Non-compliant institutions are subject to a 30% withholding tax on US-derived income emanating from, for example, interest, dividends, the disposition of US securities and pass-through payments. In addition, any foreign bank that fails to disclose the required information on its American clients – which includes natural persons, as well as partnerships, corporations, estates and trusts – faces exclusion from the US financial markets. This would effectively cut them off from the most dominant economy in the world and from the US dollar, the

MARKET CONDUCT

de facto currency of global trade. In an unparalleled development in the age of globalisation, the US has effectively succeeded in creating a law that the governments and banks of other countries are compelled to comply with, not because of the threat of legal penalties, but based solely on the power of American hegemony and the risk of exclusion from its markets. Upon its initial promulgation, the US was also under no obligation to reciprocate by providing tax information to foreign countries as it related to their citizens who held bank accounts in the US.

The introduction of FATCA was not well-received in Switzerland. "The American authorities are trying to use the banks as guardians of the clients' conscience, which is not really what we're here for," Michel Dérobert, secretary general of the Swiss Private Bankers Association in Geneva, told the press when questioned about FATCA. "Priests are better for that."

In response to Swiss resistance to FATCA, the DOJ pursued cases against a further fourteen Swiss banks that it alleged had assisted American clients to avoid paying taxes. The most significant of these turned out to be a case involving the relatively small Wegelin & Co, Switzerland's oldest bank, founded in 1741. In 2013, Wegelin pleaded guilty to having aided American citizens in evading taxes totalling at least $1.2 billion for nearly a decade. The bank agreed to pay $57.8 million to the US in restitution and fines, but the reputational damage of the indictment proved to be more detrimental than the financial penalty. Within a year, Wegelin had filed for bankruptcy. The failure of the bank prompted Switzerland to negotiate a non-prosecution agreement with the US in late 2013, under which Swiss banks voluntarily disclosed undeclared US assets on their books and paid related penalties, in a bid to "enable every Swiss bank that

[was] not already under criminal investigation to find a path to resolution". This set the stage for Switzerland's acquiescence to full compliance with FATCA, which occurred the following year. When questioned by the press about the agreement, Zeno Staub, CEO of Zurich-based Vontobel Asset Management, stressed how important it was for Swiss financial institutions to maintain a good relationship with US authorities. "The US is simply too big, too wealthy and too important," he stated.

By 2014, the US had reached intergovernmental agreements with 26 countries to implement FATCA. As of 2023, 113 countries are either completely compliant with the Act, or have agreed to work towards compliance. In this process, governments can opt to follow one of two models. In the first and most-used model, financial institutions channel American account-holder information to their national tax authorities, which hold automatic exchange of information agreements with the IRS, allowing for the systematic periodic transmission of taxpayer information. In the second model – chosen by Switzerland – financial institutions are required to send their US clients' tax data directly to the IRS after obtaining consent from their customers to do so. In cases where this consent is not provided, Swiss financial institutions are still required to report aggregate account-holder information to the IRS, which may then submit a request to the Swiss Federal Tax Administration for individual-level information. Under the agreement, Swiss financial institutions are protected from prosecution by their own government in instances where compliance with FATCA results in a violation of bank secrecy laws, which otherwise remain in effect.

Following the US's lead, at the 2013 G20 Summit in Russia, world leaders reached an agreement on sharing tax data that was formalised

MARKET CONDUCT

in 2014 through the establishment of the Standard for Automatic Exchange of Financial Information in Tax Matters. In an effort to enhance transnational financial transparency, this standard provided a single framework for facilitating the exchange of information between the tax authorities of different countries. Initially, this included the 38 members of the Organisation for Economic Co-operation and Development, but by 2023, a total of 114 jurisdictions had joined the pact, with another nine committing to meeting the standard by 2026. The standard stipulates common due diligence procedures that must be followed by financial institutions and provides for the annual automatic exchange of financial account information between participating jurisdictions. Although the US is not formally listed as a participating country, it has implemented the standard as part of its FATCA-based intergovernmental agreements, acknowledging the need for equivalent levels of reciprocal automatic information exchange with its partner jurisdictions.

The introduction of new market conduct and tax regulations for financial institutions has been accompanied by a reshuffling of the financial services regulatory structure in many countries. Historically, in most regions, a sectoral model of regulation dominated, resulting in banks being regulated separately from other kinds of financial institutions, such as insurance companies. In 1995, Dr Michael Taylor, an official with the Bank of England, first suggested that this model had become outdated, given the overlap that was frequently occurring in the work of different regulators. He proposed what is known as the Twin Peaks structure for regulation in the financial industry: one regulator to oversee prudential regulation – which is

89

concerned with the technical, financial stability of institutions – and one regulator for ensuring adequate market conduct and consumer protection. Both regulators would be responsible for banks and other financial institutions.

Since the Global Financial Crisis, the Twin Peaks model has been widely adopted around the world, with different countries currently in differing stages of its implementation. Crucially, the introduction of the Twin Peaks model has signalled a global recognition of the dual functions of financial institutions in the 21st century, which are now not only responsible for managing their own credit and liquidity levels, but which have also been progressively coerced into becoming extensions of the state in the larger fight to combat criminality and terrorism. While the case can be made against the imposition of market conduct and tax-related regulations on banks as private enterprises, it is superseded by the simple fact that, without financial institutions performing this crucial function, criminal and terrorist activities around the world would be amplified. From a geopolitical and economic standpoint, the argument is perhaps even more compelling: countries that fail to conform to international market conduct and tax-reporting standards will face significant impediments to doing business with compliant countries, becoming pariahs in an ever-more interconnected global financial landscape.

CREDIT SUISSE

At around 10pm on 21 April 2013, a vehicle pulled up in front of a police station in Sofia, the capital city of Bulgaria, and hastily ejected a ten-year-old girl, leaving her standing alone as it sped away into the night. Bewildered, but unharmed, the girl was immediately identified as Lara Banev, the daughter of Bulgarian wrestler Evelin "Brendo" Banev; she had been missing for more than a month after she was kidnapped outside her home by three masked men. Her abduction had garnered massive press coverage, occurring while her father stood accused in both Bulgaria and Italy of heading a drug cartel involved in trafficking cocaine between South America and Europe. The case had been shrouded with suggestions of clandestine links between the cartel and prominent Bulgarian politicians, leading to much conjecture that the kidnapping had been a warning to Banev, cautioning him against revealing anything incriminating to investigators. In the end, his daughter was safely returned after a ransom of half a million euro was paid, and the charges against him were dropped due to insufficient evidence. The case was reopened in 2018, but Banev – the "Cocaine King", as he was known to the Sofian press – disappeared before he could be detained. He was found guilty in absentia in both countries, and placed on Interpol's most-wanted list. In 2021, he was arrested in Ukraine, though attempts to extradite him proved futile as he held Ukrainian citizenship. Less than a year later, Banev's name resurfaced in the press, appearing side by side with that of banking behemoth Credit Suisse, when it became the first Swiss-domiciled bank to be criminally charged for failing to prevent the laundering of drug money.

In June 2022, Credit Suisse was found guilty by Switzerland's Federal Criminal Court of accepting millions of Swiss francs (SFr) in deposits between 2004 and 2008 from a group of Bulgarian clients who were registered as real estate entrepreneurs, but who were, it transpired, members of the drug cartel headed by Brendo Banev. Elena Pampoulova-Bergomi, a former Bulgarian tennis star who worked as a relationship manager at the bank at the time, was personally charged with money laundering offences after it emerged that she had routinely collected suitcases filled with large sums of cash from individuals who were known to be part of the cocaine syndicate. Once deposited at the bank, the funds were used to buy real estate in Bulgaria and Switzerland. For failing to flag or investigate what the court ruled were clearly suspicious transactions, Credit Suisse was ordered to pay a cumulative sum of SFr21 million (about $22 million) in fines and compensation to the Swiss government.

This case marked only the beginning of the reputational damage that Credit Suisse would suffer in 2022. That same year, in what became known as the "Suisse Secrets" scandal, documents were leaked to the press by an employee of the bank that provided the account details of 30,000 Credit Suisse clients, many of them linked to

CREDIT SUISSE

criminal activities, including human and drug trafficking, corporate fraud and tax evasion. Among these clients were also several dictators from autocratic regimes across the globe. Credit Suisse responded by arguing that many of the cases dated to a time before banks were required to adhere to market conduct regulations, adding that several of the accounts had since been closed. But this response did little to restore the bank's credibility in the eyes of the public, who were only too aware that it had been the same commitment to Swiss banking secrecy that had, a century before, led Credit Suisse and other Swiss banks to hold accounts for many members of the Nazi party.

The Suisse Secrets scandal highlighted the incongruity of the Swiss regulatory environment: philosophically, it still clings to a bygone era of banking secrecy, but at the same time it attempts to meet the demands of international market conduct and automatic exchange of information regulations that prioritise the need for increased transparency. The bank secrecy laws first introduced in Switzerland in 1934 remain in effect, and were even extended in 2015. This followed the leak of UBS's American account-holder information in 2007, as well as a series of smaller leaks that occurred in the years that followed, involving the divulgence of bank account-holder information to the German and French tax authorities. Today, not only do individuals and institutions who inappropriately disclose bank client information face criminal prosecution, but any third party that makes use of such information can also be charged with violating bank secrecy laws, facing up to five years in jail for doing so. In the case of Suisse Secrets, the Swiss press was obliged to ignore the leaked data or face criminal sanctions if they published anything on it, and it was therefore thanks to the international media that the story came to light. This ignited a wave of anger among Swiss journalists, who raised concerns over the degree to which bank secrecy laws violate freedom of speech in one of the most liberal democracies in the world. This is especially true in cases where the disclosure of bank information by whistleblowers is deemed to be in the public interest, potentially placing bank secrecy at odds with international human rights laws.

Despite its fierce protection of bank secrecy, Switzerland has taken steps to strengthen its adherence to market conduct regulations. This follows a review in 2016 by the Financial Action Task Force (FATF), the intergovernmental organisation that oversees the development and implementation of policies regarding anti-money laundering, combating the financing of terrorism, and countering of proliferation financing. The FATF acknowledged "the generally good quality" of the Swiss financial system in terms of its ability to guard against misuse by criminal or terrorist agents; it did, however, also identify some regulatory weaknesses, prompting the Swiss government to pass a revision to its Federal Act on Combating Money Laundering and Terrorist Financing in the Financial Sector in 2021. Among other things, the Act stipulates the specific circumstances under which Swiss financial institutions are permitted to share client information. The new provisions, which only came into effect at the beginning of 2023, focus most significantly on strengthening the legal obligation of financial intermediaries to identify the beneficiaries of any accounts they manage, and to ensure that this information remains up to date. Despite these advances, Switzerland has faced consistent criticism for taking a passive approach to market conduct regulation, implementing and strengthening its policies only when placed under international pressure to do so.

This pressure has mounted significantly in the 21st century, following a string of Swiss banking scandals, many of which involved

CREDIT SUISSE

Credit Suisse. In 2014, in the same year Switzerland yielded to the US in its acceptance of the Foreign Account Tax Compliance Act, Credit Suisse pleaded guilty to conspiring to help Americans file false tax returns. In 2017, it paid SFr5.3 billion ($5.3 billion) to the US Department of Justice to settle allegations related to its conduct in the packaging, securitisation, issuance, marketing and sale of residential mortgage-backed securities in the lead-up to the Global Financial Crisis. As part of its broader campaign to hold financial institutions responsible for their role in the Crisis, the DOJ found that Credit Suisse had made false and irresponsible representations of the risk associated with these securities, on which investors, including federally insured financial institutions, had subsequently lost billions of dollars.

In 2019, things took an almost cinematic turn when news of a spying scandal at the bank broke, prompted by a dramatic car chase through the streets of Zurich as investigators, hired by Credit Suisse, tailed the bank's head of wealth management, Iqbal Khan. Khan was leaving the bank following a personal fallout with Credit Suisse CEO Tidjane Thiam. The two men owned neighbouring properties on the shores of Lake Zurich, and Khan's ambitious construction plans threatened to block Thiam's views of the lake. Khan had subsequently accepted a position at Swiss competitor UBS, and his employer, reportedly concerned that he may try to poach Credit Suisse employees and clients, hired private detectives to follow him. Further inquiries revealed that this was not an isolated event, with the Swiss Financial Market Supervisory Authority (FINMA) finding that the bank had orchestrated espionage operations on seven of its executives between 2016 and 2019, due to similar concerns about employee and client poaching. Although Swiss banks had fought for years against the institution of regulations that compromised the sanctity of the country's bank secrecy laws by requiring them to monitor their clients more closely, Credit Suisse apparently had few qualms about violating the privacy of its own employees.

In an obvious attempt by the bank to signal to the public that a cultural change was afoot, Thiam stepped down as CEO and was replaced by Thomas Gottstein in February 2020. It would prove to be a signal with little substance, however, with Credit Suisse buckling under a torrent of controversy the following year. In February 2021, a senior banker named Patrice Lescaudron was found guilty of defrauding some of the bank's most prominent customers, including former Georgian prime minister Bidzina Ivanishvili and Russian oligarch Vitaly Malkin. For more than a decade, Lescaudron had used these misbegotten funds on a prolonged personal spending spree that included luxury houses, sports cars, Rolex watches and Chanel jewellery. He received a prison sentence for the crime, and Credit Suisse attempted to distance itself from the case by arguing that it could not be held responsible for the actions of a lone rogue actor. This argument was strongly undermined by a report compiled by FINMA's lawyers, which alleged that the bank had been made aware of the suspicious transactions in question but had failed to act on the evidence.

The following month, Credit Suisse suffered losses related to the collapse of London-based specialist finance firm Greensill Capital. With offices all over the world, Greensill primarily offered supply-chain finance services; that is, the company mediated payments between business suppliers and buyers, charging fees to pay suppliers on behalf of the bank's customers, the buyers in the transaction, who would in turn repay Greensill. To generate more profit on the

CREDIT SUISSE

transactions, Greensill was using supplier invoices as short-term assets, placing them into funds that investors could buy. The funds were sold through Credit Suisse, which persuaded a thousand of its wealthiest clients to invest, assuring them of princely returns at almost no risk. The firm collapsed in March 2021 after credit insurers withdrew cover, owing to concerns related to its exposure to the steel and commodities tycoon Sanjeev Gupta's GFG Alliance. Credit Suisse consequently lost some SFr9.3 billion ($10.3 billion) in client funds. A report later released by FINMA found that the bank had "seriously breached its supervisory obligations… with regard to risk management and appropriate organisational structures".

A few weeks later, the bank lost a further SFr5.1 billion ($5.5 billion) in a trade involving Archegos Capital, which collapsed in 2022 when its founder, Bill Hwang, was indicted and arrested on federal charges of fraud and racketeering. This marked the bank's largest trading loss in its 167-year history. An internal investigation subsequently concluded that there had been a "fundamental failure of management and controls" in Credit Suisse's investment banking arm, and a pervasive "lackadaisical attitude towards risk".

Scandal continued to plague the bank, which in October 2021 paid a settlement amount of SFr442 million ($475 million) to US and UK authorities to resolve issues related to some SFr1.2 billion in loans that it had provided to the Mozambican government between 2012 and 2016. These loans were intended to support the development of the country's tuna fishing industry, but investigations revealed that most of this money had been diverted in kickbacks to local officials and to the bankers involved in arranging the deal. The discovery of this mismanagement prompted other donors to withdraw their support of the project, which had been intended to boost the economy of one of the poorest nations in Africa. The loss of this project cost Mozambique an estimated $400 per citizen, equivalent to the country's entire gross domestic product in 2016. As a result of these scandals, the Credit Suisse share price dropped by 75% between 2011 and 2021.

In January 2022, just a few months prior to the Suisse Secrets leak, the bank underwent another change of leadership, with Gottstein replaced by former UBS executive Ulrich Körner, who was charged with developing a plan that would turn the bank's fortunes around and restore confidence in the institution. In October of that year, the CEO announced that the bank would focus primarily on boosting its more conservative wealth management arm, while unwinding much of its riskier investment banking operations. In addition, the bank intended to halt share buybacks, cut dividends, reduce its costs by roughly SFr1 billion ($1.1 billion) – with a large portion of this coming from job cuts – and raise SFr4 billion in capital to finance its restructuring. SFr2.24 billion was ultimately raised in a rights offer to existing shareholders, with a relatively small number of shares sold in the market. The balance was funded in private placements with Middle Eastern investors, most notably Saudi National Bank (SNB), Credit Suisse's largest investor, which purchased a 9.9% stake in the bank, and the Qatar Investment Authority, which gained a 5.6% stake. In January 2023, this was increased to 6.9%, making the Qatar Investment Authority the second-largest investor.

Before the plan could be announced, however, rumours began to circulate on Twitter over the first weekend of October that the bank was on the verge of collapse. "Markets are saying it's insolvent and

CREDIT SUISSE

probably bust. 2008 moment soon?" tweeted Jim Lewis, an amateur investor who posted under the moniker Wall Street Silver to an audience of over 300,000 followers. These fears were reiterated by other users, who began to discuss shorting Credit Suisse stock. The following Monday morning, the bank's shares – which had already fallen by more than 50% since the beginning of the year – dropped another 11.5%, and its bonds plummeted to record lows before rebounding slightly by the end of the day. Spreads on Credit Suisse credit default swaps also rose sharply, indicating growing investor concerns, despite reassurances from the bank that its liquidity position was sound.

With the bank's reputation undeniably stained by the string of scandals that had played out over the previous two years, the tweets pushed what was already a precarious situation into a panic, and customers began to withdraw their funds. As both a wealth management firm and a deposit-taking institution, Credit Suisse was vulnerable to two types of outflows, in the form of customer deposits, which are used to extend loans, and customer assets, which cannot be used for loan purposes. During the final quarter of 2022, some SFr111 billion ($119 billion) in customer assets was withdrawn, equivalent to 8% of Credit Suisse's assets under management at the time. By December 2022, Credit Suisse's share price had hit a new low of SFr2.77. The bank's market capitalisation, which had stood at SFr31 billion at the start of 2021 and dropped to SFr23 billion in January 2022, plunged to a low of SFr12 billion by January 2023, roughly the same as that of an average regional bank in the US. UBS, by comparison, had a market capitalisation of about SFr47 billion at the time.

Seeking to calm the panic and reassure the bank's customers, Credit Suisse chair Axel Lehmann had told the media on 1 December 2022 that customer outflows had "completely flattened out" and "basically stopped". When the bank released its financial results the following February, however, it was evident that these outflows had continued throughout December 2022 and into January 2023, albeit at a slower pace than in October and November. This prompted an investigation by FINMA into Lehmann's comments, though the Swiss regulator ultimately concluded that there were insufficient grounds to pursue supervisory proceedings against the Credit Suisse chair.

Of more concern in the financial results were the reported loss figures: in 2022, the bank had suffered its largest annual loss since the Global Financial Crisis, including a loss of SFr1.4 billion ($1.5 billion) in the fourth quarter, taking its annual loss for the year to a total of SFr7.3 billion. Alongside this, Credit Suisse was forced to delay the release of its annual report after the bank's auditor, PwC, identified weaknesses in the bank's internal controls. These related in particular to the classification and presentation of non-cash items in the consolidated statements of cash flows, which had resulted in its balance sheet and cash flow positions being understated since 2019. The findings prompted an inquiry by the US Securities and Exchange Commission, which demanded more information before the report was published. On its release, Credit Suisse indicated its agreement with the auditor, stating that "management did not design and maintain an effective risk assessment process to identify and analyse the risk of material misstatements in its financial statements". It added that it was in the process of addressing the weaknesses identified, with a plan that would focus on strengthening its risk and control frameworks.

These statements did little to pacify its investors and customers. On the day the report was released, 14 March 2023, Credit Suisse's

CREDIT SUISSE

share price dropped to SFr2.30, sparking significant selloffs in the bank's stock amid larger global panic related to the failure of Silicon Valley Bank, Signature Bank and ultimately First Republic in the US. With the bank's equity and bonds dropping to unprecedented lows, a fatal blow was dealt the following day, when Ammar Al Khudairy, the chair of Saudi National Bank, informed the press that his bank would not be providing any additional financial assistance to Credit Suisse – this coming less than a year after its significant investment in the bank. Two weeks later, Al Khudairy resigned his position citing personal reasons; the international press speculated that he had been compelled to leave as punishment for drawing unnecessary attention to SNB amid Credit Suisse's decline. Six months later, in early September 2023, the head of FINMA, Urban Angehrn, would resign from his post, citing "permanent stress levels" that had taken a significant toll on his health. He had been the head of the Swiss regulator for less than two years at the time of his resignation.

On the same day Al Khudairy confirmed that SNB would not be increasing its investment in Credit Suisse, FINMA and the Swiss National Bank released a joint statement, assuring investors that Credit Suisse met the higher capital and liquidity requirements for a global systemically important bank. Moreover, they added, the Swiss National Bank would provide a SFr50 billion ($54 billion) liquidity backstop to the bank, if necessary – but this all failed to calm the crisis of confidence. By the end of the week, Credit Suisse's shares had dropped to SFr1.85 – an overall decrease of 85% since the start of 2021 – in a downward spiral from which it would not recover. Depositors continued to withdraw their money, culminating in total outflows of SFr61.2 billion for the first quarter of 2023. Conceptually, this was not unlike the bank runs of the pre-digital era that had seen customers stampeding into failing banks to withdraw their money, as in the cases of Stockholms Banco and Banque Royale centuries before.

With the situation having become unsalvageable, Swiss president Alain Berset addressed the press regarding Credit Suisse on Sunday 19 March. "On Friday the liquidity outflows and market volatility showed it was no longer possible to restore market confidence, and a swift and stabilising solution was absolutely necessary," he stated. "This solution was the takeover of Credit Suisse by UBS."

With the collapse of Credit Suisse threatening to destabilise Switzerland's entire banking system and further disrupt international markets after the SVB-related crisis in the US, a deal was hastily brokered by Swiss regulators between Credit Suisse and its long-time rival, UBS. UBS agreed to buy Credit Suisse for SFr3 billion ($3.25 billion), paying roughly SFr0.76 a share – less than half the closing price of Credit Suisse's stock the Friday before the deal was made. The Swiss government issued an emergency ordinance to waive any regulatory and governance requirements that would stall the closing of the transaction and, to further sweeten the deal, the Swiss National Bank also agreed to provide a SFr100 billion liquidity line backed by a federal default guarantee to UBS.

Established in 1856 as Schweizerische Kreditanstalt and later rebranded with what would become one of the most recognisable names in global banking, Credit Suisse had long been regarded as one of the most stable pillars of the Swiss banking system, and a critical facilitator in driving Switzerland's economic growth in the late 19th and throughout the 20th century. It was because of Credit

CREDIT SUISSE

Suisse that the rail system that links Switzerland to trading cities and ports in both northern and southern Europe came into being; that the country's electrical grid was developed; and that the Alpine nation could support efforts to rebuild in the aftermath of World War II. The famed sanctity of Swiss banking secrecy further bolstered the attractiveness of the country's banks for international depositors, but this once-coveted confidentiality and discretion would ultimately be the undoing of Credit Suisse.

The bank's story demonstrates the severe moral shortcomings of these ideas when they are adopted to an extreme degree, especially in a modern world where the values of transparency and equality are prioritised. Forgoing any moral grounding in favour of an extreme version of capitalism is simply no longer a position banks can afford to take if they wish to build and maintain the trust of their customers.

THE SOUTH AFRICAN A2 BANKING CRISIS

In May 2001, in the "Businessman of the Week" section of *Beeld*, a South African daily newspaper, there appeared a glowing profile of Jeff Levenstein, the CEO of Regal Bank. A small bank with R1 billion ($125 million) in assets, Regal was, according to Levenstein, "the Investec of the new millennium". On 26 June 2001, just six weeks after the profile was published, the bank was taken into curatorship. In the intervening time, Levenstein had resigned as CEO under a shroud of controversy, and a devastating run on the bank had ensued. In the Commissioner's Report, published shortly after the bank's collapse, Levenstein was placed at the centre of Regal's failure. "Levenstein was not a fit and proper person to be a director and CEO of a bank or its holding company, and he carried on the business of the bank and Regal Holdings in a reckless manner," read the report. "Levenstein ran the bank with less sophistication than one would expect from the local fish-and-chips shop."

THE SOUTH AFRICAN A2 BANKING CRISIS

Regal Bank's doors first opened in 1996, and in 1999 the holding company, Regal Holdings, listed on the Johannesburg Stock Exchange (JSE). Very soon after, as the Commissioner's Report later revealed, Levenstein began manipulating the share price of the company in various ways. Almost as soon as the company's shares began trading publicly, Levenstein, aided by various members of Regal Holdings' board of directors, urged employees to borrow money from the bank to buy Regal shares. According to the South African Companies Act of 1973, this is clearly illegal; the Act stipulates that a company cannot provide financial assistance to employees for the purpose of purchasing any of its shares or shares of its holding company. Levenstein also instructed the holding company's "Incentive Trust" to buy shares off the open market, ostensibly to use as part of executives' remuneration packages. When employees wanted to sell shares, however, they were blocked from doing so – the result of an instruction that Levenstein had personally given to the finance department. The CEO also used various entities that he held influence over to buy Regal Holdings' shares, often instructing Regal Bank to lend companies money to do so. "Levenstein's main motivation for running the bank was not in the interest of its depositors, but rather to boost the holding company's share price," the Commissioner's Report concluded.

Following the collapse of Regal Bank in mid-2001, South African authorities charged Levenstein with eight counts of fraud and contravening the Companies Act. It would take eight years for justice to run its course. In 2009, following a prolonged court case throughout which Levenstein was allowed to live under house arrest, the Bloemfontein-based Supreme Court of Appeal found the ex-CEO guilty on all eight counts, and he was sentenced to fifteen years in prison for his crimes. He served the majority of his time at Zonderwater Correctional Centre in Cullinan, a small mining town in the Gauteng province of South Africa. In 2013, Levenstein's sentence was reduced to an effective eight years in prison, which meant he would be released in 2017 at the age of 66.

While the failure of Regal Bank was ultimately pinned on the criminality of one bad actor, the broader economic and regulatory conditions were – as is the case with many bank failures throughout history – already primed for a much wider banking crisis to unfold in the months following the bank's collapse. Regal Bank was, in this sense, a harbinger of a crisis that would shake the confidence of the South African banking industry to its core. In what would become formally known as the South African Small Banks Crisis of 2002/03 – though it was more commonly referred to as the A2 Banking Crisis, because the majority of those affected were A2-rated banks – 22 of the 47 banks operating in South Africa at the time would ultimately fail or deregister.

In the years preceding the A2 Banking Crisis, the US was in the midst of the dotcom bubble. It was a period in history that the chair of the Federal Reserve at the time, Alan Greenspan, portrayed as an era of "irrational exuberance", describing the largely unfounded market optimism that was pervasive throughout much of the 1990s. Billions of dollars of investments were flowing into IT firms and dotcom start-ups each year in the US, driving exponential growth in the stock market. As a result, between 1995 and 2000, the tech-heavy Nasdaq Index rocketed from a price level of under 1,000 to more than 5,000 as investors took on ever greater risks to chase ever diminishing returns.

THE SOUTH AFRICAN A2 BANKING CRISIS

The speculation was amplified by an environment of extreme tech optimism that seemed to nullify any logical argument for the otherwise implausible price-to-earnings ratios that these companies were garnering. This was true of the many dotcom companies that arrived on the scene, such as the memorable pets supply company Pets.com, which became a household name thanks to its high-profile marketing campaign and signature sock puppet mascot that made appearances in Super Bowl advertisements. Within two years of its establishment, it had been liquidated due to mismanagement. At the time, this was not uncommon and pointed to a larger trend: beneath the veneer of success of many companies, serious financial instability was looming. As businesses clambered to disguise just how precarious the situation was, there emerged a tacit acceptance of the complex financial and accounting techniques used to boost the appearance of companies' performance to attract more investment. Many of these practices were not technically illegal, but were nonetheless misleading to shareholders. Overall, there was a distinct shift in focus from business performance to company stock prices, which were boosted using any techniques available. The pursuit of free market ideals was being significantly overextended, producing a kind of hyper-capitalism in which the pursuit of profits and ever higher share prices was being justified by almost any means.

As inevitably transpires, and despite acolytes within each era of excessive exuberance claiming that "this time will be different", the dotcom bubble burst dramatically in April 2000. Having grown five-fold between 1995 and 2000, the Nasdaq Index tumbled from a peak of 5,050 in March 2000 to a low of 1,140 by October 2002, representing a decline of 77% in less than three years. In early 2001, as the market collapsed, the Federal Reserve, still under the leadership of Alan Greenspan, responded by rapidly lowering interest rates in an attempt to stabilise the economic environment and to help the market recover. Between January and December 2001, the Fed decreased the Federal Funds Rate from 6% to 1.75% – the lowest it had been since the 1960s.

When the US started lowering interest rates in early 2001, the South African Reserve Bank (SARB) saw it as an opportunity to likewise drop the country's interest rates, moving in lockstep with the US and thereby lowering the cost of money for the average South African consumer. This had been the SARB's policy for some time, since moving in a synchronised manner with US interest rates aided in preserving South African financial assets' relative attractiveness in the global market. This applied especially as it relates to carry trades, where investors seek to profit from higher interest in one country compared to another. Over the course of 2001, the SARB reduced the overnight policy rate, or repo rate, from 12% to 9.5%. While this decision was intended to preserve South Africa's general competitiveness in the international market, by guarding the export market against any undue pressure resulting from a weaker US dollar, it ironically resulted in a significant destabilisation of the South African rand.

As the SARB lowered interest rates – in a fearful global economic environment induced by the bursting of the dotcom bubble and aggravated by the 9/11 terrorist attacks in the US in 2001 – South African government bonds became relatively less attractive compared to safe-haven assets such as US Treasuries. As a result, the rand rapidly depreciated. A substantial outflow of foreign investment from South African assets ensued, with the perceived risk of these assets significantly increasing in relation to their perceived value. In response, the rand weakened dramatically against the US dollar, falling from R7.79 per dollar in January 2001 to R12.13 by December, a 56% depreciation in a single year. In combination, the decline in the rand's value and a generally gloomy global economic outlook put severe pressure on the South African banking industry.

In the latter half of the 1990s, many South African banks, especially the smaller A2 banks, had significantly increased their unsecured lending portfolios, primarily in the form of personal loans with no collateral, often granted to vulnerable consumers. This type of lending was highly profitable for banks, which could charge higher interest rates on unsecured loans, and was relatively low risk at the time due to the prevailing regulations. Until 2001, interest payments on unsecured loans were permitted to be deducted from government employees' payrolls prior to their salaries reaching their bank accounts. These "payroll loans" virtually guaranteed that banks would be paid the interest on these loans, and the market for this product grew massively in the late 1990s. In June 2001, however, this practice was halted by Minister of Finance Trevor Manuel, who noted that he was "gravely concerned at the low level of take-home pay of many employees", with almost 70,000 government employees taking home less than R600 a month, equivalent to less than $100 at the time. The extension of payroll loans to government employees, the minister noted, was a primary cause of the problem. The government's intervention significantly affected the profitability of the banks dealing in these loans, and substantially changed the risk-reward calculation of this practice. Despite this, the growth of unsecured lending still increased strongly throughout 2001. In particular, Saambou Bank and UniFer, the micro-lending subsidiary of the Absa Group, both had substantial exposure to this type of loan by early 2002.

In the years to that point, Saambou – the seventh-largest South African bank at the time – had grown its loan book substantially, mostly in the form of unsecured loans, with its personal loan portfolio increasing by 85% in the twelve months ending in March 2001. Signs of weakness at the bank started to emerge in October that year, however, when Saambou published a statement prior to the release of its interim results, noting that it expected to post a R5 million loss on its bottom line for the six months ending in September 2001. The losses, Saambou stated, were largely the result of a significant increase in loan loss provisions and R35 million in expenses related to setting up its "20twenty" internet banking initiative. Upon release of its interim results in late October, it was revealed that Saambou's loan loss provisions had more than doubled from the comparable period the year before, increasing from R110 million to R291 million.

The scrutiny of Saambou intensified shortly after the interim results were released, when news broke that the JSE would be investigating several of the bank's directors, including CEO Johan Myburgh, in relation to potential insider trading. On 15 August 2001, less than two months before the profit warning, Myburgh had sold 200,000 of his Saambou shares worth R2.4 million ($280,000) and representing 15% of his total stake in the bank. This occurred shortly after Charles Edward, the bank's executive director for personal banking, had sold 1.145 million shares, equating to R12.6 million. While the combination of insider trading allegations and growing concerns related to unsecured loan losses weighed heavily on Saambou's share price, which declined by 20% following the announcement of the JSE's probe, the majority of the bank's depositors were not yet panicking. This would change in mid-January the following year,

THE SOUTH AFRICAN A2 BANKING CRISIS

when an announcement by the Absa Group sent a shockwave of fear through the market.

On 15 January 2002, Absa revealed that its micro-lending subsidiary UniFer had understated its loan loss provisions for the six months ending in September 2001 by a staggering R1.5 billion, resulting in total loan loss provisions of R1.8 billion ($258 million) – more than six times the amount originally declared. Two months prior, UniFer had announced in an interim report that it had grown its loan book by 63%, from R3.4 billion to R5.6 billion, in the six months to September 2001. In the same report, the micro-lender stated that its provisions for loan losses in that period had more than doubled from same period the previous year, increasing from R106 million to R222 million. Despite this concerning increase in loan losses, UniFer's CEO, Gavin Kretzschmar, noted that the company's balance sheet was strong, saying to the press, "the group is solid". Just two months later, however, Absa, which held a 61% stake in UniFer, revealed that the micro-lender had grossly misrepresented the actual condition of its balance sheet, which was deteriorating at a rapid rate.

Following the announcement, the South African media quickly concluded that if UniFer was experiencing significant loan losses on its unsecured loans portfolio, other banks with similar exposures may be experiencing equally drastic losses on theirs. Various newspaper articles speculated that Saambou was facing a comparable deterioration in its assets, since its clientele overlapped significantly with UniFer's. Although Saambou still claimed that its financial position was secure and that it had capital levels well above regulatory requirements, many of its depositors had started to lose trust in the bank's leadership team. After the events of late 2001, including disastrous interim results and ongoing investigations into insider trading, the flurry of media speculation about the bank's instability pushed depositors over the edge.

In response to Absa's announcement, Saambou depositors started withdrawing their money, fearing the bank could be in an equally precarious position to UniFer. Ironically, the rush of withdrawals that ensued was accelerated by the fact that many of Saambou's more sophisticated customers, with larger balances and longer-term deposits, had moved onto the bank's newly created internet banking platform, allowing them to withdraw their deposits and give notice on their savings more easily than before. The effect was the same as that of a run, with long-term deposits falling drastically in the next few weeks. In the last fortnight of January 2002, Saambou's retail deposits fell by R861 million, equivalent to 9% of total retail deposits. By mid-February, the outflow of funds had reached over 20% of total retail deposits, with more than R1 billion being withdrawn in the span of just two days at the peak of the panic. From early February, Saambou's share price also started to drop. On 6 February alone, the share price declined by 46% during intraday trading. Throughout the month, deposits continued to be pulled from the bank, and Saambou's liquidity position became increasingly difficult to sustain.

To cover the widening liquidity gap and survive on a day-to-day basis, Saambou leaned heavily on the interbank lending market, quadrupling its short-term borrowing facilities from R250 million to R1 billion that February. But given the bank's rapidly deteriorating financial position, other banks became reluctant to roll over their short-term lending agreements with Saambou, fearing an imminent collapse. On Saturday 9 February, with other banks no longer willing to lend to Saambou on the interbank market and with

THE SOUTH AFRICAN A2 BANKING CRISIS

deposit withdrawals expected to continue, the SARB took the bank into curatorship. At the time of its collapse, Saambou had been in operation for sixty years.

Five days later, the finance minister made a statement rationalising the decision to refuse a bailout for Saambou. Committing any financial assistance to Saambou would "not be prudent", Manuel noted, since the bank's financial position was so weak that any attempt to prop it up would ultimately prove futile. The announcement signalled to the market that the SARB was unwilling to provide financial support to save smaller banks in the case of their imminent collapse. Six years later, a similar signal would be broadcast by US regulators, when they announced that they would not be bailing out Lehman Brothers in September 2008. In both cases, the decision sent panicked investors and depositors scrambling to safeguard their money, believing that their own banks would likely not be rescued in the event of a potential future failure. Bank runs on other South African A2 banking entities, including Board of Executors (BOE), TA Bank, Cadiz, FirstCorp, PSG Investment Bank and International Bank, followed in the weeks after the announcement.

Of these bank runs, the BOE run was the most devastating and the most systemically destabilising. One of the oldest banking institutions in the country, dating back to 1838, BOE was the fifth-largest bank in South Africa at the time, holding 6.5% of total banking assets. Between February and June 2002, depositors withdrew R10 billion ($1.3 billion) from the bank, equating to over 20% of total deposits. Taking a similar approach to Saambou prior to its collapse, BOE attempted to bolster its liquidity position with interbank borrowing, but in the fearful atmosphere that pervaded the market, this source of funding could not sustain it for long. Unlike Saambou, however,

113

when BOE was teetering on the edge of collapse in March 2002, the SARB stepped in to stabilise the much larger, more systemically important bank.

While the SARB propped up BOE with significant liquidity assistance and a full guarantee of its deposits, other smaller banks continued to crumble, including Brait Bank, Corp Capital, SECIB and Unibank. In total, almost half of all the banks operating in South Africa at the time deregistered between 2002 and early 2003, many being absorbed by the largest players in the industry, including Absa, FirstRand, Standard Bank and Nedbank. BOE eventually merged with Nedbank in early 2003, making it the largest bank to deregister as a result of the crisis. Overall, the merger was a success for the Nedbank Group, which increased its market share in the South African banking industry from 14% to 22% following the acquisition, thus securing its position as one of the biggest banking groups in the country for years to come.

Studies undertaken in the years following the South African A2 Banking Crisis have shown that – in contrast to the common perception of bank stability – those banks that failed held, on average, more capital than those banks that survived. This proved to some extent that in the case of severe economic distress, higher capital levels are not necessarily enough to save a bank from collapse. Instead, these studies identified that the level of short-term interbank lending that smaller banks used to fund their operations was a much stronger indicator of failure. In general, while there was little difference between the asset mix of these banks, it was the banks that relied most heavily on interbank funding on the liability side of

THE SOUTH AFRICAN A2 BANKING CRISIS

their balance sheets that ultimately failed. This phenomenon would be demonstrated again some years later, albeit on a much larger scale, in the failure of the UK's Northern Rock, which also relied heavily on short-term interbank funding. The Northern Rock bank run in September 2007 was the first bank run in the UK in 150 years, and proved to be an early warning sign of the devastation to come for the global banking industry in the years that followed.

When the dust had settled after the 2007/08 Global Financial Crisis, several studies echoed the insights revealed by the research that had analysed the bank failures of South Africa's A2 Banking Crisis. In one such study, which examined the financial statements of the 1,000 largest banks worldwide in 2007, researchers found that the banks that were more reliant on the interbank market prior to the Global Financial Crisis were the banks that would be more likely to fail during the Crisis. Of the 106 banks that failed or were bailed out worldwide in the period from 2008 to 2010, the study found that one ratio – customer loans to deposits – was a far clearer indicator of failure than any other.

In its liability structure, a bank depends on deposits made by customers – whether corporate or individual deposits – or interbank lending to meet its obligations. The inference can therefore be made that the higher the percentage of total loans to customer deposits, the more reliant banks are on the interbank market to meet this demand. In this way, the ratio of total loans to customer deposits serves as a proxy for a bank's reliance on interbank funding, as well as indicating to some degree which banks are likely to come under the greatest liquidity pressure in a particularly stressed economic scenario. Over the years, this stressed scenario has changed, but many of the same principles still apply.

WHY BANKS FAIL

In the Global Financial Crisis, the interbank market – essentially comprised of a small group of very interconnected traders who controlled, and to some extent continue to control, the amount of liquidity extended to individual banks – seized up completely. Panic and fear caused this handful of traders to stop rolling over funding to desperate banks. This caused dozens of banks, especially those highly reliant on the interbank market, to fail instantaneously. In recent years, the pervasive nature of technology, particularly in the form of social media and electronic banking, has added another element of risk to the banking system. Amplified by the power of social media, rumours and bad news travel faster than ever before, reaching millions of users across the globe at lightning speed. In addition, depositors can, if they so wish, instantly withdraw their funds from a bank with the click of a button, rather than queueing outside of their local bank branch or ATM. In this sense, technology has transformed the phenomenon of a bank run from being a physical event that may take days or weeks to play out, to an electronic event that can happen in a virtual instant. In 2023, this was the fate of SVB, with many of its large, well-informed depositors withdrawing their money from the bank electronically, spooked by rumours on Twitter that the bank may be facing liquidity problems.

In many ways, the manner in which the A2 Banking Crisis played out in 2002 was a precursor to what would occur five years later during the Global Financial Crisis. Once again, it would not be a lack of capital, but rather an acute paralysis of the interbank market, that would trigger the sudden death of some of the largest and most prestigious financial institutions across the world. And in many cases, it was those banks that relied most heavily on the interbank market for their survival that were crushed instantaneously under the pressure. In the years since the Crisis, banking regulators have focused their energy on raising capital requirements, as well as raising liquidity requirements through the introduction of the liquidity coverage ratio and the net stable funding ratio – but these efforts largely address the symptoms and not the underlying cause.

Perhaps, in an alternate universe, things may have turned out differently if Hank Paulson, Ben Bernanke and Timothy Geithner, the men at the helm of the US financial system for many years prior to and during the Global Financial Crisis, had taken a moment to learn the lessons from a small banking crisis that occurred in 2002, in a relatively small country with an economy roughly the size of Michigan's at the time. Or perhaps, as Geithner argues in his book *Stress Test: Reflections on Financial Crises*, published in 2014, regulators should not be judged too harshly by the public in times of crisis. No matter how many times they seem to get it wrong, "You can't judge a decision by how it turns out, only by whether it made sense given the information available at the time."

The problem with Geithner's assessment is that, in most cases, regulators *do* have the relevant information available to make the correct changes. Yet, time and again, they fail to do so, because the regulation of banking has become geopolitically fractured, excessively mathematical and technical, too focused on regulating for the symptoms of the last crisis, and in many cases politically entangled or, even worse, overly sensitive to the whims of the market. There is no clearer example of this than in the failure of the Federal Reserve to manage monetary policy in an effective manner since the Global Financial Crisis.

THE SOUTH AFRICAN GREYLISTING

In February 2023, South Africa was officially placed on the Financial Action Task Force's (FATF) list of "Jurisdictions Under Increased Monitoring", commonly known as the "grey list". Following a twelve-month monitoring period, South Africa and Nigeria were the two newest inclusions on the global money laundering and terrorist financing watchdog's list. They joined 24 other nations already there, including South Sudan, the Democratic Republic of Congo, Haiti, Mozambique, Syria and the Cayman Islands.

The countries on the grey list are those that the FATF has deemed to have "strategic deficiencies in their regimes to counter money laundering, terrorist financing and proliferation financing" – the latter related to the financing of the development and distribution of weapons of mass destruction, whether nuclear, chemical or biological. South Africa, which became a full member of the FATF in 2003, was just the third G20 nation to be placed on the grey list, following the inclusion of Argentina and Turkey in 2009 and 2021 respectively.

THE SOUTH AFRICAN GREYLISTING

While Argentina had made enough progress to be removed from the list in 2014, Turkey remained on at the time of South Africa's inclusion.

The FATF, or Groupe d'action financière (GAFI), was established at the G7 Summit in Paris in 1989 to address the growing problem of money laundering, particularly as it related to drug trafficking. Leaders of the G7 mandated this new task force with examining money laundering techniques and trends across the globe, reviewing the actions that had already been taken at a national and international level to combat money laundering, and defining the measures that needed to be taken. As an independent intergovernmental body, the FATF was not created to be a formal international organisation, such as the United Nations, but rather as a technical and policymaking body. To establish and maintain the operations of the task force, its members agreed to fund it through annual contributions, based on the relative size of each member country's economy. It was also decided that the FATF's secretariat – the permanent staff who manage its day-to-day operations – would be housed administratively at the headquarters of the Organisation for Economic Co-operation and Development (OECD) in Paris, though the FATF and the OECD are separate organisations.

At the time of its creation, the FATF had sixteen members. These included the 1989 G7 Summit participants, as well as eight additional countries to increase the FATF's reach. At first, its scope was limited to anti-money laundering, but its mandate was expanded to include combating the financing of terrorism in 2001, following the 9/11 terrorist attacks. In 2012, in response to the rising threat of the funding, development and propagation of weapons of mass destruction, emanating from countries such as Iran and North Korea, the FATF's mandate was expanded again to include the countering of proliferation financing. By 2023, the FATF was comprised of 36 member countries and two regional organisations: the European Commission and the Gulf Cooperation Council. The Russian Federation was previously a full member of the FATF, but its membership was finally suspended on 24 February 2023 – a full year after its invasion of Ukraine and, coincidentally, on the same day that South Africa was greylisted – with the FATF citing that Russia's "continuing and intensifying war of aggression against Ukraine" runs counter to its principles of promoting security.

As a key part of its mandate, the FATF has developed a series of guidelines for nations to follow, collectively known as the "FATF Recommendations", that are generally recognised as the global standard for anti-money laundering (AML), counter-terrorist financing (CTF) and counter-proliferation financing (CPF). In 1990, the FATF published its first report detailing these guidelines, containing forty recommendations in relation to AML best practices. Over the years, these guidelines have been updated and supplemented to form what has been called the "Forty Plus Nine Recommendations", including nine special proposals on global CTF and CPF standards. The FATF's recommendations specify legal, regulatory and operational measures for countries to detect, prevent and prosecute crimes related to money laundering, terrorist financing and the funding of weapons of mass destruction. In this sense, the FATF does not work at an institutional level to implement these measures, but rather at a national and international level, guiding countries in building a more robust national framework, within which individual institutions, including banks, public and private companies, and government agencies, must operate.

To promote the global adoption of the recommendations, in addition to its 36 country members, the FATF also relies heavily

THE SOUTH AFRICAN GREYLISTING

on its network of associate members. These associate members include international organisations such as the United Nations and the International Monetary Fund, as well as FATF-style regional bodies (FSRBs), which monitor the FATF's standards across their regions. These FSRBs include, among others, the Asia/Pacific Group on Money Laundering, the Financial Action Task Force of Latin America, the Middle East and North Africa Financial Action Task Force, and the Eastern and Southern Africa Anti-Money Laundering Group. In combination, the FATF global network spans more than 200 countries across the world.

The network of associate members plays an important role in the ongoing assessment of country-level compliance with the FATF's Forty Plus Nine Recommendations. In what are known as "Mutual Evaluations", the FATF works alongside member countries to conduct peer reviews, in conjunction with teams from associate members. The aim of a Mutual Evaluation process is to provide an in-depth analysis of a country's systems, benchmarked against the FATF's Recommendations, as well as to provide focused action points, or "Recommended Actions", to address deficiencies. In April 2019, South Africa began its third Mutual Evaluation, with previous assessments having occurred in 2003 and 2009.

South Africa's 2019 Mutual Evaluation assessment was led by a team from the IMF, assisted by officials from the Eastern and Southern Africa Anti-Money Laundering Group and representatives from other FATF member countries. Upon completion of the two-year process in May 2021, the FATF adopted the findings of the assessment and began compiling South Africa's Mutual Evaluation Report, which was released six months later. "The main domestic money laundering (ML) crime threats are consistently understood by the key authorities," noted the report, "but the understanding of their relative scale, ML vulnerabilities and the threats from foreign predicates is limited." As a result of South Africa's geographical location and status as a financial hub on the African continent, the report noted that the country has been, and continues to increasingly be, vulnerable to the threat of money laundering and terrorist financing activities, by both local and foreign entities. Additionally, the report highlighted that South Africa has a relatively high volume and intensity of crime, more than half of which generates financial proceeds for the entities involved in these crimes, primarily through tax evasion, bribery, corruption, fraud and the trafficking of illegal goods.

In total, the Mutual Evaluation Report of October 2021 detailed 67 Recommended Actions for South Africa to strengthen its national systems, processes and institutions. A key area that required significant corrective action was South Africa's systems and processes associated with the identification and monitoring of beneficial ownership. This relates to the recognition of a person who ultimately benefits from the ownership of a commercial entity, such as a company or a financial asset, even if the entity is not registered in that person's name. In terms of combating money laundering, the misrepresentation of beneficial ownership, often through the use of shell companies and complex financial structures, has over time allowed criminals and sanctioned individuals to conceal the proceeds of their crimes from authorities. A prominent example of the problem arose in Antigua in 2022, when the beneficial owner of an 81-metre superyacht that had been abandoned for months in Falmouth Harbour could not be identified. As authorities attempted to work out who in fact owned it, the

THE SOUTH AFRICAN GREYLISTING

yacht piled up hundreds of thousands of dollars of costs for docking and maintenance, which was ultimately paid for by the Antiguan government. With an estimated value of over $80 million, the vessel was rumoured to be owned by Russian oligarch Andrey Guryev, one of many superyachts that were discovered in a global hunt for sanctioned oligarchs' assets following the invasion of Ukraine.

Several other weaknesses were also identified in South Africa's law enforcement and legal systems in relation to identifying, charging and convicting entities for financial crimes. Specifically, the report noted that South Africa had "suffered from a sustained period of state capture, which helped to generate substantial corruption proceeds, and undermined key agencies with roles to combat such activity". It also stated that compared to its risk profile, the nation's conviction rate of money launderers was low, again citing that "ML cases relating to state capture have not been sufficiently pursued". On something of a positive note, in what was otherwise a sobering assessment, the report recognised that South Africa's large banks fundamentally understood their money laundering risks and were largely compliant with global standards. The report also noted, however, that the nation's smaller financial institutions, in general, "are focused on compliance, not on identifying and understanding risks". Following the publication of the Mutual Evaluation Report, South Africa was granted one year to make substantial progress in implementing the Recommended Actions set out by the FATF. Failure to adequately address the deficiencies identified by the report would result in South Africa being greylisted.

Since 2000, the FATF has maintained both a grey list and a black list that identifies countries that have been deemed to have weak measures to combat money laundering, terrorist financing and proliferation financing. The organisation publishes an update of each

123

list three times a year. For countries on the black list, officially called "High-Risk Jurisdictions Subject to a Call for Action", the FATF calls on all members to apply enhanced diligence and counter-measures to protect themselves and other nations from their ongoing operational deficiencies s. These nations are identified as a serious threat to the safety of the international financial system and are not actively engaged with the FATF in addressing their deficiencies. As of 2023, there were just three countries on the black list – North Korea, Iran and Myanmar – each of which has been shut out of the international financial system, essentially becoming economic pariahs. In comparison, countries on the grey list are considered to have weaknesses in their AML, CTF and CPF systems but are recognised as actively working with the FATF to address these shortcomings, and are therefore subject to increased monitoring. As of June 2023, the FATF had reviewed 125 countries and placed 98 of these nations either on their grey list or black list. Of these 98 countries, 72 had successfully enacted the necessary reforms to rectify their vulnerabilities by June 2023, resulting in their removal from the lists. One such nation was South Africa's island neighbour Mauritius, which managed to remove itself from the grey list in a mere ten months, following its listing in February 2020.

In the twelve-month monitoring period, from October 2021 to October 2022, South African authorities did indeed make progress in strengthening the nation's AML, CTF and CPF systems and processes, particularly through two significant legislative interventions. The first of these interventions made changes to the Companies Act through the passing of the General Laws (Anti-Money Laundering and Combating Terrorism Financing) Amendment Act of 2022. The amendment required companies to file and update beneficial ownership information with the Companies and Intellectual Property Commission on a periodic basis. In another legislative amendment, related to the Financial Intelligence Centre Act of 2001, the mandate of the Financial Intelligence Centre (FIC) was expanded to allow for more effective monitoring and detection of financial crimes by bringing additional categories of institutions and businesses under its scope. These institutions included co-operative banks, crypto service providers, trust service providers and payment clearing service operators. Additionally, in 2020, the South African government established the Fusion Centre, a local multidisciplinary initiative comprising various law enforcement and investigative bodies, with the aim of improving information sharing to enforce regulations more effectively. Located at the FIC headquarters in Centurion, the Fusion Centre proved to be successful in this endeavour to some degree, recovering approximately R1.75 billion, or $92 million, in criminal assets by early 2023.

Despite South Africa's efforts to bolster its systems, the FATF announced at a plenary session in February 2023 that the country would be placed on the grey list. While the FATF acknowledged that South Africa had made some headway, successfully reducing the number of Recommended Actions from 67 to fifteen by the time of the greylisting, South Africa had not demonstrated sufficient compliance with the Forty Plus Nine Recommendations. To be removed from the grey list, the FATF prescribed an eight-step action plan. Most critically, the plan required South African authorities to improve the supervision of smaller financial institutions with regard to anti-money laundering; to ensure the timely and accurate reporting of beneficial ownership information; to demonstrate a sustained increase in investigations and prosecutions of financial crimes;

to implement a comprehensive national strategy for the counter-financing of terrorism; and to introduce an effective framework to enforce targeted sanctions on identified individuals and entities. South Africa committed to resolving the eight strategic actions by January 2025, at which time the FATF would decide whether the country has made enough progress to be removed from the grey list.

While most analysts agreed that the impact of South Africa's greylisting would not be economically devastating in the short term, neither severely affecting growth nor trade relations in the near future, the long-term implications were expected to be more significant, especially if the country did not manage to remove itself from the list by 2025. "Greylisting is not the end of the world for South Africa," said Investec Chief Economist Annabel Bishop in March 2023, "but it comes at an unfortunate time. It represents more bad news heaped onto the worsening energy crisis and other critical failings in areas such as transport and water, which are essential to a functioning economy." Bishop also noted that the longer South Africa stays on the grey list, the more likely rating downgrades on South African debt instruments become, which would significantly increase the cost of capital.

The more harmful consequences of South Africa's greylisting are not easily quantifiable in economic terms. Beyond the immediate and burdensome impacts that the country's financial institutions will have to weather, such as increased administrative and bureaucratic hurdles when dealing with international financial entities, the reputational damage from being placed on the grey list alongside war-torn nations such as South Sudan, Burkina Faso and Syria is likely to be more severe.

PART IV

"Since I've become a central banker, I've learnt to mumble
with great incoherence. If I seem unduly clear to you,
you must have misunderstood what I said."
– Alan Greenspan, former chair of the Federal Reserve

"A little humility never hurts."
– Ben Bernanke, Alan Greenspan's successor

BAD ACTORS AND
THE PROBLEM OF HUBRIS

At 5.46am on 17 January 1995, an earthquake registering 7.3 on the Richter scale hit the Hanshin region of Japan. Lasting only twenty seconds, it left more than 6,000 people dead and 40,000 injured. It also caused roughly $100 billion worth of structural damage, particularly in the city of Kobe, close to the epicentre. But the aftershocks of the Kobe earthquake travelled further afield than anyone could have imagined: they rippled – at least metaphorically – as far as London, where the natural disaster ultimately resulted in the collapse of Barings Bank, the second-oldest merchant bank in the world.

At the centre of the bank's collapse was one of its star employees, Nick Leeson, an aggressive trader who, at the age of only 25, had been appointed the general manager of Barings' offices in Singapore, heading up the front- and back-office operations as both the chief trader and head of settlements operations. By 1993, after just three years in this position, Leeson had racked up profits amounting to

BAD ACTORS AND THE PROBLEM OF HUBRIS

£10 million, accounting for almost 10% of Barings' total profits that year. Leeson's job was to execute arbitrage trades between derivative contracts that were listed on both the Osaka Securities Exchange and the Singapore International Monetary Exchange. The bank's strategy was simple and conservative: buy on one exchange and sell on the other, making a profit on the price difference. Emboldened by his early successes, Leeson began to take a more aggressive approach, making unauthorised directional bets on futures contracts by buying and holding them, as opposed to continuing the far safer arbitrage strategy that had worked well until then. Sometimes these bets paid off, but sometimes they didn't. When his luck failed, Leeson hid the losses in one of Barings' error accounts – account 88888. By the end of 1994, Leeson had, unbeknown to his employers, lost Barings £208 million.

In a desperate attempt to negate the losses, Leeson placed a massive bet, known as a short straddle, on the Tokyo Stock Exchange's Nikkei market index. A short straddle involves the selling of both call options and put options with the same strike price and the same expiration date. The strategy is commonly used when a trader believes the underlying asset will not move significantly higher or lower before the expiration of the option contracts. The maximum profit that such a trade can make is equivalent to the premiums collected by writing the options, but the potential loss is unlimited. In Leeson's case, he had placed a $6.68 billion bet that the Japanese stock market would not move significantly overnight, selling more than 70,000 put and call options in total. By this stage, however, his luck had run completely dry: he executed his plan on 16 January 1995, the day before the Kobe earthquake. Instead of the minimal market movement he needed, there was an almighty, wholly unforeseeable movement of first the Earth and then the markets, with the natural disaster sending the Nikkei plummeting. In total, Leeson lost $1.3 billion – over twice Barings' available trading capital – and by the end of February, the bank had been taken into receivership. It was eventually sold to Dutch investment group ING for the nominal sum of £1, assuming all of Barings' liabilities and forming the subsidiary ING Barings.

As soon as news of his disastrous trade emerged, Leeson fled Singapore, leaving only a note reading "I'm sorry" on his empty desk at Barings. Not long after, the young trader was caught at the airport in Frankfurt and extradited back to Singapore, where he pleaded guilty to two fraud-related charges. Leeson was sentenced to six-and-a-half years in prison, though he would only serve four as a result of a colon cancer diagnosis. Ironically, his jail time served to boost his infamy in a way that proved highly beneficial later in his life. His autobiography, *Rogue Trader*, was published while he was in prison, and was subsequently made into a movie starring Ewan McGregor, which premiered in Singapore in 1999, shortly before Leeson's release. He went on to appear in *Celebrity Apprentice Ireland* and the UK's *Celebrity Big Brother* TV series, and he became a sought-after guest speaker at corporate events, where he highlights the importance of sound risk management programmes and corporate ethics.

Leeson's story, though shocking, is not uncommon. Over the years, countless individual bad actors have been blamed for bringing financial firms to the brink of failure or, at the very least, for inflicting untold reputational damage on their employers. In 2008, to take another example, a rogue trader by the name of Jérôme Kerviel lost French securities firm Société Générale €4.9 billion after making unauthorised and false trades. While he was sentenced to three years in prison and ordered to pay a hefty fine, he ultimately spent only 110 days behind bars and his fine was reduced to €1 million. Four

BAD ACTORS AND THE PROBLEM OF HUBRIS

years later, JPMorgan Chase & Co found itself in a similar position to Société Générale, having to explain to its investors how a single trader by the name of Bruno Iksil had managed to lose the bank $6.2 billion. Iksil became known in the press as "The London Whale" because of the size of the damage he had inflicted on the bank. As a result of Iksil's actions, JPMorgan had paid $920 million in penalties by 2013 for misstating its financial results and failing to ensure internal controls were in place to prevent financial fraud by its traders. Although the Federal Reserve appeared to be pursuing an enforcement action against Iksil, it decided to stop proceedings in 2017.

The year after the London Whale first made headlines, another bad actor by the name of Tom Hayes was found guilty of manipulating the London Interbank Offered Rate (LIBOR) while working as a trader, first for UBS and then for Citigroup. He was sentenced to fourteen years in prison. At the time, LIBOR influenced the bulk of the world's debt security markets, the face value of which was upwards of $350 trillion. While Hayes was the one who was imprisoned, he by no means acted alone, as his manipulation of LIBOR between 2006 and 2010 necessitated the use of a large network of traders, brokers and bankers to be successful. Nonetheless, Hayes was identified as the mastermind, and therefore bore the subsequent punishment.

In other cases, the influence of bad actors has had implications that stretch far beyond their own organisations. Take, for example, Robert Citron, treasurer of the wealthy Orange County municipality in California, who lost $1.64 billion on derivatives trades in December 1994. Citron had bought complex securities, including a novel derivative known as a step-up double inverse floater, which he was introduced to by a Merrill Lynch bond salesman named Michael Stamenson. Inverse floaters carry a high degree of interest rate risk and are considered volatile investments – a fact that Stamenson did not explain to Citron. When interest rates began to rise, the value of Citron's highly leveraged securities declined rapidly, resulting in the largest municipal bankruptcy in history at the time. In April 1995, Citron pleaded guilty to six felony counts that included lying to investors and falsifying financial records. During legal proceedings, Citron's lawyers argued that Stamenson took advantage of him, claiming he had the maths capability of a seventh grader, he was in the bottom 5% of the population in terms of his ability to think and reason, and he had advanced dementia. Orange County sued Merrill Lynch for $2 billion, and Merrill ultimately paid $400 million to end the legal battle. Despite this, Merrill maintained that it had not misled anyone, and that it had always operated with the utmost integrity. Citron served one year in jail and was fined $100,000.

In the same year that Orange County went bankrupt, Procter & Gamble (P&G) sued Bankers Trust for $195 million. In this instance, there was no single bad actor, but accusations of institution-wide malfeasance. P&G argued that Bankers Trust had purposefully obfuscated the degree of risk associated with two complex interest rate swaps and encouraged a false sense of safety through various lock-in clauses. While a court ruling was expected to side with Bankers Trust, they ultimately chose to settle the case, agreeing to pay P&G $35 million. This was largely owing to the fact that more than 6,500 recordings of conversations between Bankers Trust employees had been leaked to the press, documenting their extreme and distasteful profit-driven ethos and mockery of P&G. While their actions were not technically illegal, they had eviscerated the public's trust and destroyed their credibility as a firm – to such an extent that they had even tarnished the reputation of the investment banking industry at

BAD ACTORS AND THE PROBLEM OF HUBRIS

large. This was exacerbated a few years later, in 1999, when Bankers Trust pleaded guilty to diverting $19.1 million of unclaimed customer funds onto their own books in order to prop up their financial position.

Meanwhile, 1998 saw the revered Long Term Capital Management (LTCM) hedge fund brought to the brink of failure. The individual actors in this case may not have been bad in the criminal sense, but they were highly prominent and filled with the type of Icarian hubris that can produce similarly disastrous results. They were financial savants and Nobel Prize-winning economists, including John Meriwether, Myron Scholes, Robert Merton and David Mullins, who had created the top-secret and highly complex quantitative modelling techniques that were LTCM's claim to fame. Using these techniques, the hedge fund purported to model market risk so accurately that they all but nullified any inherent risk within its investment strategies, making large losses almost impossible and large profits inevitable. In August 1998, however, their modelling successes came crashing down after the Russian rouble collapsed, with global repercussions. Following the dissolution of the Soviet Union in 1991, the Russian economy had already been subject to extreme economic instability, and when speculators targeted a government-set exchange rate for the rouble, the collapse of the currency resulted in the nation defaulting on its domestic debt and issuing a moratorium on repayment of foreign debt. With the US and European stock markets plummeting, LTCM lost $553 million on 21 August 1998 alone, more than ten times the maximum single-day loss predicted by the fund's revered "quants". In the following month, it lost almost $2 billion. The firm, which was deemed to be "too big to fail", was ultimately rescued by the Fed, which brokered a $3.65 billion bailout with some of the largest Wall Street banks. There is to this day no evidence of illegal activity in the actions of LTCM, but the individuals involved did play an outsized role in proceedings, and came to personify yet another catastrophic event within the financial community.

Ten years later, in the midst of the Global Financial Crisis, many of the salient features of LTCM's demise would manifest again, this time on a much larger and more destructive scale. Perhaps the most infamous instance within the broader Crisis was the collapse of Lehman Brothers, led by CEO Dick Fuld. Despite using an accounting gimmick called the "Repo 105" to obscure the fact that the firm was overleveraged, Lehman Brothers filed for bankruptcy on 15 September 2008, reporting debt that was $129 billion larger than its assets. In the wake of Lehman's collapse, Fuld came under immense scrutiny from authorities, who wanted to know how the giant investment firm had found itself in such a disastrous position. Fuld would, however, never be convicted of any charges. Repo 105 accounting was not illegal – rather, it exploited an accounting standard loophole – and the court could not convincingly argue that Fuld, or any Lehman executive, knowingly committed fraud.

The individual stories described in this chapter are a small sample of the recent actions of bad actors and particularly prominent bankers and money managers across the global financial system. There are many, many more. And while their actions were in most cases undeniably reckless and often grossly unethical, their stories reflect a general tendency to pin the failures and misconduct of entire financial firms on individual employees. Historically, this has worked to divert attention away from the fact that incentivisation for irresponsible behaviour is often entrenched at multiple levels of the institutions themselves, and more widely throughout the financial system.

For one, individual bad actors are often publicly shamed but are rarely held accountable for their actions, generally receiving ineffective slaps on the wrist rather than meaningful fines or sentences. While Hayes, with a fourteen-year sentence, was an exception, the likes of Iksil and Fuld escaped punishment altogether, and Leeson leveraged his prison experience into a successful new career. There is, quite simply, not a strong enough incentive for certain types of risk-takers *not* to chance their arms with other people's money – this is, at core, another form of moral hazard.

Second, and more fundamentally, the elevation of profit at all costs has become an academically sanctified way of thinking within the broader financial markets and banking industries. This is thanks largely to the work of Milton Friedman, another Nobel Prize-winning economist, and the acolytes of the Chicago School of Economics – his contemporaries and students who emerged from mathematically inclined schools of economics at Ivy League universities. The result has been, since the 1970s, the justification of an ideology of avarice that reduces the human condition to profit and the bottom line, and that validates the relentless pursuit of financial gain, providing little motivation for institutions to revise risky or irresponsible practices.

Meanwhile, the devastating losses incurred when disaster inevitably strikes are felt most severely by ordinary citizens – the customers, depositors and taxpayers. When a bad actor is singled out and blamed for malfeasance, this disguises the incentives that are embedded in the system, overlooks the significant culture of risk-taking, and undervalues the dimension of human dignity, which has become ideologically excluded from our economic and financial infrastructures.

THE CREATION OF THE FEDERAL RESERVE

On a summer's evening in 1781, James Armistead Lafayette, a slave working as a spy for the British during the American War of Independence, moved hastily through the barracks of the Redcoats stationed in New York, and requested a meeting with General Henry Clinton. Lafayette claimed he had intercepted a letter carried by a courier from George Washington, leader of the American rebels, to one of his allies, detailing his plans to mount an attack on New York, using every available soldier in the middle states. The news was of paramount importance to Clinton, who was preparing to send 6,000 of his troops to attack the French army, which was about to sail into Huntington Bay off the north side of Long Island to support the American army. Acting on the intel from Lafayette, the British general ordered his troops to remain in New York, where they waited for an American attack that would never come. Unbeknown to Clinton, Lafayette was in fact a double agent working for the Revolutionary Army, and the information he had supplied had been false, concocted

THE CREATION OF THE FEDERAL RESERVE

specifically to divert the British in New York, while Washington's forces moved south to Yorktown. On the 19th of October 1781, the American army, with the help of its French allies who entered America unobstructed, triumphed in what became known as the Battle of Yorktown. While American independence had been declared more than five years earlier, in July 1776, Yorktown marked the last major conflict of the war and the true beginning of US independence.

Two years later, Britain formally acknowledged the sovereignty and independence of the United States of America. Although a triumph for the Founding Fathers and all those who had supported the bid for freedom from British rule, the newly established nation faced significant challenges, many of them economic in nature, including the need to stabilise the monetary system, repay war debts, and stimulate commercial and industrial activities after eight years of conflict. The solution offered by Alexander Hamilton, the first secretary of the Treasury under the new Constitution, was the establishment of a national bank, modelled on the Bank of England. This bank would issue paper money, safeguard public funds, facilitate commercial transactions, and act as the government's fiscal agent by collecting taxes and paying sovereign debts. Hamilton's plans were, however, met with strong opposition. England's attempts to place the monetary systems of its colonies under the supervision of the Bank of England were still fresh in the minds of the Founding Fathers, who had regarded this move as an act of oppression that had contributed directly to the War of Independence.

Thomas Jefferson, the primary author of the Declaration of Independence, was particularly opposed to the idea of a national bank, voicing concerns that such an institution may create a financial monopoly that undermined the authority of existing state banks.

He also feared that the national bank may, over time, adopt policies that favoured financiers and merchants, who tended to take on the role of creditors in financial agreements, over plantation owners and farmers, who were generally the debtors. This would only concentrate wealth and power among a few, at the expense of the nation as a whole. Nonetheless, Hamilton's idea was eventually accepted by Congress and Senate, who recognised that drastic steps were required to stimulate economic growth. The Bank Bill was passed into law in February 1791, and the Bank of the United States, later known as First Bank, opened its doors before the end of the year.

Headed by a board of 25 directors, First Bank grew over the following decade to include a total of eight branches. It opened with a capitalisation of $10 million – $2 million of which was provided by the government, and the remaining $8 million by private investors – making it the largest corporation of any type in the US at the time. The bank operated with a dual mandate, servicing the financial needs of the government by holding its deposits, making its payments, and helping it to issue debt to the public, while also offering commercial banking services to businesses and individuals. It did not act as a lender of last resort for other banks, however, nor did it hold their reserves or set monetary policy in the manner that central banks do today. This was in large part due to the structure of the monetary system at the time.

The Coinage Act of 1792 established America's system of gold and silver coins, or specie, but there existed no national paper money until 1861. Instead, private state banks issued their own banknotes, backed by specie, and alongside these, the national bank also began to issue its own notes. As the use of these notes became more widespread, the Bank of the United States began to practise a rudimentary form

THE CREATION OF THE FEDERAL RESERVE

of monetary control, exerting some influence over the country's overall money supply, and subsequently the level of interest charged to borrowers. This influence was most clearly demonstrated in the national bank's dealings with state banks. In the course of its business, the national bank would receive state-issued banknotes, and when it wished to decrease money supply, it would present these notes to the state banks to be redeemed for gold and silver coins. It would then hold this specie, limiting the number of notes state banks could issue by deliberately depleting their reserves. When it wished to increase money supply, this specie was then used to back the new notes that were issued.

The central bank's existence was short-lived, with policymakers ultimately deciding not to renew its twenty-year charter when it came due in 1811. By this time, the US had undergone a broader transition of political power, with Alexander Hamilton's pro-bank Federalist Party having been unseated by Thomas Jefferson's Democratic-Republican Party. Those who had opposed the creation of the bank, echoing Jefferson's concerns about centralised financial control, maintained their position. Five years later, however, plans for a national bank resurfaced.

During the War of 1812, fought between the US and Great Britain over British violations of American maritime rights, international trade had been severely disrupted, stymieing economic activity and drastically reducing government revenues, which were primarily earned through trade tariffs on imports. After a period marked by significant increases in production and trade prior to the onset of the war, the US suddenly entered a period of decline: by 1814, exports had declined from $61 million in 1811 to $7 million, and imports had dropped from $53 million to $13 million. The knock-on effect of this was a general downturn of the economy, and the US became heavily indebted as it struggled to fund the war. This was substantially worsened by the lack of a central bank through which the government could issue debt, collect revenues or pay its bills.

In response, a coalition of 150 businessmen from New York City signed a petition that was submitted to Congress, urging policymakers to establish a second national bank that would, they hoped, bring stability to the financial system, thereby protecting their business interests, while also helping to raise war finances and increase the value of government issues of debt. It was also suggested that, with the creation of a national bank, the country could move towards uniform paper money, the issuance of which would be centrally controlled. "A national bank would be the best and perhaps the only adequate resource to relieve the country and the government from the present embarrassments," wrote Secretary of the Treasury Alexander Dallas in his 1815 annual report. Despite this, advancing the idea in Congress was a slow process, much as was the case for the first national bank. But as the US economy continued to suffer in the aftermath of the war, to such an extent that many state banks stopped redeeming their notes for specie owing to a depletion of their reserves, policymakers were forced to acknowledge that the establishment of a second national bank was the only possible solution. By this time, financing the war was no longer a primary driving force for the bank's establishment, but the government still required such an institution to manage its war debt, re-establish trade and stabilise the currency.

In April 1817, the new Bank of the United States, also known as Second Bank, opened for business in Philadelphia. It had a capitalisation of $35 million, 20% of which was provided by the

THE CREATION OF THE FEDERAL RESERVE

government and 80% by private investors, and a twenty-year charter. Second Bank had a similar structure and function to its predecessor, though its reach was far greater than that of First Bank, as it operated with a network of 25 branches, compared to the original's eight. This proved paramount in supporting the economic growth of the country in two ways. First, the national bank facilitated the extension of credit to farmers and businesses, boosting their outputs and providing funds to stimulate exports of the goods produced. Second, it provided the critical financial infrastructure required to support the movement of money between branches as needed to provide loans, ensuring credit was made available where it was most needed, and in the quantities required. The branches also took in revenues from the sale of federal land, and collected customs duties emanating from foreign trade. While it did not formally set monetary policy, the bank could, by managing its lending policies, manipulate the supply of money and credit in the economy to some extent, and therefore also the rate of interest charged to borrowers. As before, however, Second Bank did not regulate state banks, nor did it hold the reserves of, or act as a lender of last resort to, other financial institutions.

Second Bank was not an immediate success. In a bid to stimulate economic growth, the bank initially extended too much credit, and then rapidly restricted it, leading to a financial panic. As public animosity towards the bank began to mount, its officials made the decision to decrease drastically the number of notes in circulation, with state banknotes exchanged for specie in such a significant quantity that many of these institutions were forced into bankruptcy, owing to insufficient reserves. Recession and a sharp increase in interest rates followed, with prices of farm produce plummeting and unemployment beginning to rise, but over time the situation began to stabilise. Despite this, public suspicion of the bank did not abate, because it had demonstrated that it had the power to drain specie from state banks seemingly at will, and consequently to unilaterally regulate money supply. This did not sit well with the new president of the Unites States, Andrew Jackson, who took office in 1828.

Jackson's distrust of Second Bank was born out of a general distaste and wariness for the entire banking industry, which had been ignited more than two decades before during a contentious land deal. In the deal, Jackson had accepted promissory notes in payment for a piece of land that he sold, but when the buyers went bankrupt, the paper he held was rendered worthless, and he incurred significant losses. As a result, Jackson advocated that only specie should qualify as an acceptable medium of exchange. He also saw the extension of credit as dangerous, believing that people should live within their means rather than borrowing money to pay for what they wanted. On a philosophical level, the new president also believed that the national bank exerted too much influence over state banks, limiting their ability to function as free agents, and more generally, that it concentrated power in the hands of too few private citizens and lacked an efficient system of regulatory oversight. In sum, it was able to function beyond the purview of governmental control, which Jackson felt posed a potential threat to state influence in the financial sphere, while also creating the perfect conditions for monopolisation.

A battle between Jackson and the bank's officials ensued, during which the bank's influence was drastically reduced. Ultimately, in 1834, the House of Representatives voted not to re-charter the bank, indicating their agreement with Jackson's assertion that such an institution was "unauthorised by the Constitution, subversive to the rights of States, and dangerous to the liberties of the people".

THE CREATION OF THE FEDERAL RESERVE

For almost eighty years, the US operated in what became known as the Free Banking Era, during which state banks proliferated and operated with minimal regulation. The payments system rapidly deteriorated, rendered inefficient by more than 7,000 different state banknotes in circulation, which were prone to counterfeiting. The period was marked by frequent bank failures and regional financial panics, as well as five significant national panics, which took place between 1873 and 1907. The last of these would be the most severe, proving beyond any doubt the need for a centralised banking system.

Several events occurred in the lead-up to the Panic of 1907. A year and a half earlier, the devastating San Francisco earthquake had triggered significant payouts from British insurers, and to stem the flow of money from the UK into the US, the Bank of England had raised its discount rate. As money started to flow back to the UK, the US stock market fell, and by May 1907 America was in a recession. Later that year, monetary conditions tightened even further when the country experienced its customary surge in demand for currency and credit from farmers over the autumn period, as they harvested and shipped their crops. With no central bank in the US available to provide alleviation during this seasonal rise in demand, it was common practice for banks to individually increase interest rates. Already in a precarious position, the US financial system was then dealt a final, crippling blow in October 1907 when two bankers, Charles Morse and Fritz Heinze, tried and failed to corner the stock of copper mining company United Copper.

Morse and Heinze incurred a heavy loss, and the circulation of this news incited a run on all the banks and trusts associated with them. This panic was quickly contained within the banking sector, thanks to the role of the New York Clearing House Association.

143

Prior to 1853, banks operating in New York had to perform their clearing processes manually; that is, a bank would record its exchanges with corresponding banks and then send porters to these banks to settle all transactions and exchange cheques for cash on a weekly basis. With the number of banks growing rapidly at the time, the idea of a centralised clearing house was adopted, where certificates replaced the use of actual cash in the exchange process. This led to the establishment of the New York Clearing House Association, the country's first clearing house, which acted as a central bank and played a key role in preventing financial panics. It issued loan certificates that were backed by banknotes held by member banks, effectively creating a quasi-currency that helped to stabilise the monetary system.

When the panic hit in 1907, the New York Clearing House Association acted as intended: it vouched for the solvency of its members, and bank runs were quickly halted. But the Clearing House provided no relief for US trusts, because trust companies were excluded from its membership. Instead, the panic intensified when news broke two days later that Morse had been associated with Charles T Barney, the president of Knickerbocker Trust, the second-largest trust in the country. Trust companies emerged in the US in the late 1800s, acting as executors and trustees for funds owned by individuals and companies. By the turn of the century, however, demand for these services was dwindling, and to survive they began to engage in more general financial activities: taking deposits, providing loans and making investments. In doing so, trusts effectively began to operate like commercial banks, though they were far less regulated and often significantly more leveraged than banks. This had both positive and negative implications for the economy.

THE CREATION OF THE FEDERAL RESERVE

Trusts played a key role in providing liquidity by routinely extending short-term loans to New York equity markets, such as the New York Stock Exchange. At this time, nationally chartered commercial banks were prohibited from making uncollateralised loans or guaranteeing payment of cheques written by brokers on accounts with insufficient funds. But trusts did not require collateral for the loans they extended in equity markets, which were repaid by the end of the business day. Brokers could therefore take a short-term loan from a trust and use it to purchase securities, which were then used as collateral for an overnight call loan from a bank, which was in turn used to purchase stock. The proceeds of these activities were then used to pay back the initial loan from the trust. This process supported daily transactions on exchanges, but it carried with it inherent risk. While trusts played an important role in the financial system, they generally had a low volume of cheque clearing compared to banks, and consequently held much lower cash reserves relative to deposits – usually around 5%, compared to 25% for commercial banks. As was the case with commercial banks, however, trust company deposit accounts were demandable in cash, making these institutions vulnerable to runs on deposits. And in October 1907, while the banks were saved by the safety net of the Clearing House, the trusts were in freefall. Panic broke out on Wall Street.

At the time, President Theodore Roosevelt was reportedly away on a hunting trip in Louisiana, and – in lieu of a central bank or a president – there was only one man with enough power to bring the panic to an end: financier JP Morgan. Morgan was a wealthy and prominent businessman who had partnered with various bankers early in his career to form his own company, which, through its provision of financial services, had subsequently endowed its founder

WHY BANKS FAIL

with a significant share in all the largest industries in the US at the time, including rail, electricity and steel. Morgan, who had been away on holiday in Virginia when the panic erupted, raced back to New York and immediately assembled at his home the presidents of the largest banks, together with other prominent financiers, to devise a response. In his private study, he convinced them that there was only one thing to do: to stabilise the markets, they had to provide credit to those trusts deemed solvent, while insolvent trusts would be left to fail. With Morgan leading, the bank presidents, the US Treasury and the Clearing House worked together to save the viable trusts. The US would remain stuck in a recession until June the following year, but a total financial collapse had been averted.

The take-charge attitude of the leaders of the financial sector ultimately saved the country from economic disaster, and yet in the wake of the Panic of 1907, rather than applauding their efforts, the public began to view these men with great suspicion. For many, the fact that the bankers – and JP Morgan in particular – had possessed the power to rescue Wall Street from failure ignited concerns that a small, elite group of bankers and business leaders had gained altogether too much influence over the US financial system. Public trust had, it seemed, reached an all-time low, and this prompted support for policy changes that would reform the financial system and go some way to limiting the degree to which wealth and power could collect in such a small pool of beneficiaries. As these changes were debated in Congress, the idea of creating a central bank was inevitably raised again, but America's resistance to the establishment of such an institution remained as strong as ever. Lawmakers in the agricultural South were particularly suspicious of a central bank, which they believed would disproportionately benefit the urban commercial

THE CREATION OF THE FEDERAL RESERVE

hubs in the North. The major banks in the North, meanwhile, wanted to ensure that they were supported by a lender of last resort – but they wanted to take charge of this entity themselves, rather than leave it in the hands of government. Although the American Civil War had ended in 1865, long-standing tensions between the North and the South were reignited as arguments over the issue raged on with no clear way to appease all parties. There was, however, one undeniable point of agreement: the need for an institution that could prevent repeated bank failures in the US.

In immediate response, the Aldrich-Vreeland Act was passed in 1908, enabling national banks to establish national currency associations to issue emergency currency. The Act also established the National Monetary Commission, which was led by Nelson Aldrich and made up of members of Congress who travelled to Europe to observe the banking systems there. The commission was impressed with how well the central banks in European countries operated, though the challenge of trying to implement such a system in the US remained.

By 1910, lawmakers were still stuck in a stalemate on the issue of a central bank. It was at this point that Aldrich decided to assemble a small group of men whom he believed were capable of developing a solution that would provide a compromise between the clear necessity for a central bank and the deeply ingrained distrust of such an institution. The group included Aldrich's private secretary, Arthur Shelton; Henry Davison, a partner at JP Morgan & Co; Abram Piatt Andrew, assistant Treasury secretary; Frank Vanderlip, president of National City Bank; and Paul Warburg, a partner at the investment bank Kuhn, Loeb & Co. To avoid drawing unnecessary public attention, they left their homes under the guise of embarking on a duck-hunting trip and boarded the train for Jekyll Island off

147

the coast of Georgia. It was at this meeting – which the attendees would deny took place for at least thirty years after the fact – that the foundations of the Federal Reserve system were laid. Instead of a single central bank, a network of central banks would be created, which would accept assurances of future customer payments to businesses as collateral for cash. A bank in the South that found that its cash supplies were running low when farmers made withdrawals during the harvest season could, for example, go to its central bank and gain access to cash, with a loan to a farmer serving as collateral. A national board of directors would be appointed to set the interest rate and therefore exert some control over credit for the entire country. The bank would also issue Federal Reserve Notes, or US dollar bills, as legal tender, consolidating the complex and disordered system of paper money that had prevailed in the US up until this point.

Aldrich presented the plan to Congress, which ultimately conceded to the plan for a central bank system. Arriving at the final version of the Federal Reserve Act was not an easy process: a long and aggressive battle was fought between the banks and government for control over the new system. Nonetheless, in December 1913 the Federal Reserve came into being, providing a key source of stability to the US banking system, which quickly became the dominant centre of the global financial system. To insulate decisions made regarding monetary policy from undue political influence, the Federal Reserve was structured in two parts: a centralised authority based in Washington that is known as the Board of Governors, which includes both the Treasury secretary and representatives approved by Senate, and a network of twelve Federal Reserve Banks, which were established in cities throughout the country deemed to be of economic or political importance. To this day, the Board of Governors and the

THE CREATION OF THE FEDERAL RESERVE

presidents of the twelve Federal Reserve Banks jointly oversee the US banking system. Critically, policy and operational decisions made by the Fed do not require approval from Congress or the US president, and the Fed's operations are self-funded through interest earned on US government securities, interest on loans to financial firms, and fees charged to banks. Congress does, however, retain the power to change the laws governing the Fed and its structure.

History had repeatedly proven the need for a central banking system in the US, and the version established after the Panic of 1907 provided a compromise between a fierce American sense of independence and the undeniable benefit of having a bank of last resort and the guiding hand of central command. It would go on to provide tremendous advantages throughout the remainder of the 20th century as US economic growth accelerated, especially in the decades following the end of World War II. It has also served as an important counterweight at moments when the banking system has faced significant pressure to capitulate to politically motivated agendas. Most importantly, the establishment of the Federal Reserve worked to restore trust in the financial system after the Panic of 1907. This trust has been severely tested on multiple occasions through the years, most obviously during the Great Depression and more recently since the Global Financial Crisis. Nonetheless, in their conceptualisation as independent institutions that act in the public interest, central banks remain an indispensable anchor for the banking system, without which, as history has shown, chaos and panic ensues.

CRYPTOCURRENCIES AND THE PROLIFERATION OF VARIETY

"Economists are, at this moment, called upon to say how to extricate the free world from the serious threat of accelerating inflation which, it must be admitted, has been brought about by policies that the majority of economists recommended or even urged governments to pursue. We have indeed at the moment little cause for pride: as a profession we made a mess of things." So said the renowned Austrian-British economist Friedrich Hayek.

Addressing the crowd that had gathered for a lavish banquet to celebrate his acceptance of the Nobel Memorial Prize in Economics, one could be forgiven for thinking that Hayek was speaking in the year 2023, rather than in 1974. Then, as has been the case recently, the Western world was witnessing a sharp uptick in the price of goods and services. While the US, the UK and Europe had all entered the 1960s with inflation rates below 2%, by the time Hayek delivered his speech, inflation had climbed above 5% in the UK

CRYPTOCURRENCIES AND THE PROLIFERATION OF VARIETY

and Europe, and had surpassed 10% in the US for the first time in 27 years.

The radical solution that Hayek offered was the denationalisation of money. As an avid advocate of free-market capitalism, the economist had long argued for the minimalisation of state intervention in the financial system, based on the core belief that the economy was simply too large and too complex to be managed effectively through central planning. The idea that governments and central banks could understand and preside over such a complex system with a high degree of confidence was no more than a delusion, he suggested. In two influential books published in 1976 and 1978, Hayek applied this thinking to monetary policy, arguing that government monopoly over the issue of money and the centralisation of monetary control under central banks had proven ineffective. History had repeatedly shown that traditional policies related to money supply and the setting of interest rates had led to recurrent cycles of inflation and deflation. Hayek believed that as long as governments and central banks continued to intervene in the monetary system – printing money to stimulate economies out of downturns or increasing interest rates to combat inflation – the world would be doomed to perpetual cycles of boom-and-bust.

With inflation targeting by central banks proving problematic in Hayek's estimation, and commodity-backed currencies having failed with the demise of Bretton Woods and the gold standard, he proposed a new alternative: a system in which government-issued currencies would be replaced by a number of currencies issued by private institutions. This idea stemmed from the belief that money should be thought of as no different to any other commodity which, according to free-market thinking, could be better supplied through competition between private issuers than by a government monopoly. In this denationalised monetary system, Hayek envisaged that the market would determine which currencies became the most widely used, leading to some kind of natural restriction on the number of currencies concurrently in circulation. Price stability was expected to be the most important factor in this, as currency appreciation is generally unfavourable for debtors in transactions, while currency depreciation is unfavourable for creditors.

According to Hayek's monetary model, private institutions would take responsibility for issuing and regulating their own private currencies and, owing to the necessity for price stability, they would be induced to limit the quantity they issued, or risk depreciating their currency and losing business to another issuer. "The inferior quality money would be valued at a lower rate and, particularly if it threatened to fall further in value, people would try to get rid of it as quickly as possible," wrote Hayek. "The selection process would go on towards whatever they regarded as the best sort of money among those issued by the various agencies, and it would rapidly drive out money found inconvenient or worthless." Essentially, Hayek believed that market forces would ensure that only the most stable currencies, the purchasing power of which remained relatively constant over time, remained in circulation. Thus a solution to the problems of excessive money supply and subsequent inflation would be provided.

Although Hayek's ideas garnered much academic interest, his proposal remained no more than a thought experiment, with the economist himself acknowledging in the 1980s that a denationalised monetary system would likely never be more than a utopian dream, owing to the political pushback that would prevent it from ever coming to fruition. "I don't believe we shall ever have good money

CRYPTOCURRENCIES AND THE PROLIFERATION OF VARIETY

again before we take it out of the hands of government," Hayek lamented in an interview in 1984, while acknowledging that control of monetary policy could not be wrestled away violently. This did not necessarily mean, however, that there was no way to establish a denationalised monetary system. "All we can do is by some sly, roundabout way introduce something they can't stop," he noted. His words would prove to be prophetic.

A little over two decades later, in the midst of the Global Financial Crisis, with trust in the global financial system at an all-time low, a white paper appeared online entitled "Bitcoin: A Peer-to-Peer Electronic Cash System", outlining the concept of a completely denationalised and decentralised monetary system. Disillusioned with the failings of the incumbent economic system, advocates of the new cryptographic system sought to bring into the world a transparent and decentralised form of monetary exchange that would bypass traditional financial institutions. Bitcoin was by no means the first cryptocurrency in existence, but it was the first to gain widespread appeal, tapping into a zeitgeist of rapidly diminishing institutional trust. While central banks and governments were responding to the Crisis by printing large quantities of money, substantially increasing money supply as a result, these cryptographers had created a new, alternative network of exchange that by design eliminated the need for official institutions, such as central banks to issue money, and private banks to oversee and effect transactions. This system based itself in a counter-cultural ethos that further stoked the popularity of cryptocurrency among those who had lost faith in the presiding financial system.

The same philosophy underscored interest in the broader idea of decentralised finance, driving the development of many different types of cryptocurrencies, as well as the blockchain technologies that enable transactions between them, and theoretically between them and the traditional world of financial products. In fact, the ideology of crypto acolytes was, and remains, to use blockchain and mass consensus-based authentication to seamlessly facilitate transactions between crypto and traditional world assets and counterparties, evading the use of the traditional banking infrastructure altogether.

Enthusiasm for cryptocurrencies only accelerated as the overall amount of money available in the financial system – whether dollars, euros or pounds – radically increased throughout the post-Crisis and Covid-19 years. For crypto purists, the actions of central banks were further proof of the mismanagement of money by central authorities, bolstering the theoretical case for Bitcoin, Ethereum and other cryptocurrencies. And for financial speculators, it was an opportunity to make sizable profits. By 2022, the cryptocurrency market had exploded, reaching a peak market capitalisation of some $3 trillion, before it stabilised around $1 trillion in 2023.

There has been a dangerous tendency to conflate the popularity of cryptocurrencies as an asset class that people can invest in with their viability as alternative currencies – their potential, in other words, to function as competing, privately issued currencies in a digitised 21st century version of the denationalised currencies that Hayek imagined. Demand for any speculative asset is driven by the subjective value placed on it by society, whether it is a work of art that costs very little to produce or a rare classic car that is technically inferior to modern mass-produced vehicles. Similarly, the demand for cryptocurrency has been driven by the popular appeal of decentralised finance combined with an abundance of money that found its way into the stock markets, and the potential to make significant profits

CRYPTOCURRENCIES AND THE PROLIFERATION OF VARIETY

through online trading. Its popularity is not, however, indicative of the market having reached some kind of consensus on its practical use as an alternative currency in the manner described by Hayek.

The ability to conduct transactions using cryptocurrency is based on blockchain technology, the technical infrastructures on which authenticated transactions are recorded. When a transaction is initiated, a record containing all the information pertaining to the transaction is generated and stored as data in a "block", which houses the records of a batch of pending transactions. This block of transactions is then broadcast to a network of cryptocurrency "miners", so that it can be immutably recorded. In the traditional monetary system, this function is taken for granted, since bank account holders simply trust their banks and the money in which they are transacting; other than basic fraud and accounting checks, automated steps within the banking system authenticate these transactions almost immediately.

In the case of cryptocurrency, the authentication process is decentralised; it is carried out by having many multiples of miners solve a cryptographic function that enshrouds the block of transactions. This involves solving an arbitrary mathematical problem that has been designed so that there is no analytical way of solving it – the answer can only be determined through a laborious process of trial and error. Miners are presented with an equation in which certain inputs and the output are known, and they must then compete with one another to be the first to determine certain unknown numbers that will solve the equation. In the original cryptographic formulation, these were two prime numbers, but there are other mathematical functions that can be used, as long as they are difficult to solve and necessitate "brute force" to find the input factors. To demonstrate the scale of this exercise, computers on the Bitcoin network tested roughly 390 quintillion answers per second in 2023.

It is only through a system of mass consensus that a transaction can take place. This consensus is achieved not by having miners verify individual transactions, but rather by proving that they have done the brute-force work of solving the cryptographic problem associated with a particular block of transactions. To ensure that there will be people who volunteer to undertake this tedious process, a reward is offered to the first miner who solves the mathematical problem and publishes the block of authenticated transactions, usually in the form of a portion of a cryptocurrency coin. At any given time, then, there are thousands of miners, or groups of miners who pool resources, working on the same block of transactions in the hopes of being the first to solve the same mathematical problem. This approach is integral to the system of consensus on which the authentication of transactions relies – and it is why cryptocurrencies are supposedly trustless. Once the mathematical problem is solved, the transactions are executed, and the block is effectively sealed off, ensuring that the data cannot retrospectively be altered and that a public record of every transaction is maintained indefinitely. A new block of pending transactions is then created and added to the closed block, so that a chain of blocks is formed. This "blockchain" forms the public ledger.

It is the mathematical problem that miners must solve that provides intrinsic value to a cryptocurrency, and crypto proponents often argue that these cryptographic functions are comparable to gold in the system of gold-backed currencies that once prevailed, offering the security and stability of a currency supported by something less

CRYPTOCURRENCIES AND THE PROLIFERATION OF VARIETY

fragile and more unassailable than trust. The energy intensity and human labour of mining cryptocurrencies has also been likened to the process of mining gold out of the ground, but a key difference between these two endeavours is that gold need only be extracted once to be used as a store of value and a medium of exchange. It would be profoundly inefficient if a unique gold nugget had to be mined for every dollar ever used in any transaction at any point in time. And yet this is essentially what occurs in the blockchain system. For every block of transactions that takes place and is secured, a cryptographic problem must be solved by thousands of crypto miners through the tedious proof-of-work system, the equivalent of mining the same commodity again and again. Not only is the crypto system inefficient as a means of exchange, but because every transaction must be confirmed by mass consensus, an excessive expenditure of computational power and human potential is also required every time a transaction takes place. This is surely not what Hayek had envisioned as a superior form of financial intermediation.

In addition to this problem, by design, cryptocurrencies allow for transactions to be conducted anonymously and without the need for an official financial intermediary. These features of a decentralised structure are often cited by advocates as being the critical strength of cryptocurrencies, but they may also be viewed as a severe structural shortcoming, most obviously because they enable illicit transactions. Banks, by comparison, are subject to market conduct regulation, which has become a critical area of oversight in the financial system. In fact, it is now considered as important as, if not more so than, the rules governing capital adequacy, and failure to adhere to these regulations can attract substantial fines and reputational damage, as was witnessed in the case of Credit Suisse. It is precisely because banks are required to monitor all transactions that simply eliminating the prevailing monetary system in favour of a decentralised system creates issues far more complex and dangerous than is generally acknowledged. Converting to a monetary system that is devoid of any kind of regulatory oversight would be a societal regression, as has been demonstrated in recent years, with the decentralised and unregulated nature of cryptocurrency having repeatedly been shown to help facilitate tax evasion, money laundering and the financing of crime.

In addition to their inefficiencies and lack of market conduct regulation, cryptocurrencies have an even deeper fundamental flaw: an apparent inevitability within the nature of cryptographic and blockchain technology to produce a proliferation of variety. This is the problem that is most pertinent in the context of this book, and the hardest to solve, as it undermines the very justification for the existence of cryptocurrencies.

While there were certainly many different currencies in circulation during the 20th century, at the time of the gold standard all currency varietals were linked, at least in theory, to the same precious metal, which was globally recognised as being a store of value. By comparison, there are no barriers to entry in the crypto market. Anyone who wishes to create a new blockchain or a new cryptocurrency can do so with the right software and a modicum of technical knowledge. This presents the opportunity for an infinite number of different cryptocurrencies to be created, a phenomenon that is already well underway.

At the start of 2021, there were roughly 4,000 cryptocurrencies with a combined market capitalisation of $700 billion. By 2022,

CRYPTOCURRENCIES AND THE PROLIFERATION OF VARIETY

there were 9,000 cryptocurrencies with a market capitalisation of $3 trillion. In 2023, there were estimated to be more than 20,000 different cryptocurrencies in existence, each operating according to its own protocols, which govern its systems of release and circulation. They had a combined market capitalisation of around $1 trillion, following the crash of the crypto market in late 2022. In such a system, the problem of maintaining a stable value – precisely what Hayek was trying to solve – becomes clear, as has been seen in the volatility of the prices of this ever-increasing variety of cryptocurrencies.

In the case of cryptocurrency, market dynamics have not worked as Hayek imagined they should in a system of privately issued currencies. According to his prediction, the competition between cryptocurrencies should be pared down as public interest becomes concentrated on the most stable and viable currencies, provided theoretically by issuers who are under pressure to continually serve their customers better. Instead, there has been a proliferation of variety in cryptocurrencies, driven by a rather different set of market motivations. This is evidenced by the fact that in many instances cryptocurrencies are created without any real intent to function as a currency, exemplified by the popularity of "memecoins", cryptocurrencies that are created expressly to generate interest, and investment, by capitalising on social trends related to viral moments and internet jokes. As one example, hours after actor Will Smith slapped Chris Rock while he was presenting at the Academy Awards in 2022, a memecoin called "Will Smith Inu" appeared. It garnered more than $3 million in trading before collapsing to nearly zero within a week. Even more tellingly, the original memecoin, Dogecoin, was expressly created as a joke parodying the frenzy surrounding Bitcoin, but it too received a staggering amount of interest from investors who wished to be in on the joke, with the price of the token climbing 600% between 2013 and 2021. Although it failed to break the $1-per-unit mark, the market interest betrayed the underlying forces at play, which were memorably captured in a tweet by the coin's creator in 2022: "Current 'meme' coins aren't even memes. They're made by people trying to get rich off of other people trying to get rich."

The modern introduction of cryptocurrencies supposedly solves one existential problem within the financial system – the failure of trust in centralised authorities – while introducing another. The proliferation of cryptocurrencies is in many ways reminiscent of medieval times, before the issuance of gold and silver coins was centralised, when any nobleman who owned precious metal reserves could mint and issue his own unique set of coins. This system quickly became unmanageable, hindered by the existence of too many different currencies in circulation concurrently, with no stable system of exchange existing between them and no consensus on their value. A similar story played out in the US in the period before the Civil War. Banks issued their own private currencies, but the inefficiency and costs associated with tracking the exchange rates and conducting payments in multiple currencies with multiple prices eventually led to the establishment of a uniform currency and a central banking system, even in a country that was highly sceptical of the centralisation of monetary control. Any comparison between national currencies backed by gold and cryptocurrency are made spurious by the fact that there are an infinite number of varietals of crypto, whereas there is only one gold – Au – on the periodic table. It has to be acknowledged, however, that during the Nixon Shock, the dollar replaced gold as the world's reserve currency, becoming a guiding benchmark for money for the next half century, until recently, when the Fed radically altered

CRYPTOCURRENCIES AND THE PROLIFERATION OF VARIETY

the way it executed its monetary policy. This is one of the key reasons for the prevailing drive for alternative forms of money.

There is one obvious and deeply ironic solution to the critical shortcomings faced by cryptocurrencies. The imposition of a centralised regulator would help bring order to the chaos, solving the problem of the potential for infinite cryptocurrencies on an infinite number of public ledgers, while implementing some kind of market conduct over the system as a whole. But this simply leaves us back at square one. If the entire philosophical rationale for cryptocurrencies is to create a trustless system that bypasses national sovereignty and the entire traditional financial system, then this centralised solution to making it viable undoes its purpose in the first place. Thus, in avoiding the oversight of a central authority, the proliferation of cryptocurrencies is the modern equivalent of maintaining the system of couriers and travelling paperwork that was necessary to enable bills of exchange in the 14th and 15th centuries, knowing that this system is slow, laborious and prone to fraud and manipulation.

Either way, there is no future for cryptocurrency as real-world money. Rather than a workable alternative to fiat money, it is merely an expression of societal distrust and regression – and so the conundrum of resolving centralised regulation remains.

DOOMSDAY STRESS-TESTING

Since the passing of the Federal Reserve Reform Act of 1977, the Federal Reserve has functioned under a "dual mandate", targeting both maximum employment and price stability. A long-standing criticism of this approach argues that these are, at times, contradictory or competing economic goals, and it is telling that most nations' central banks typically have a single mandate: to keep inflation within a specific target range. The South African Reserve Bank is a case in point. The merits of the argument for single versus dual mandates notwithstanding, this is a debate that masks – or, perhaps, evolves into – a second major criticism of the Fed as it is run today: that its monetary policy has become largely reactionary and in thrall to market forces.

Since the Global Financial Crisis, the Fed has swiftly and consistently come to the rescue of the markets, specifically the bond and stock markets, by altering interest rates and increasing money supply to ease investors' pain at even the slightest intimation of a downturn. This was most obviously witnessed in what became

DOOMSDAY STRESS-TESTING

known as the taper tantrum of 2013. After three successive rounds of quantitative easing (QE), spanning 2008 to 2013, and with the US economy finally showing signs of heating up following the Crisis, the Fed announced, in May 2013, that it would begin "tapering" its asset-buying programme at some unspecified point in the future. This would involve slowing the rate of purchases of government bonds and mortgage-backed securities over time before eventually halting them altogether. In the days following the announcement, the Dow Jones and the Nasdaq dropped significantly, and yields on US government bonds rose sharply. By September 2013, with bond yields continuing to climb and stock markets remaining stagnant, the Fed had buckled, announcing that it would hold off on tapering and extend its asset-purchase programme even further.

As alluded to by American economist Allan Meltzer at the time, the relationship between the Fed and the markets was increasingly resembling one in which the tail was wagging the dog. "Excessive concern for short-term changes causes the Federal Reserve to respond to events over which it has little control and largely ignore longer-term changes that it can influence," wrote Meltzer in May 2013. "One can appreciate the political and market pressures that Federal Reserve policymakers, especially the chairman, face. That is the reason for independence, but it requires determination to resist the pressures." Contrary to this sensible appeal, the Fed has displayed remarkably little stomach for resisting the pressure. Ultimately, in the six years from the start of QE1 in late 2008 to the end of QE3 in late 2014, it increased its balance sheet from $900 billion to $4.5 trillion – a five-fold increase after decades of stable and diligent management.

After the discontinuation of QE3, the Fed managed to reduce the size of its balance sheet slightly, to under $4 trillion, by September

2019. In that same month, however, due to a confluence of events squeezing liquidity, interbank lending rates doubled from 2.5% to over 5% in a single day. Reminiscent of the worst days of the Global Financial Crisis, the volatility in the repo market concerned policymakers to such an extent that the Fed announced it would be further expanding its balance sheet by reigniting its asset-purchase programme to facilitate liquidity in the interbank market. In the months that followed, the $4 trillion mark was once again breached. Then in March 2020, when the first wave of the Covid-19 pandemic hit American shores, the Fed's monetary policy entered a new phase, unleashing an unprecedented torrent of money, the size and scale of which the world had never before experienced. In a matter of just two years, the Fed's balance sheet doubled once more to beyond $8 trillion.

In recent years, the Fed appears to have completely redefined its role in society. It has left the taps of money supply wide open, and the previously well-understood idea of monetary economics, centred around gradually dripping liquidity into the market only when required, has been disposed of entirely. By 2022, the Fed had created a monster: a financial system flooded with money, leaving the stock markets and bond markets addicted to QE. This tidal wave of money supply brought with it wild swings in asset prices, with stock markets reaching all-time highs on a weekly basis and the prices of all manner of speculative investments skyrocketing, from luxury watches and superyachts to cryptocurrencies and NFTs. And in its wake came the return of real inflation, the extent of which had not been experienced since the early 1980s. As this happened, Fed chair Jerome Powell continued to deny that inflation was becoming embedded in the system, erroneously claiming that it was merely a "transitory" phenomenon. When it was no longer possible to deny its

DOOMSDAY STRESS-TESTING

stickiness, Powell was forced to rapidly raise rates. Following eleven consecutive increases from March 2022 onwards, the Federal Funds Rate reached 5.5% in August 2023 – its highest level in 22 years – at which point the rate was finally held steady the following month.

At this juncture, with interest rates at record highs and US unemployment at record lows, as well as with workers striking for significant wage increases across numerous industries, there remains the strong possibility that core inflation could be embedded in the system for some time to come. One scenario that could alter this trend would be a severe and painful correction of the markets, which would only serve to further undermine the public's trust in the global banking system.

Thomas Jefferson demonstrated great prescience at the turn of the 18th century in his objection to a national bank, on the grounds that it would, over time, adopt policies that favoured "financiers and merchants" – this is effectively what we are seeing today. The general public, whose trust the entire banking system depends on, not only in the US but the world over, has over the past two decades significantly lost faith in the institution of banking; in fact, in the entire financial infrastructure, and to some extent in money itself. The public may not know this, but it is the pre-eminent guardian of money – the institution tasked with caretaking this complex and existentially important system, the Federal Reserve – in which it has truly lost faith.

On 28 June 2023, the Board of Governors of the Federal Reserve released the results of their annual bank stress tests, stating confidently that the US banking system was well positioned to weather even the most severe economic storm. "Today's results confirm that the banking system remains strong and resilient," said Vice Chair for Supervision Michael Barr. Hours later, the *Financial Times* reported that even in a "doomsday economic scenario" the stress tests proved the banking system had more than enough capital to survive an "economic catastrophe".

The confidence expressed by the Fed in June 2023 seemed somewhat surreal, given that the US banking system had just experienced three of the four largest commercial bank failures in its history. That March, the federal authorities had prevented a systemic failure of trust, and thus a subsequent domino-like failure of banks, only by guaranteeing all deposits at Silicon Valley Bank, even those above the $250,000 federal deposit insurance threshold, and signalling that the same would be done elsewhere if required. Despite this near-catastrophe, Barr was proclaiming that the US banking system was "strong and resilient", and he was doing so based on the results of an annual stress test conducted on just 23 of the approximately 4,500 banks operating across the United States.

Officially known as Comprehensive Capital Analysis and Review, stress tests were introduced in 2011 as a direct response to the social and economic carnage caused by the Global Financial Crisis. Designed to measure whether banks have sufficient capital buffers to withstand severe economic downturns, they include hypothetical scenarios, decided on by the Fed, that simulate adverse economic and financial conditions, such as recessions, market disruptions and shocks, against which banks' balance sheets are assessed. Originally, all banks with more than $50 billion in assets were subject to annual testing, but that threshold was raised to $250 billion in 2018, following a regulatory rollback under the Trump administration. This substantially decreased the number of banks being tested on an annual basis.

DOOMSDAY STRESS-TESTING

As part of the stress-testing regime, participating banks are required to submit detailed financial information and risk management data to the Fed. This includes information on their balance sheets, capital adequacy, risk exposures and risk management practices. The Fed then estimates the potential impact on the banks' capital levels, and evaluates whether they have sufficient capital to continue lending and operating even under severe economic conditions. Any banks found to have insufficient capital are instructed to cut back on their dividend payments and share buyback programmes in order to build up their capital buffers.

In the 2023 stress test scenario, the Fed simulated what it termed a "severe global recession", involving a 40% decline in commercial real estate (CRE) prices, a 38% decline in residential real estate prices, and a brutal increase in the unemployment rate, from its historically low level of 3.6% at the time to a peak of 10% in the theoretical scenario. Under these conditions, the Fed calculated that the 23 banks tested would have to absorb a projected $541 billion in total losses, comprising $424 billion in loan losses, a significant proportion of which was attributed to a sharp increase in defaults that would occur in a theoretical collapse of the CRE market.

Since 2020, with the pandemic radically altering where people work and live, there has been a very real concern that commercial real estate prices, particularly office and downtown real estate, will come under growing pressure, eventually triggering a severe financial crisis. Evidence of this downward spiral in CRE prices was widespread by 2023, with waves of defaults occurring at what were previously deemed prestigious addresses. Before the pandemic, for example, the Bay Area in San Francisco was home to the third-highest concentration of Fortune 500 companies in the US, but there has been a mass exodus of commercial activity since, as well as a pronounced increase in homelessness and crime, further accelerating the decline in property prices.

Somewhat disconcertingly, while the Fed's post-pandemic stress-testing regime has focused extensively on a sharp decline in commercial real estate prices, the tests have failed to capture the true risk of this problem. In its 2023 report, the Fed itself noted that only 20% of all office and downtown CRE loans were held by the 23 large banks that were subject to testing that year. The vast majority of these assets were held by smaller banks – institutions that fall outside of the ambit of the annual stress tests. It is astonishing to conclude that the Fed knowingly fails to capture 80% of the risk related to what it deems to be one of the greatest threats to the US banking system.

Besides this inherent intellectual blind spot bedevilling the Fed's post-pandemic stress tests, there is an additional fundamental problem embedded in them: the handling of the spectre of inflation. As a result of extremely loose monetary policy, exacerbated by supply chain disruptions and the war in Ukraine, among other factors, the US and Europe have experienced their highest rates of inflation in more than four decades. By March 2022, the sharp and sustained increase in prices had forced the Fed to raise interest rates rapidly in an attempt to stamp out the flames of inflation; however, similar rates were not reflected in the Fed's worst-case economic scenario in 2023. Instead of keeping interest rates elevated, the expectation was that if a recession were to occur, interest rates would again be cut to near zero, where they had been for many years, in order to stimulate economic growth. For large banks, this would hypothetically, and counterintuitively, nullify one of the biggest risks that US banks face in a post-pandemic, high-interest-rate environment: the billions of dollars of unrealised losses on their bond portfolios.

DOOMSDAY STRESS-TESTING

In the pandemic era, a rush of new deposits entered the banking system as a result of a broad range of centralised initiatives: stimulus cheques, business loans, the forgiving of student debt, and the generally excessive printing of money, much of which found its way into the pockets of the already wealthy. In response to this massive inflow of deposits, many banks concluded that the smartest way to invest the new funds was to purchase apparently low-risk US government debt, resulting in a significant increase in their bond holdings between 2020 and 2022. As a general rule, the value of bonds – including government debt, such as US Treasuries – declines when interest rates rise, since higher interest rates erode the value of the future coupons and capital repayments of these bonds. At the time, interest rates remained low and bond prices were trading at historically high levels, as they had consistently done in the low-interest-rate environment that dominated the post-Crisis era.

Traders and treasury officers who were responsible for managing their banks' interest rate and liquidity risks have largely avoided criticism for buying bonds, since they were ostensibly investing excess cash in one of the safest assets available, US government debt. In reality, however, this was plainly an injudicious call. Despite rare examples in Europe and Japan over the past few decades, real interest rates have seldom dropped below zero. Thus, by investing in US government bonds when interest rates were at or near zero, these treasury officers were entering a trade that essentially had no upside potential. At best, these bonds would retain their value if interest rates did not move. More realistically, they would lose significant value when interest rates inevitably increased from their historically low levels – and this is exactly what happened from early 2022 onwards.

169

By the first quarter of 2023, the Fed's rate hikes had resulted in $515 billion of unrealised losses on the balance sheets of banks across the US; that is, theoretical losses that had not yet been realised through a sale or a transaction. Of the four largest banks in the US, three had accumulated a similar amount of unrealised bond and mortgage-backed securities losses by early 2023: $40 billion each for JPMorgan Chase & Co and Wells Fargo, and $25 billion for Citigroup. However, the second-largest bank in the country, Bank of America (BofA), had managed to rack up a staggering $100 billion in unrealised losses.

Like SVB, BofA had pumped much of the $670 billion in new deposits it received in the pandemic era into government bonds and mortgage-backed securities. And as was the case with SVB, this strategy encountered serious problems when the Fed began to raise rates. Unlike SVB, however, which was forced to sell its bonds and realise the losses because of a liquidity squeeze, BofA was under no obligation to account for the loss in value as "realised losses" at the time of the stress test in 2023. Barring a severe liquidity crunch or a run on the bank, BofA could therefore nurse these unrealised losses on its books until the bonds reached maturity, avoiding any actual losses – an approach supported by an accounting treatment termed the "mixed measurement model".

Under the mixed measurement model, assets that are not explicitly categorised as available-for-sale (AFS) or held-for-trading (HFT) are classified as held-to-maturity (HTM), and their unrealised gains or losses are not recognised. As a result, banks can hold billions of dollars of unrealised losses on their bond and mortgage-backed securities portfolios without these losses ever affecting their income statements or balance sheets, as long as these assets are demarcated as HTM.

DOOMSDAY STRESS-TESTING

The only scenario in which the losses on HTM assets would need to be realised is if a bank was forced to sell these bonds or securities at a loss in the case of a severe liquidity crisis, such as a bank run.

The mixed measurement approach has been criticised by various industry experts, including the Chartered Financial Analyst (CFA) Institute. "We do not support a Mixed Measurement Model," noted the institute in 2010, when it argued for the abolition of the differing accounting treatment of assets based on a company's intent. "A financial instrument's value is not different because it will be held by one financial institution and sold by another. Such reporting flexibility creates differences in appearance but not actual valuation." In 2023, following the collapse of SVB, the CFA Institute reiterated its belief that the HTM classification should be eliminated, stating that all financial instruments should be measured at fair value in financial statements, especially in the case of banks. The institute also criticised the Fed and US banking regulators for not identifying the risk related to bond losses at an earlier stage. "The Fed's own actions should have alerted banking regulators to the emergence of such losses and their impact on bank business models," said the institute in relation to the Fed's rapid interest rate hikes. "This should have been predictable since the value of fixed instruments always declines when rates rise."

Considering this criticism, the Fed's decision to drop interest rates to near zero in its 2023 "doomsday" scenario seems disingenuous. Instead of keeping rates high and testing the resilience of the $515 billion in unrealised bond and mortgage-backed securities losses in the US banking system – an amount that is nearly equivalent in size to the total $541 billion of predicted losses in the 2023 "extreme" stress test – the Fed chose to nullify these unrealised losses by hypothetically dropping interest rates. Indeed, many banks actually benefited from the doomsday scenario; none more so than BofA, the institution holding one-fifth of the entire US banking system's unrealised losses. The senselessness of this outcome was highlighted when, upon receiving the results, BofA's own risk management team expressed surprise that the bank had performed far more positively than their own calculations had estimated it would. Ironically, then, in the "severe global recession" scenario simulated by the Fed, what seemed to be one of BofA's biggest weaknesses – $100 billion in unrealised losses – turned out to be a major benefit.

"In the stress tests, the Fed thought the problem would be falling GDP; defaults on commercial real estate loans; and a spike in unemployment," noted Thomas Hogan, the former chief economist at the Senate Banking Committee, contemplating the Fed's post-pandemic approach. "Instead, we got the opposite of that: a good economy, low joblessness and few defaults. The things the Fed thought would be a problem are good now. And the thing they deemed not to be important, the risk of a big rise in rates, is causing the failures in the financial system."

Despite the glaring incongruity between its theoretical worst-case scenario and the post-pandemic economic reality, the Federal Reserve boldly proclaimed that the US banking system was safe and sound upon the conclusion of the 2023 stress test. All the banks that were subject to testing were deemed to have sufficient capital to continue operating and lending to households and businesses, even in a severe recession. As a result, many of the largest banks in the US, including JPMorgan, Morgan Stanley, Citibank, Wells Fargo and even Bank of America, had the opportunity to inform their shareholders that they would be increasing their previously stated dividend payments, since they were technically overcapitalised according to the Fed.

DOOMSDAY STRESS-TESTING

Years of loose monetary policy, seemingly motivated by the performance of the stock market rather than the broader economy, were a principal driver of the erosion of public trust in the financial system. Now that the taps of quantitative easing have been closed, at least for the time being, an opportunity has arisen to earn back some of that much-needed trust. And yet if the execution of its annual stress tests reflects its approach, the Federal Reserve appears to be spurning the opportunity to inspire public trust once again.

Considered in context of their real-world implications, its doomsday stress-testing scenarios are not nearly as severe as they are made out to be, and certainly do not capture the true risk in the US banking system. If anything, the stress tests may actually do more harm than they prevent, inadvertently promoting further distrust and moral hazard in an already fragile financial system.

PART V

"We've come through a terrible crisis. The American people have paid a very high price. We simply cannot return to business as usual. That's why we're going to ensure that Wall Street pays back the American people for the bailout. That's why we're going to rein in the excess and abuse that nearly brought down our financial system. That's why we're going to pass these reforms into law."
– Barack Obama, 21 January 2010

"We have comprehensively promoted major-country diplomacy with Chinese characteristics... and unswervingly opposed any unilateralism, protectionism and bullying. We have promoted the construction of a new type of international relations, actively participated in the reform and construction of the global governance system. China's international influence, appeal and shaping power have been significantly improved."
– Xi Jinping, 16 October 2022

THE POWER OF THE DOLLAR

Held in Glasgow, Scotland in November 2021, the 26th United Nations Climate Change Conference of the Parties (COP26) was plagued by large protests that decried the lack of meaningful progress in the fight against global climate change. Amid the generally gloomy mood that pervaded the proceedings, there was, however, one small glimmer of hope – for South Africa, at least. On 2 November, British Prime Minister Boris Johnson announced that, in partnership with the US and the European Union, the UK would provide South Africa with $8.5 billion to decarbonise its coal-intensive energy system. This would involve various funding mechanisms, including grants, concessional loans and risk-sharing partnerships with private institutions.

"This game-changing partnership will set a precedent for how countries can work together to accelerate the transition to clean, green energy and technology," said Johnson. The message of support was reiterated by US President Joe Biden. "By assisting and responding to the needs of developing countries, rather than dictating projects from afar, we can deliver the greatest impact for those who need it the most," he said. While the announcement created great excitement and some much-needed positive press for COP26 at the time, the promise never materialised – or at least not as hoped.

A year later, at COP27 in Sharm El-Sheikh, Egypt, South African President Cyril Ramaphosa pleaded, cap in hand, with the UK and its partners to follow through on their financial pledge to help South Africa decarbonise. In particular, Ramaphosa rued the fact that the majority of the funding promised in Glasgow – over 97% – had been offered in the form of loans from commercial institutions with draconian repayment terms, rather than as unconditional grants. "At present, multilateral support is out of reach of the majority of the world's population due to lending policies that are risk-averse and carry onerous costs and conditionalities," said Ramaphosa. "The commitments that were made must be honoured, because failing to honour these commitments breaks trust and confidence in the process."

The hesitancy displayed by the US, the UK and the EU in following through with their funding pledges to South Africa was not the first failure of its kind. In 2009, for instance, the group of developed nations present at COP15 in Copenhagen, Denmark had resolved to increase the financing provided to developing nations to combat climate change to $100 billion a year by 2020. When the deadline arrived, only a part of the $100 billion had been mobilised, and the timeline was summarily moved out to 2023. These examples of broken promises form part of a wider trend, illustrating the extent to which the G7 and its allies – the old guard of global democratic values – are losing their grip on a changing world order.

THE POWER OF THE DOLLAR

Thirty years ago, the US and its allies were at the peak of their powers, setting the rules and standards that other nations were required to follow; in the decades since, their role as global leaders has lost significant appeal. In the Cold War era, the equation was simple: nations were either with the US or against it. Today, in a world where the US and China stand at opposite ends of the ideological spectrum, the geopolitical landscape is far more complex.

In what Alec Russell of the *Financial Times* has called an "à la carte world", middle powers across Asia, Latin America and Africa, including the likes of South Africa, no longer have to choose between one side or the other; they can cherry-pick the economic and political arrangements that suit them best at the time. "As the post-Cold War age of America as a sole superpower fades, the old era when countries had to choose from a prix fixe menu of alliances is shifting into a more fluid order," wrote Russell in August 2023. In this à la carte world, non-democratic regimes are free to woo developing nations to join their ranks, often through trade and infrastructure deals, exemplified most obviously by China's trillion-dollar Belt and Road Initiative.

Three decades ago, by comparison, at the G7 Summit in Paris in 1989, US global hegemony had reached its crescendo. It was a time when the US was the undeniable leader of the world – politically, economically, militarily and culturally. The US was refining and exporting its unique brand of capitalism, deeply rooted in consumerism, to every corner of the globe, from Africa to Asia, South America to Australia, and everywhere in between. This was a time when Madonna was the "Material Girl", Tom Cruise was in every cinema, and Michael Jackson's "Man in the Mirror" was blaring on every radio from Hungary to Hanoi. With the fall of the Berlin Wall in 1989, the evolution of American exceptionalism was seemingly fully fledged. It was "the end of history", as Francis Fukuyama wrote at the time. "What we may be witnessing is not just the end of the Cold War, or the passing of a particular period of post-war history, but the end of history as such," wrote Fukuyama in 1989. "That is, the end-point of mankind's ideological evolution and the universalisation of Western liberal democracy as the final form of human government." Liberty, individualism and democracy were no longer positions to be debated. The ideals of democracy had defeated the collectivism of communist ideology, and they would now be sanctified and protected at all costs – and the US would be their chief protector.

A key facilitator of this hegemony was the dominance of the US dollar in the global financial system, dating back to the 1940s. In 1944, the Bretton Woods Agreement established the US dollar as the world's reserve currency. Backed by the world's largest gold reserves and the economic and military might of the US, the dollar became the obvious choice for use in international trade between nations, and commercial and financial agreements around the globe were increasingly being settled in dollars. This process was accelerated by the significant reconstruction challenges that Europe and Japan faced after World War II, which led them to rely on the dollar for trade and investment. Additionally, the establishment of powerful international post-war institutions such as the International Monetary Fund and the World Bank served to solidify the dollar's dominance. Not only did these global institutions conduct all their lending to Asian, Latin American and African nations in US dollars, converting them to loyal US trade partners and consumers for the US industrial machine in the process, but they also served to export the ideals of democracy to these embattled economies.

THE POWER OF THE DOLLAR

The resilience of the dollar would be tested in 1971, when President Richard Nixon announced the suspension of dollar-to-gold convertibility, effectively ending the Bretton Woods System and initiating an era of floating exchange rates. This shift did not, however, diminish the dollar's global status. Rather, it transformed it into a fiat reserve currency with its value determined by market forces. Fortunately for the US, several factors converged to ensure the dollar continued its dominance for decades to come. At the time of the abolition of Bretton Woods, the US economy was by far the largest in the world, with an annual GDP of $1.1 trillion in 1971, representing more than a third of the global economy. The USSR had the second-largest economy at the time, two-and-a-half times smaller, at $433 billion. This US dominance would persist for decades. Even in the era of fiat money, and despite the US's numerous self-inflicted political wounds, the dollar has maintained its status as the world's unchallenged reserve currency. That is, until fairly recently.

Since the 1970s, for central banks across the globe, the combination of political stability, market depth and market liquidity has made the dollar the foreign reserve currency of choice. As of 2019, 62% of all central banks' foreign reserves were held in dollars. The two primary reasons for central banks to hold these foreign reserves are to prove that they have enough hard currency – such as dollars, euros or pound sterling – to pay international debts; and to stabilise their local currencies. In a scenario where a nation's local currency may be faltering, for example, a central bank can use its foreign reserves to buy the local currency on the open market, thereby increasing its demand and stabilising its price.

In the global foreign exchange (forex) market, where the relative prices of the world's currencies are determined, the US dollar has dominated for many decades. Of the $2 trillion of daily transactions executed in the global foreign exchange market in 2022, the top three most traded pairs – EUR/USD, USD/JPY and GBP/USD – all included the US dollar. In the past, the supremacy of the dollar in the forex market, and in the global financial system more generally, proved to be a powerful economic and geopolitical weapon for the US and its allies. If a nation was cut off from using the currency, it could almost instantaneously become an economic pariah. By the end of the 20th century, however, this was changing. While the dollar largely maintained its dominant global status, the geopolitical landscape that lay beneath it was shifting.

Where the US and its allies once held the power to completely ostracise a nation through economic sanctions by cutting it off from the dollar, this was no longer the case by the second decade of the 21st century. The clearest example of this diminishing economic and geopolitical might was witnessed in the largely unsuccessful sanctions imposed on Russia following its invasion of Ukraine in 2022.

On 28 February 2022, shortly after Vladimir Putin authorised the full-scale invasion of Ukraine, the US and its allies, including France, Japan, Germany and the UK, froze $300 billion of the Central Bank of Russia's foreign reserves being held outside of Russia. "The unprecedented action we are taking today will significantly limit Russia's ability to use assets to finance its destabilising activities, and target the funds Putin and his inner circle depend on to enable his invasion of Ukraine," proclaimed Treasury Secretary Janet Yellen.

The rouble-dollar (RUB/USD) exchange rate quickly spiked, from 83 roubles per dollar on 27 February to a peak of 135 on 10 March.

THE POWER OF THE DOLLAR

"As a result of our unprecedented sanctions, the rouble was almost immediately reduced to rubble," US President Joe Biden tweeted on 26 March, nearly a month after the invasion. But this was somewhat disingenuous, as the rouble had made a startlingly quick recovery, settling in the mid-80s range by the end of that same month. After Biden's proclamation of victory, the rouble strengthened even further, far surpassing its pre-war level to reach 52 roubles per dollar by late June 2022. A year and a half after the invasion began, with the war still grinding on, in August 2023, the rouble was trading at 90 roubles per dollar, close to where it was trading prior to the war.

In the years leading up to the war, Putin had anticipated the use of sanctions against Russia and enacted various measures to limit the potential damage on the country's economy. The first of these actions was for the Central Bank of Russia (CBR) to significantly decrease its foreign reserves held in US dollars – from around 50% of its total foreign currency reserve portfolio in 2017 to 22% the following year. Over the same period, the CBR increased its holdings of Chinese yuan to 15% of its total foreign reserves – much larger than the average of all other central banks at the time. To further reduce Russia's vulnerability, Putin increased the nation's trade surplus – meaning that, on a net basis, it was exporting more than it was importing – to a record high by early 2022. This significantly aided in continuing the flow of foreign income into the country prior to the invasion.

Despite the grand geopolitical posturing of Western governments, their sanctions clearly did not work as intended. As an early indication of the challenge, it was galling for the US that its own allies in Europe, particularly Germany, had become so dependent on Russian oil and gas that they continued to buy large quantities long after the invasion. Of more significant longer-term concern was the ease with which Russia circumvented sanctions by using the many financial channels that its allies such as China, India and countries in the Middle East afforded it. China, for example, drastically increased its imports of Russian oil, gas and coal, from $57 billion the year before the invasion to $88 billion the year of the invasion. Similarly, India's purchases of Russian oil rose significantly in 2022, from a low base of 2% of the nation's total oil imports in late 2021 to nearly 20% in early 2023. Pakistan, Turkey and Bulgaria also started buying more Russian oil after the invasion of Ukraine.

Ironically then, not only did the sanctions fail to "reduce the rouble to rubble", but they had another important unintended geopolitical consequence: they weakened the US's grip on global power even further, and strengthened the economic and political bonds between various autocratic regimes, pseudo-democracies and historically excluded countries.

BRICS AMBITIONS, DE-DOLLARISATION AND SOUTH AFRICA'S PLACE IN THE GLOBAL ORDER

The global shift from US hegemony has become more apparent in recent years in the ever-closer bonds between the nations that comprise the BRICS alliance: Brazil, Russia, India, China and South Africa. The term "BRICs" was first coined in 2001 by then-Chairman of Goldman Sachs Asset Management Jim O'Neill, in a research paper called "Building Better Global Economic BRICs". The paper highlighted the fact that in the coming decade, the real GDP growth in the largest emerging market economies – represented by Brazil, Russia, India and China – would exceed that of the G7. "Over the next ten years," the paper noted, "the weight of the BRICs and especially China in world GDP will grow, raising important issues about the global economic impact of fiscal and monetary policy in the BRICs." Eight years later, in July 2009, leaders from Brazil, Russia, India and China officially met at the first BRIC Summit to discuss a mutually beneficial alliance.

Out of that inaugural summit, held in Yekaterinburg, Russia, emerged a loose agreement by the members to partner in various economic ventures, including infrastructure and development projects. The following year, South Africa joined the bloc as its fifth member state, expanding the acronym to BRICS. The inclusion of South Africa, a relative economic minnow, provided the group with representation on the African continent, without which a comprehensive "Global South" alliance would have been incomplete. As of 2023, the five BRICS nations have a combined total population of 3.2 billion people, representing 42% of the global population, and together their economies account for over a quarter of the world's total GDP, at $28 trillion of the $100 trillion total. Of the combined BRICS GDP, however, China's $18 trillion economy contributes by far the largest share, representing almost two-thirds of the bloc's combined economic heft.

Many economic commentators, mostly from the US and the UK, have criticised BRICS, describing the group as a melange of five seemingly unaligned and uncoordinated nations that have achieved little since their first meeting in 2009. "The BRICS' weaknesses as a policymaking forum are evident," wrote Alan Beattie of the *Financial Times* in August 2023. "The club has insufficient unity of purpose and little ability to enforce decisions." Even Jim O'Neill, the economist who coined the term BRICS, declared that the group had "never achieved anything". "Quite what they attempt to achieve beyond powerful symbolism, I don't know," he said. Despite his clear disdain for the idea, O'Neill also alluded to the reason that the BRICS allegiance had persisted over the years and had not simply faded away as many had expected. "The dollar's role is not ideal for the way the world has evolved," said O'Neill. "You've got all these economies who

BRICS AMBITIONS, DE-DOLLARISATION AND SOUTH AFRICA'S PLACE IN THE GLOBAL ORDER

live on this cyclical never-ending twist of whatever the Fed decides to do in the interests of the US."

Since the 1970s, the US has benefited geopolitically from the power of the dollar as the world's reserve currency. Based on its growing collective economic weight, the BRICS group was originally formed as an attempt to create a general geopolitical alliance to act as a counterbalance to the US and its allies. As a direct result of the seizure of Russia's foreign dollar reserves following the invasion of Ukraine, the alliance has been galvanised by the idea of an alternative reserve currency. In June 2022, it was Vladimir Putin himself who announced that the alliance was working on developing a new reserve currency based on a basket of currencies of its member countries. The real commonality uniting BRICS, therefore, "is scepticism about a world order they see as serving the interests of the United States and its rich-country allies who promote international norms they enforce but don't always respect," according to Reuters Chief Southern African Correspondent Tim Cocks, writing in August 2023. This is the essential sentiment that has bonded together five vastly different nations, with different geographical locations, governing systems and ideologies.

In April 2023, Brazil's President Lula da Silva voiced his support for a common BRICS currency. "I am in favour of creating, within the BRICS, a trading currency between our countries," he said on a trip to Spain, "just like the Europeans created the euro." Economic commentators have scoffed at the idea that this disjointed group of emerging economies could produce a common currency in any way resembling the euro. In February 2023, the *Financial Times* called it a "flawed idea" with many "practical challenges". O'Neill weighed in at the time, calling it "ridiculous".

As the next BRICS Summit edged closer, tensions escalated. At the Summit for a New Global Financing Pact held in Paris in June 2023, leaders of developing nations, including South Africa, Brazil and China, reiterated their disappointment in the commitment of developed nations to follow through with their financial pledges. The summit, which was set up to "mobilise financial support for developing and low-income countries facing the challenges posed by excessive debt, climate change and poverty", seemed to highlight the fact that many developing countries were willing to jeopardise, or at least minimise, their historical relations with the G7 powers in favour of new, less restrictive relations with non-G7 nations.

This sentiment was passionately articulated at the same summit by President Cyril Ramaphosa, who announced that he was, once again, discouraged by the broken promises of developed nations to developing nations. "There have been times when we feel like we were beggars," said Ramaphosa. "At the time it felt like there would just be droppings from the table, and yes, we will give you that and that. But let me tell you something, that generated a lot of resentment." Similarly, Lula da Silva again advanced the idea of a non-dollar dominated world, led by the BRICS. "Some people get scared when I say that we need to create new currencies for trade," he said. "If it's up to me, it'll happen at the BRICS meeting."

The tensions in Paris set the stage for the 15th BRICS Summit, to be held in South Africa just two months later.

On 22 August 2023, as ordinary citizens of Johannesburg listened to military jets roaring overhead and found their usual routes to work blockaded by police vehicles and security guards, leaders from the

BRICS AMBITIONS, DE-DOLLARISATION AND SOUTH AFRICA'S PLACE IN THE GLOBAL ORDER

BRICS nations gathered in South Africa's most populous city to discuss what they imagined to be the path to a better future. Two particularly salient points were on the agenda: the de-dollarisation of the global financial system and the potential expansion of the BRICS group to include new member states. On the first day of the summit, the group's de-dollarisation ambitions were firmly restated by Lula da Silva's loyal ally, Dilma Rousseff. Rousseff, who had also been president of Brazil, but was impeached in 2016 in relation to illegal campaign funding allegations, was now acting in her role as the head of the New Development Bank (NDB), formerly the BRICS Development Bank. Whereas the NDB had until then mainly issued loans in Chinese renminbi, Rousseff announced that it intended to begin lending in South African rands and Brazilian real, as part of a grander plan to reduce the bloc's reliance on the US dollar.

Set up in 2015 and headquartered in Shanghai, China, the NDB's original mandate was to facilitate loans between BRICS nations for various infrastructure and development projects. Rousseff's statements at the summit seemed to signal that the NDB would be the institution to spearhead a move by the BRICS alliance away from the dollar. "Local currencies are not alternatives to the dollar; they're alternatives to a system," said Rousseff. "So far the system has been unipolar. It's going to be substituted by a more multipolar system."

In acutely differentiating the NDB from the World Bank and the International Monetary Fund, Rousseff described the institution's lending practices as unconditional, as opposed to the loans offered by its Western counterparts, which dictate stringent reform agendas and policy adjustments that often include reining in government spending and bolstering anti-corruption efforts. "We repudiate any kind of conditionality," Rousseff explained. "Often a loan is given upon the condition that certain policies are carried out. We don't do that. We respect the policies of each country."

The other globally significant outcome of the Johannesburg summit was the announcement that six new members had been invited to join the bloc: Argentina, Egypt, Ethiopia, Iran, Saudi Arabia and the United Arab Emirates. In the lead-up to the summit, the expansion of the group had been a point of contention among the existing BRICS members. While South Africa and China were in support of the idea, Brazil and India were opposed to including new members, fearing that an expansion of the bloc would dilute their influence and strengthen China's control over the group even further. As many as 22 other developing nations had signalled their intention to join the group. If all the aspiring countries were eventually to be included, the combined economic force of the group would represent up to 45% of global GDP.

The day before the start of the summit, a casual reader of *The Star*, a South African daily newspaper, might have sensed the repositioning of South Africa's place in the global order merely by scanning the front page that day. An article written by Xi Jinping, accompanied by a prominent portrait of the Chinese president, sat alongside an article by President Ramaphosa, which clearly signalled the latter's support for increasing BRICS membership and South Africa's alignment with China in this regard. "For its efforts to be more effective, BRICS needs to build partnerships with other countries that share its aspirations and perspectives," wrote Ramaphosa. "An expanded BRICS will represent a diverse group of nations with different political systems that share a common desire to have a more balanced global order." Below Ramaphosa's contribution was an ostensible piece of journalism, though it read more like an advertorial, apparently

BRICS AMBITIONS, DE-DOLLARISATION AND SOUTH AFRICA'S PLACE IN THE GLOBAL ORDER

announcing the "Second Season" of a series of books containing Xi Jinping's "Greatest Quotes", published by China Media Group.

Any delegates attending the summit, or indeed any businessperson flying through Johannesburg's OR Tambo International Airport, where the newspaper is made freely available in the airport's lounges, would have observed President Ramaphosa clearly supporting Xi Jinping's vision of "a more balanced global order". *The Star* is one of South Africa's oldest newspapers – dating back to 1887, as it declares on its front page – and thus signals an apparent authority in its reporting. The many delegates and businesspeople who read that particular issue may not have been aware that it is now owned by Iqbal Survé, a notorious South African businessman with intimate ties to South Africa's ruling ANC party. Among other controversies, he was dragged to court by the South African Public Investment Fund in 2021 in an attempt to claw back more than R4 billion in squandered investments provided to his various companies. Accordingly, these delegates and businesspeople may not have been aware that the newspaper is widely regarded as a mouthpiece for certain factions of the South African government.

Whatever the people of South Africa may or may not want, the message from the corridors of power was clear: South Africa has chosen to fall in line with Chinese ambitions.

CONCLUSION

"Economic control is not merely control of a sector of human life which can be separated from the rest; it is the control of the means for all our ends. And whoever has sole control of the means must also determine which ends are to be served, which values are to be rated higher and which lower; in short, what men should believe and strive for."
– Friedrich Hayek, *The Road to Serfdom* (1944)

"The Republic of South Africa is one, sovereign, democratic state founded on the following values: human dignity, the achievement of equality, and the advancement of human rights and freedoms."
– Constitution of the Republic of South Africa, 1996

CONCLUSION

Banking can be thought of as the brain of the body economic, directing funding and capital to all other industries, which form the limbs and organs. Through its life-giving functions, banking has made the advancement of civilisation possible, driving the wave of industrialisation and invention that took hold from the Renaissance to the Industrial Revolution and beyond. In essence, banking exists beneath and between industries, directing the extension of credit and capital that have allowed the global economy to evolve and grow in size and complexity in recent centuries.

Given this fundamental role in society, it is one of the great metanarratives of our world that banking is safe, stable and secure. But this is an illusion. Despite its indispensable role in the upliftment of the human condition, the facts defy this broadly held misconception. In my career alone, I have witnessed multiple bank failures in South Africa and across the world, from working as an equity trader in the early 2000s at a bank that failed during the A2 Banking Crisis, to witnessing the failure of banking clients in the teeth of the Global Financial Crisis, to observing the recent failures of Silicon Valley Bank, Signature Bank, First Republic Bank and Credit Suisse. The history of banking demonstrates that beneath the veneer of stability, the business of banking is inherently risky.

By design, banks have a fundamental vulnerability: they extend more credit for longer terms than they have available deposits. In general, without this feature, and unless they radically alter their business models, banks would fail to be meaningfully profitable. Whether as a result of reputational damage, mismanagement, the actions of bad actors or inadequate regulatory oversight, banks always face the existential risk that their depositors may suddenly choose to withdraw their funds en masse. Almost without exception, this is the reason that banks actually fail, often instantaneously, as has been experienced repeatedly throughout history.

This risk of bank runs, which is encapsulated in the term "liquidity risk", is an inherent feature of the banking business model, which therefore depends, more so than any other industry, on public trust. When the bonds of this trust are broken, there is a certain inevitability to the wave of bank failures to come. This risk of failure resulting from a loss of trust is indelibly intertwined with the nature of banking, and it is therefore a risk that will persist into the future.

Over the past few decades, there has been an accelerated erosion of trust – in financial institutions, in financial regulators, in money itself, and in the global financial ecosystem as a whole. The glorification of hyper-capitalism is partly to blame for this, but so too are the problems inherent in central banking and in centralised government-led monetary regimes more generally. While these problems are not new, they have become particularly pronounced in recent times. But most people cannot articulate what exactly it is they have lost faith in. The answer is that they have lost faith in the guardian of the world's reserve currency, the Federal Reserve.

Since 2008, central banks, and specifically the Federal Reserve in the US, have printed extraordinary amounts of money, initially to ease the pain caused by the Global Financial Crisis, itself the result of the overextension of credit and of poor monetary policy, then in response to the Covid-19 pandemic. Having underestimated the impact of a decade and a half of unprecedented money printing, the Fed then implemented a series of rapid interest rate increases, in early 2022, in response to the inevitable inflation that had followed.

CONCLUSION

The result was a destabilisation of currency markets across the world, the export of inflation, and ultimately some of the largest bank failures in history.

Meanwhile, in an effort to mitigate the riskiness of banking in the wake of the Crisis, regulators enforced a raft of stringent and restrictive capital and liquidity requirements on banks that, while intended to safeguard the financial system, compromise their ability to operate and profit as private enterprises. By increasing the quality and quantity of capital that banks must hold, these regulations have made banks less attractive investments, which makes it even more difficult for them to raise capital. Besides constraining the business model of banking in this way, these regulations are attempting to address what are really the symptoms of bank failures rather than the cause, which is the failure of trust.

As the watchdogs of the financial system, regulators, who should continually be alert to systemic risk, have also demonstrated poor oversight. This was particularly evident in the execution of the Fed's 2023 stress-testing protocols. While these are meant to act as a worst-case crash test for individual banks in the US, they were intrinsically flawed, undermining the intent and usefulness of this critical undertaking.

The conundrum of central banks is that their role in bringing some kind of order to the potential chaos of the financial world is necessary, as is their intervention in manias, crises and panics – but it is a role that is beset with difficult decisions and unintended consequences. Often the medicine is as bad as, or even worse than, the initial illness.

While the Fed has been criticised for attempting to follow a dual mandate, the deeper problem lies in its insistence on appeasing the markets rather than safeguarding the broader American economy.

WHY BANKS FAIL

Rather than acting in the interests of the American population as a whole, the Fed has shown itself to be strongly preoccupied with the opinions of an elite group of traders – a few hundred people around the world who control the bond market, specifically trading US debt.

While congressional hearings were held in the wake of the Global Financial Crisis to try to glean an understanding of its root causes, no individuals in the US Treasury or inside the Federal Reserve system were held accountable for creating an environment that resulted in such calamity. Following this, the Fed was then allowed to apply its own self-corrections, mainly through the deployment of extremely loose monetary policy for persistent periods of time. In the process, it can authentically be argued that the actions of the Fed have significantly eroded the very trust it is charged with protecting. This must be addressed.

The Fed should ignore short-term market disruptions and so meaningfully assume its role as the protector of the American banking and monetary systems, and by extension, the global financial system as a whole.

History demonstrates that central banking is non-negotiable for the sustainability of sophisticated economies all around the world. More recently, the history of banking also reveals an increasingly intimate connection between global financial markets and geopolitics. Today, the dynamics of our contemporary geopolitical system indicate the critical importance of the global banking infrastructure and the immense strain that it is under.

In a world where the Federal Reserve acts without constraint, excessively and consistently opening the taps of money supply in

CONCLUSION

an overreactive and irrational manner, the viability of the entire fiat currency system, led by the US dollar, has been called into question. This, in turn, has led to several misguided attempts to create an alternative monetary system, best exemplified in the proliferation of cryptocurrencies, which attempt to circumvent traditional financial institutions in favour of a decentralised system of exchange.

Following the seizure of Russia's foreign reserves in the wake of the invasion of Ukraine in 2022, the urge to find monetary alternatives has now manifested in the efforts of the BRICS group to create a new common currency. The hegemony and supremacy of developed nations, once led by the US in a unipolar world, has waned significantly over the past few decades. The US dollar remains the global reserve currency for the time being, both because of the deep and sophisticated nature of US markets, as US Treasury Secretary Janet Yellen justifies it, and because of the sheer unadulterated size of the US economy. But the self-serving interests of the Fed are now driving other countries to seek alternative forms of financial intermediation. This has been fuelled by the disingenuity and unreliability of the G7 nations in particular, whether it be in the form of unfulfilled promises made at annual summits or stringent clauses limiting the financial aid provided to developing countries by institutions such as the World Bank and the International Monetary Fund.

Developed nations have largely failed in their obligation to assist vulnerable, emerging economies that have repeatedly requested assistance, and the resulting breakdown of geopolitical trust has critically undermined the global project of democracy. The past three decades of monetary policy, as practised in the West, have led to financial crises, extreme market volatility, bank runs and now inflation that has spread worldwide. It has become increasingly apparent that the actions of central banks in liberal democracies have severely undermined global public trust.

Traditionally democratic nations, including South Africa, are now turning for support to autocracies such as China, which offer supposedly unconditional solutions to their financial needs. After all is considered, there is something quite postmodern about the fact that the 1990s poster child of US-led capitalism, Goldman Sachs, unwittingly conceptualised the idea of the BRICS alliance – originally as an investment strategy – and that it would later become the collective name adopted by a group of nations intent on undermining the US-dominated world order. We are now witnessing a dangerous shift towards an ideologically multipolar world.

It is tempting to argue that a fairer balance of power may emerge in a world where multiple value systems can find a way to co-exist, despite their contradictions. There is, however, a stronger argument that moral relativism ultimately fails, often catastrophically, as demonstrated by the history of communism in the second half of the 20th century. Specifically, it should be self-evident to most observers that a mutual scepticism of the US and its allies is insufficient common ground to bond nations with diametrically opposed ideologies – that there must also be some form of multilateral contract, based on shared values, which is predetermined and agreed upon.

Without such parameters in place, each country risks compromising the principles that guide not only its formal constitution, but its ethical stance on myriad social, political and economic issues. The implications of this for banking manifest most sharply in the global project of market conduct. In the 21st century, banks have

CONCLUSION

been progressively coerced into becoming extensions of the state, through the dominance of the US dollar, nullifying their status as truly independent, private firms. Any impairments to their business have, however, been outweighed by the benefits of developed nations essentially co-opting most other countries, barring certain extreme outliers such as North Korea, into the grand project of making the world safer. They have achieved this by putting legal and functional guardrails in place throughout the global financial system to identify and isolate tax evaders, money launderers, criminals and terrorists. Since the 9/11 attacks, market conduct regulations have made the role of banks in society more important than ever before, and it is reasonable to conclude that the world *is* a safer, better place as a result. Market conduct has shown that barriers of entry into the financial world are very effective – far more effective than building actual walls. But unless governed by a multilateral agreement based on a shared set of values, multipolar projects are unlikely to regulate all financial institutions in a manner that can similarly protect citizens. After all, without a shared set of values there would be no agreement on what "good" versus "bad" conduct would be. The purpose of market conduct itself would therefore be evaded.

The South African banking community, along with the banking communities of other developing nations, finds itself in an ideological bind. If the country does veer towards a BRICS currency in a multipolar world, we will have effectively undone decades worth of hard work to integrate our banking systems with those of the global liberal order. It is worth noting, at this juncture, that the South African banking system is legitimately recognised to be one of the most sophisticated and best-regulated banking systems on Earth.

WHY BANKS FAIL

While a US dollar-dominated world order may have its downsides, it is surely better than the alternative currently being offered – a loose alliance of non-aligned countries that in many cases conduct themselves in a way that conflicts with our values. And for those who argue that an alternative reserve currency outcome is unlikely, it should not be forgotten how quickly six European nations collaborated to create an alternative currency in the 1970s, in the wake of the Nixon Shock. This ultimately led to the failure of the Bretton Woods System, which demonstrates the significant global consequences at stake.

There are several actions that can be taken to rectify the current state of the global financial system. The answers lie neither in creating an entirely new, decentralised and ultimately ungovernable system, nor in throwing in lots with an alternative financial system based on little more than opposition to US dominance. Rather, it requires a rational and sober addressing of the shortcomings of the current system.

The Federal Reserve needs to actively recover public faith and credibility. To start, its annual stress-testing should immediately be revised; in particular, how the scenarios are conceived. As a minimum requirement, an institution outside of, and independent of, the Fed should be defining them. This could be done, for instance, as an annual function under the US Senate Banking Committee, ensuring it remains independent of the US Treasury and the Fed. It makes no sense to have the Fed mark its own homework.

From this impartial standpoint, stress-testing could also be designed to be more globally oriented, rather than focusing on an entirely US perspective, rendering the stress tests more systemically

CONCLUSION

useful to the international banking system. It would be possible to test for a variety of potential consequences – for example, the impact of exported inflation from the US – taking into account both global *and* US interests.

As part of the revision of the Fed's stress-testing regime, two obvious weaknesses must be addressed. The first is the mixed measurement model of accounting, which uses a technical shortcut to sidestep critical areas of risk related to unrealised losses on banks' bond and mortgage-backed securities portfolios. This model needs to be substantially revised. The second is the rollback of laws that took place in 2018, which saw the minimum balance sheet requirement for testing raised to $250 billion, critically diluting the effect, and thus the point, of the stress tests. To capture the true risks embedded in the wider banking system, the threshold should be returned to $50 billion or lowered even further. This is particularly relevant for the impact of a potential commercial real estate downturn, of which the 2023 stress test captured only 20% of the risk to the US banking sector.

The fact that, in 2018, a large swathe of the US banking system was suddenly released from a raft of regulatory, capital and liquidity obligations, owing to the successful lobbying of Congress by various interested parties, is testament to the need for immediate global alignment and the implementation of a single set of banking rules around the world, as unrealistic and unlikely as this may sound. This would include a streamlining of current regulatory governance practices across all central banks, through the creation of unified standards – including capital adequacy, liquidity ratios and stress-testing practices – ultimately reducing the fallibility of individual regulators. Arguments that this alignment is already in place are countered by the recent failures of US and European banks, the

WHY BANKS FAIL

Fed's nonsensical stress-testing, and the serious contemplation of an alternative reserve currency.

As a key element of a more aligned system of global regulations, a better balance must be achieved between the desire for sufficient capital buffers in banks, and the desire for banks to be able to produce attractive returns on equity. Although banks do regularly report strong profits, their ability to generate returns on shareholder equity in relative terms is hindered tremendously by the amount of capital they are required to hold under the capital adequacy regulations enforced following the Global Financial Crisis. While the capital adequacy buffer is in theory a good idea for protecting against loan losses and market risk, it inadvertently makes the financial system as a whole more dangerous and prone to failure. The fact that systemically important financial institutions, of which Credit Suisse was one, are required to hold more capital than other financial institutions, thereby making them less attractive investments, is patently counterintuitive. Put simply, the capital buffers as they currently stand are too high, making banking an unattractive business for investors. Achieving a better balance between capital adequacy and return on equity for banks must be prioritised.

From this cohesive global regulatory standpoint, ideas for a more feasible monetary system can emerge, with a particular focus on the development of a global system of exchange in which currencies are once again based on a tangible store of value. This would be something akin to the gold standard, in which there would be some kind of hard limit to the amount of money that a central bank can print at its own behest.

To help restore trust in the financial system, there are legitimate and consistent calls for a sense of accountability to be enforced upon

CONCLUSION

the financial fraternity through the stronger prosecution of bad actors. This argument is compromised by the contemporary prevalence of elite protectionism, which was vividly illustrated in 2016 with the release of the Panama Papers. In that instance, millions of leaked documents revealed the names of thousands of prominent businesspeople, politicians and celebrities around the world who were shown to be evading tax. A more recent and chilling example of this protectionism was revealed in the case of the Sackler family – the owners of Purdue Pharma, the company that introduced OxyContin to the world – who knowingly produced a highly addictive drug, fuelling an opioid crisis that has caused the death of more than 640,000 US citizens, and faced no prison time for their actions. Today, the rule of law can be evaded with relative ease by the wealthy and powerful. In such a world, it is difficult to make the practical case that there should be harsher penalties for individuals sitting at the helms of banks when they experience liquidity crises in the midst of a general panic, or for the regulators who created the frothy environment in the first place. Rather than specifically targeting the financial sector in isolation, one viable solution would be the creation of a fast-track prosecution process for all kinds of elite and corporate criminal behaviours, specifically those that abuse the liberal capitalist system and continue to undermine trust in its institutions.

There is a critical challenge that underscores all the recommendations here: they cannot be undertaken on a global level without some degree of ideological alignment. This problem was starkly highlighted in late September 2023, when Ukrainian President Volodymyr Zelensky described the United Nations Security Council as "ineffective" while directly addressing the council at UN headquarters in New York. His statement referred to the fact that Russia, the country that invaded Ukraine without provocation in 2022, remained one of only five permanent members of the Security Council, along with China, France, the UK and the US. As such, it maintained its veto powers to override and block decisions voted for by other members, including the intervention of the UN in the war in Ukraine, for example. Zelensky's observation is a recent and particularly pertinent example of a long-standing criticism of the UN, though it is increasingly relevant.

Currently, the world stands at a crossroads. "Neither global co-operation nor western domination look feasible," wrote Martin Wolf of the *Financial Times*, in a bleak contemplation of the current geopolitical moment. "What might follow? Alas, 'division' might be one answer and 'anarchy' another."

To avoid either outcome, the US and its allies should be held accountable for their unfulfilled financial promises and pledges to developing nations. Lending developing nations money at extortionate rates, with rafts of invasive conditions, is accelerating the pace with which these nations will turn towards alternatives, irrespective of ideology. The developed world has a responsibility to give more generously from its riches, both to ensure its own safety and freedoms, and to ensure the future safety and freedoms of others.

The importance of this for South Africa cannot be overstated. As the country continues to be seduced by non-democratic regimes that court it with trade deals and promises of a new global system of exchange, it drifts into dangerous moral territory. Should the BRICS group expand and become a functioning economic entity, as it intends to – criticisms of its viability notwithstanding – South Africa will find itself increasingly entangled and doing business with

CONCLUSION

countries that disregard the rights of individual citizens. Countries that pursue illegal wars; sponsor terrorism; commit war atrocities; condone mass executions and torture; practise religious persecution; subjugate women; persecute homosexuals and other minorities; build and propagate "re-education" camps to subdue entire ethnic populations; and suppress freedom of speech and the right to protest, even murdering journalists when it is deemed expedient. These examples are starkly at odds with the values and norms that underpin the very Constitution of South Africa, including human dignity, universal adult suffrage, individual freedom and the rule of law. It was these democratic values that dragged the country, by some miracle, out of the clutches of a violent, repressive and racist regime into a world where equality and individual freedoms could exist.

In building ever stronger ties with non-democratic nations, South Africa will find it increasingly difficult to uphold the values that constitutionally define it and, as this happens, South Africa's banks, which have historically been held to the highest global standards of governance, will find themselves in an increasingly delicate position. In a multipolar world, the years devoted, not only to building robust systems for market conduct and transparent financial governance, but also to the project of democracy, are in danger of being squandered. South Africa finds itself at the epicentre of this complex debate.

ADDENDUM

A select list of prominent bank and financial institution
failures throughout history.

DATE	BANK	COUNTRY	REASON
1345	House of Bardi	Italy	King Edward III defaulted on loan
1345	House of Acciaioli	Italy	King Edward III defaulted on loan
1345	House of Peruzzi	Italy	King Edward III defaulted on loan
1494	House of Medici	Italy	Mismanagement and excessive lending
1656	Stockholms Banco	Sweden	Bank run related to issuance of banknotes
1720	Banque Royale	France	Bank run related to the Mississippi bubble
1856	Royal British Bank	UK	Fraud and bank run
1866	Overend, Gurney and Company	UK	Risky investments and market disruptions
1873	Freedman's Savings Bank	US	Panic of 1873 and bank run
1893	Marine National Bank of New York	US	Losses related to speculative investments
1893	Reading Railroad Bank Syndicate	US	Failure related to the Panic of 1893
1907	The Knickerbocker Trust	US	Bank run related to the Panic of 1907
1907	Trust Company of America	US	Bank run related to the Panic of 1907
1907	Lincoln Trust Company	US	Bank run related to the Panic of 1907
1927	Bank of Taiwan	Taiwan	Shōwa Financial Crisis
1927	Tokyo Watanabe Bank	Japan	Shōwa Financial Crisis
1930	Bank of Tennessee	US	Losses related to 1929 stock market crash
1931	Bank of the US	US	Failed merger and bank run
1974	Bank Herstatt	Germany	Foreign exchange settlement losses
1974	Franklin National Bank	US	Mafia connection, bank run
1984	Continental Illinois National Bank and Trust	US	Bad loans and run on bank
1988	First Republic Bank Corporation	US	Savings and Loan Crisis
1988	American Savings and Loan	US	Savings and Loan Crisis
1989	MCorp	US	Texas energy price crash
1989	Gibraltar Savings and Loan	US	Savings and Loan Crisis
1989	Western Savings and Loan	US	Savings and Loan Crisis

ADDENDUM

1989	Lincoln Savings and Loan Association	US	Savings and Loan Crisis
1990	Edington Bank	UK	Real estate losses
1990	British & Commonwealth Merchant Bank	UK	Real estate losses
1990	Authority Bank	UK	Real estate losses
1990	CenTrust Bank	US	Savings and Loan Crisis
1990	Empire of America Savings	US	Savings and Loan Crisis
1990	MeraBank	US	Savings and Loan Crisis
1990	Alpha Bank Limited	South Africa	Fraud, taken into curatorship
1991	Bank of New England Trust Company	US	Savings and Loan Crisis
1991	Connecticut Bank & Trust	US	Savings and Loan Crisis
1991	Maine National Bank	US	Savings and Loan Crisis
1991	Sparebanken Rogaland	Norway	Credit losses and bank run
1991	Sparebanken Midt-Norge	Norway	Credit losses and bank run
1991	Christiania Bank og Kreditkasse	Norway	Norwegian financial crisis
1991	Bank of New England	US	Embezzlement and loan losses
1991	Chancery Bank	UK	Property market exposures
1991	SKOP	Finland	Mismanagement and bad investments
1991	Spar- und Leihkasse Thun	Switzerland	Real estate loan losses and bank run
1991	Fokus	Norway	Norwegian financial crisis
1991	Bank of Credit and Commerce International (BCCI)	Luxembourg	Fraud and mismanagement
1991	Cape Investment Bank	South Africa	Fraud and loan losses
1991	Pretoria Bank Limited	South Africa	Mismanagement and failed merger
1991	Southeast Bank	US	Savings and Loan Crisis
1991	Great American Bank	US	Savings and Loan Crisis
1991	Connecticut Bank & Trust Co	US	Savings and Loan Crisis
1992	HomeFed Bank	US	Savings and Loan Crisis
1994	**Banco Español de Crédito**	Spain	Mismanagement and loan losses
1994	Sechold Bank	South Africa	Liquidity problems
1994	Banco Latino	Venezuela	Real estate exposures and bank run
1994	Banco Consolidado	Venezuela	Real estate exposures and bank run
1994	Prima Bank	South Africa	Liquidity problems due to NPLs
1994	Tokyo Kyowa	Japan	Overleveraged, mismanagement
1994	Anzen	Japan	Overleveraged, mismanagement
1995	**Barings Bank**	UK	Fraud and trading losses
1995	Cosmo Credit Cooperative	Japan	Bad loans and bank run

WHY BANKS FAIL

1995	Hyogo Bank	Japan	Bad loans and bank run
1995	Kizu Credit Cooperative	Japan	Bad loans and bank run
1995	Kansallis-Osake-Pankki	Finland	Credit losses, merged to become Merita Group
1995	Union Bank of Finland	Finland	Credit losses, merged to become Merita Group
1996	Community Mutual Bank	South Africa	Liquidity problems and mismanagement
1997	Yamaichi Securities	Japan	Bankruptcy related to fraud allegations
1997	Sanyo Securities	Japan	Bad debts related to Asian financial crisis
1997	Hokkaidō Takushoku Bank	Japan	Bad debts related to Asian financial crisis
1997	Kwong Yik Bank Berhad	Malaysia	Asian financial crisis, merged with RHB Bank
1997	Banco Río	Argentina	Acquired by Banco Santander
1997	Islamic Bank	South Africa	Mismanagement and improper accounting
1998	Long-Term Credit Bank of Japan	Japan	Bad debts related to Asian financial crisis
1998	Nippon Credit Bank	Japan	Bad debts related to Asian financial crisis
1998	Bank Bumi Daya	Indonesia	Government-mandated merger
1998	Bank Dagang Negara	Indonesia	Government-mandated merger
1998	Bank Ekspor Impor Indonesia	Indonesia	Government-mandated merger
1998	Bank Pembangunan Indonesia	Indonesia	Government-mandated merger
1998	Abrar Finance Berhad	Malaysia	Government-mandated merger
1998	BestBank	US	Mortgage loan losses
1998	Banco Patricios	Argentina	Argentine banking crisis
1998	**Long-Term Capital Management (LTCM)**	US	Russian financial crisis, bailed out
1999	New Republic Bank	South Africa	Bank run and curatorship
1999	National Bank of Keystone	US	Mortgage loan losses
1999	FBC Fidelity Bank	South Africa	Mismanagement and liquidity problems
1999	Pacific Thrift and Loan	US	Mortgage loan losses
1999	**Bankers Trust**	US	Fraud, sold to Deutsche Bank
1999	Sime Bank Berhad	Malaysia	Government-enforced merger
2000	Ban Hin Lee Bank	Malaysia	Government-enforced merger
2000	United Merchant Finance Bhd	Malaysia	Government-enforced merger
2000	Perdana Finance Bhd	Malaysia	Government-enforced merger
2000	Cempaka Finance Bhd	Malaysia	Government-enforced merger
2000	Sabah Bank	Malaysia	Government-enforced merger
2001	**MBf Finance Berhad**	Malaysia	Government-enforced merger
2001	BSN Commercial Bank	Malaysia	Government-enforced merger
2001	**Regal Bank**	South Africa	Mismanagement and fraud

ADDENDUM

2001	Real Africa Durolink (RAD)	South Africa	Trading loss, bought by PSG
2002	**UniFer**	South Africa	Unsecured loan losses, deregistered
2002	**Saambou Bank**	South Africa	Mismanagement and loan losses
2002	**BOE Bank**	South Africa	Bank run, A2 Banking Crisis
2002	**Cadiz Investment Bank**	South Africa	Bank run, A2 Banking Crisis
2002	**FirstCorp Merchant Bank**	South Africa	Bank run, A2 Banking Crisis
2002	International Bank of Southern Africa	South Africa	Bank run, A2 Banking Crisis
2002	**PSG Investment Bank**	South Africa	Bank run, A2 Banking Crisis
2002	TA Bank of Southern Africa	South Africa	Bank run, A2 Banking Crisis
2002	Arab-Malaysian Finance Berhad	Malaysia	Government-enforced merger
2002	Banco General de Negocios	Argentina	Fraud, liquidated
2002	**Brait Merchant Bank**	South Africa	Contagion, A2 Banking Crisis
2002	**Corp Capital Bank**	South Africa	Contagion, A2 Banking Crisis
2002	Old Mutual Bank	South Africa	Contagion, A2 Banking Crisis
2002	**SECIB Bank**	South Africa	Contagion, A2 Banking Crisis
2003	Southern Pacific Bank	US	Unsuccessful capital raise
2003	Securities Investment Bank	South Africa	Contagion, A2 Banking Crisis
2003	**Unibank**	South Africa	Contagion, A2 Banking Crisis
2003	Cape of Good Hope Bank	South Africa	Incorporated under Nedbank
2003	African Merchant Bank	South Africa	Contagion A2 Banking Crisis
2003	Den Norske Bank	Norway	Merged with Gjensidige NOR
2003	**Asia Wealth Bank**	Myanmar	Myanmar bank crisis
2003	Yoma	Myanmar	Myanmar bank crisis
2004	Gensec Bank	South Africa	Loan losses, deregistered
2007	American Freedom Mortgage	US	Subprime mortgage crisis
2007	New Century	US	Subprime mortgage crisis
2007	American Home Mortgage	US	Subprime mortgage crisis
2007	Ameriquest Mortgage	US	Subprime mortgage crisis
2007	NetBank	US	Subprime mortgage crisis
2007	Miami Valley Bank	US	Subprime mortgage crisis
2008	Sachsen LB	Germany	Fraud, subprime mortgage losses
2008	**Northern Rock**	UK	Mortgage losses and bank run
2008	**Bear Stearns**	US	Subprime losses and bank run
2008	**Countrywide Financial**	US	Subprime losses, sold to BofA
2008	**IndyMac Bank**	US	Alt-A losses and bank run
2008	Alliance & Leicester	UK	Loan losses and bank run
2008	Roskilde Bank	Denmark	Real estate loan losses
2008	Silver State Bank	US	Subprime mortgage crisis

WHY BANKS FAIL

2008	Fannie Mae	US	Subprime mortgage crisis
2008	Freddie Mac	US	Subprime mortgage crisis
2008	Derbyshire Building Society	UK	Subprime mortgage crisis
2008	Cheshire Building Society	UK	Subprime mortgage crisis
2008	**Merrill Lynch**	US	Subprime losses, sold to BofA
2008	**Lehman Brothers**	US	Subprime mortgage crisis
2008	**Washington Mutual**	US	Subprime losses and bank run
2008	Fortis	Netherlands	Poor acquisitions, nationalised
2008	Bradford & Bingley	UK	Mortgage loan losses
2008	HBOS	UK	Mismanagement and mortgage loan losses
2008	**Wachovia**	US	Subprime losses, sold to Wells Fargo
2008	Landsbanki	Iceland	Overleveraged and nationalised
2008	Icesave	UK	UK subsidiary of Landsbanki
2008	Glitnir	Iceland	Overleveraged and nationalised
2008	Kaupthing	Iceland	Overleveraged and nationalised
2008	BankWest	Australia	Subsidiary of HBOS
2008	Sovereign Bank	US	Exposure to Fannie Mae
2008	Royal Bank of Scotland Group	UK	Poor acquisitions and subprime crisis
2008	**UBS**	Switzerland	Global Financial Crisis, bailed out
2008	**Citigroup**	US	Global Financial Crisis, bailed out
2008	**Bank of America**	US	Global Financial Crisis, bailed out
2008	**JPMorgan Chase & Co**	US	Global Financial Crisis, bailed out
2008	**Goldman Sachs**	US	Global Financial Crisis, bailed out
2008	**Morgan Stanley**	US	Global Financial Crisis, bailed out
2008	**Wells Fargo**	US	Global Financial Crisis, bailed out
2008	**ING Group**	Netherlands	Global Financial Crisis, bailed out
2008	**Société Générale**	France	Global Financial Crisis, bailed out
2008	Barnsley Building Society	UK	Mortgage loan losses
2008	National City Bank	US	Mortgage loan losses
2008	Commerce Bancorp	US	Mismanagement and loan losses
2008	Banco Português de Negócios	Portugal	Mismanagement and accounting irregularities
2008	Scarborough Building Society	UK	Mortgage loan losses
2008	Parex Bank	Latvia	Loan losses, nationalised
2008	London Scottish Bank	UK	Loan losses in unsecured lending
2008	Downey Savings and Loan	US	Mortgage loan losses
2009	Anglo Irish Bank	Ireland	Mortgage loan losses, nationalised
2009	Bank of Antigua	Antigua	Ponzi scheme, nationalised
2009	Straumur Investment Bank	Iceland	Loan losses, nationalised
2009	Dunfermline Building Society	UK	Mortgage loan losses

ADDENDUM

2009	Cape Fear Bank	US	Mortgage loan losses
2009	New Frontier Bank	US	Mortgage loan losses
2009	American Sterling Bank	US	Mortgage loan losses
2009	American Southern Bank	US	Mortgage loan losses
2009	Stanford Bank Venezuela	Venezuela	Bank run, nationalised
2009	Banco de Venezuela	Venezuela	Bank run, nationalised
2009	**Colonial Bank**	US	Mortgage loan losses
2009	Hypo Alpe Adria Bank	Austria	European debt crisis
2009	Philippine American	Philippines	Credit crunch and loan losses
2009	SPB	Iceland	Overleveraged and liquidated
2009	Dresdner Bank	Germany	Acquired by Commerzbank
2009	DSB Bank	Netherlands	Bank run triggered by rumours
2009	FBOP Corp	US	Mortgage loan losses
2009	Guaranty Bank	US	Mortgage loan losses
2009	BankUnited	US	Mortgage loan losses
2009	AmTrust Bank	US	Mortgage loan losses
2009	United Commercial Bank	US	Mismanagement and fraud
2009	California National Bank	US	Subprime loan losses
2009	Corus Bank	US	Commercial mortgage loan losses
2009	First Federal Bank of California	US	Mortgage loan losses
2009	Imperial Capital Bank of La Jolla	US	Mortgage loan losses
2009	Swedbank	Sweden	Baltic loan losses, bailed out
2009	SEB	Sweden	Baltic loan losses, bailed out
2010	Chesham Building Society	UK	Mortgage loan losses
2010	Banco Privado Português	Portugal	Fraud, liquidated
2010	EuroBancshares	US	Mortgage loan losses
2010	CajaSur	Spain	Credit crunch and loan losses
2010	Ambac	US	Ratings downgrades, liquidity crunch
2010	Chelsea Building Society	UK	Fraud, merged with Yorkshire Building Society
2010	WesternBank	US	Mortgage loan losses
2010	Amcore Bank	US	Mortgage loan losses
2010	Presbyterian Mutual Society	UK	Uninsured deposits and bank run
2011	BankMeridian	US	Mismanagement and loan losses
2011	EON Bank	Malaysia	Merged with Hong Leong Bank Group
2011	ATEbank	Greece	Greek debt crisis
2011	Banco Filipino	Philippines	Liquidity crisis and loan losses
2011	CatalunyaCaixa	Spain	European debt crisis
2011	Dexia Bank	Belgium	Greek debt exposure and bank run
2012	Bankia	Spain	European debt crisis

WHY BANKS FAIL

2012	Western German State Bank	Germany	Securitised credit losses
2012	Toender Bank	Denmark	Real estate losses and under-provisioning
2013	**Wegelin & Co**	Switzerland	Reputational damage
2013	Sparekassen Lolland	Denmark	Insolvent, merged with Jyske
2013	SNS Reaal	Netherlands	Real estate loan losses, nationalised
2013	Monte dei Paschi di Siena	Italy	Fraud, bailed out
2013	TT Hellenic Postbank	Greece	Greek debt crisis
2014	Jiangsu Sheyang Rural Commercial Bank	China	Bank run triggered by rumours
2014	Corporate Commercial Bank	Bulgaria	Bank run triggered by murder accusations
2014	**African Bank**	South Africa	Mismanagement and unsecured lending losses
2015	Doral Bank	US	Legal battle with Puerto Rican government
2016	Intermarket Banking Corporation	Zambia	Liquidity crisis and bank run
2016	Twiga Bancorp	Tanzania	Bad loans and bank run
2016	Crane Bank	Uganda	Legal troubles, deregistered
2016	Imperial Bank	Kenya	Bad loans and fraud
2017	Home Capital Group	Canada	Bank run triggered by fraud accusations
2017	Veneto Banca	Italy	Bad loans and weak capital
2017	Banca Popolare di Vicenza	Italy	Bad loans and weak capital
2018	Banco Finansur	Argentina	Liquidity problems, nationalised
2018	**VBS Mutual Bank**	South Africa	Mismanagement, fraud and liquidity problems
2019	**Mercantile Bank**	South Africa	Acquired by Capitec, deregistered
2020	Almena State Bank	US	Inadequate board oversight and poor asset quality
2021	**Greensill Capital**	UK	Credit insurers withdrew cover
2021	**Archegos Capital Management**	US	Overleveraged, defaulted on margin calls
2022	PJSC Sberbank	Czech Republic	Bank run following Russia's invasion of Ukraine
2023	Silvergate Bank	US	FTX (crypto) exposure and bank run
2023	**Silicon Valley Bank**	US	Poor risk management, bond portfolio losses, bank run
2023	**Signature Bank**	US	Bank run related to crypto exposures
2023	**Credit Suisse**	Switzerland	String of scandals leading to a crisis of confidence
2023	**First Republic Bank**	US	Ratings downgrades, uninsured deposits, bank run

NOTES

PREFACE

Becker flies to Hawaii – Donlevy, K. "Ex-Silicon Valley Bank CEO Greg Becker jets to Hawaii after collapse". *New York Post* (2023); Styles, R. "Aloha suckers! Silicon Valley Bank's failed CEO Gregory Becker escapes to his $3.1million Hawaiian hideaway". *Daily Mail* (2023)

$209 billion in assets – "California Financial Regulator Takes Possession of Silicon Valley Bank". California Department of Financial Protection and Innovation (2023)

Largest bank failure since 2007/08, second-largest in US history – French, D. "SVB is largest bank failure since 2008 financial crisis". *Reuters* (2023)

Becker-SVB history – Lang, H. "Who is Greg Becker, the former head of failed Silicon Valley Bank?" *Reuters* (2023)

SVB collapse – "Silicon Valley Bank's collapse reveals regulatory flaws". *Financial Times* (2023); Son, H., Goswami, R. and Vanian, J. "Here's how the second-biggest bank collapse in U.S. history happened in just 48 hours". *CNBC* (2023)

"We have been […]" (Gregory Becker) – Titcomb, J. "Inside Silicon Valley Bank's collapse as chief begged tech giants not to panic". *The Telegraph* (2023)

Customers withdrew $42 billion of SVB's total deposits ($175 billion), 24% of total deposits – "Order Taking Possession of Property and Business in Matter of Silicon Valley Bank". California Department of Financial Protection and Innovation (2023)

Becker and Beck sell shares – Weinstein, A. "SVB CEO Sold $3.6 Million in Stock Days Before Bank's Failure". *Bloomberg* (2023); Dukakis, A. "SVB execs sold millions of their company stock in lead-up to collapse, federal disclosures show". *ABC News* (2023)

Payroll companies – Thibodeau, P. "How the SVB collapse upended payroll for thousands". TechTarget (2023)

INTRODUCTION

During the A2 Banking Crisis of 2002/03, and in the years that immediately followed, 22 banks ultimately failed or deregistered – Tjiane, N. "Curatorship of Banks as a Measure to Rescue Failing Banks". University of Pretoria (2015)

Of the top 1,000 banks, 106 failed (10.6%) – Monocle Research Team. "The Art of Failure: Predicting Financial Distress Pre-Crisis". *Monocle Quarterly Journal* (2016)

WHY BANKS FAIL

PART I
SILICON VALLEY BANK

SVB history – Sulek, J. "How a poker game launched Silicon Valley Bank's four-decade ride on the tech wave". *Mercury News* (2023); Smith, S. "Silicon Valley Bank oral history panel". Computer History Museum (2023)

SVB Group (NASD:SIVB) added to S&P 500 (2018) – "Take-Two Interactive Software, SVB Financial and Nektar Therapeutics Set to Join S&P 500; Others to Join S&P MidCap 400 and S&P SmallCap 600". S&P Global (2018)

SVB balance sheet and bond portfolio – Lavier, F. "Analysis: Silicon Valley Bank's Bankruptcy". Lazard Frères Gestion (2023)

SVB subsidiaries – SEC filing. "SVB Financial Group Annual Report on Form 10-K". SEC (2022)

Stress test – Schroeder, P. "Explainer: How does the Fed stress test US banks?" *Reuters* (2023); "Stress Tests". Federal Reserve (2022)

Stress test rule change – On 10 October 2019, the Federal Reserve finalised a rule to exempt firms with total assets of less than $100 billion from the supervisory stress test (84 Fed. Reg. 59032 Nov. 1, 2019)

"unnecessarily" (Gregory Becker) – "Statement of Gregory Becker Chief Executive Officer SVB Financial Group, Inc On Behalf of Silicon Valley Bank". US Senate Committee on Banking, Housing, and Urban Affairs (2015)

"increase the likelihood [...]" (Congressional Budget Office) – "Comments on Economic Growth, Regulatory Relief, and Consumer Protection Act". Senate Committee on Banking, Housing, and Urban Affairs (2018)

"transitory" (Jerome Powell) – Staff writer. "Fed's Powell floats dropping 'transitory' label for inflation". *Reuters* (2021)

SVB the sixteenth-largest US bank – Russell, K. "3 Failed Banks This Year Were Bigger Than 25 That Crumbled in 2008". *The New York Times* (2023)

Fed rate hikes (2022) – "Federal Funds Effective Rate (FEDFUNDS)". Federal Reserve Bank of St Louis (2023)

SVB losses – "SVB Financial Group Announces Proposed Offerings of Common Stock and Mandatory Convertible Preferred Stock". SVB Financial Group (2023); Weil, J. "Banks Lose Billions in Value After Tech Lender SVB Stumbles". *The Wall Street Journal* (2023); Griffith, E. "Silicon Valley Bank's Financial Stability Worries Investors". *The New York Times* (2023)

89% of SVB's deposits uninsured – Schroeder, S. "After Silicon Valley Bank's shutdown, uninsured depositors face tense wait". *Reuters* (2023)

SVB share price – Yahoo Finance (2023)

Founders Fund – Chapman, L. "Thiel's Founders Fund Withdrew Millions From Silicon Valley Bank". *Bloomberg* (2023)

Depositors withdrew $42 billion, over 20% of SVB's total deposits ($175 billion) – "Order Taking Possession of Property and Business in Matter of Silicon Valley Bank". California Department of Financial Protection and Innovation (2023)

Signature Bank closed (12 Mar 2023) – Lang, H. "Signature Bank becomes next casualty of banking turmoil after SVB". *Reuters* (2023)

212

NOTES

First Republic Bank closed (1 May 2023), sold to JPMorgan Chase & Co – "Failed Bank Information for First Republic Bank, San Francisco, CA". Federal Deposit Insurance Corporation (2023)

Combined assets of SVB, Signature and First Republic: $532 billion – Goldberg, M. "The 7 largest bank failures in US history". Bankrate (2023)

"Its senior leadership [...]" (Michael Barr) – "Review of the Federal Reserve's Supervision and Regulation of Silicon Valley Bank". Federal Reserve (2023)

THE MEDICIS: BANKERS OF THE RENAISSANCE

Discovery of Michelangelo's work (1975); Medici Chapels (1520) – Poggioli, S. "This Room is Thought to Have Been Michelangelo's Secret Hideaway and Drawing Board". *NPR* (2018)

Florence established as a republic (1115) – Gardener, E. *The Story of Florence*. JM Dent & Co (2011)

Medici history; Cosimo's death (1464); bank history (1397-1494); 1527 revolt; Pazzi Conspiracy (1478); Medici return to Florence (1512); Florentine banking houses: 71 (1399), 33 (1460), 8 (1516) – De Roover, R. *The Rise and Decline of The Medici Bank*. Borodino Books (1963); Simonetta, M. "The Medici Meltdown". *Forbes* (2008); Moy, C. "Economic History of the Medici Family". *The Economic Historian* (2020)

Merchant banks – Kohn, M. "Merchant Banking in the Medieval and Early Modern Economy". Dartmouth College (1999)

Shakespeare, W. *The Merchant of Venice* (1598)

Dostoevsky, F. *Crime and Punishment* (1866)

Bills of exchange – Kohn, M. "Bills of Exchange and the Money Market to 1600". Dartmouth College (1999)

4,500 US banks (2023) – Federal Deposit Insurance Corporation (4,672 banks in March 2023)

FREQUENCY OF BANK FAILURES

King Edward III's default (1343) – Mount, H. "The art of the Medicis is a lesson in absolution for bankers". *Financial Times* (2011); Kunal, T. "The Crash of the European Financial System in 1345". The Financial Engineer (2013)

Stockholms Banco (1656) – "First banknotes in Europe". Sveriges Riksbank; Högberg, S. "Sweden's first banknotes". *Scandinavian Economic History Review* (2011)

Commercial paper crisis (1763) – Schnabel, I. and Song Shin, H. "Liquidity and Contagion: The Crisis of 1793". *Journal of the European Economic Association* (2004)

British crises (1772-1773; 1810-1890) – Kenny, S., Lennard, J. and Turner, J. "The macroeconomic effects of banking crises: Evidence from the United Kingdom, 1750-1938". *Explorations in Economic History* (2021); "The Credit Crisis of 1772". Hansraj College (2021)

US panics (1792-1905); Panic of 1893 (600 bank failures); Treasury Reserves $190 million-$100 million (1890-1893) – Richardson, G. and Sablik, T. "Banking Panics of the Gilded Age". Federal Reserve History (2015); Carlson, M. "Causes of Bank Suspensions in the Panic of 1893". *Explorations in Economic History* (2005); Klitgaard, T. and Narron, J. "Crisis Chronicles: Gold, Deflation, and the Panic of 1893". Federal Reserve Bank of New York (2016); Stevens, A. "Analysis of the Phenomena of the Panic in the United States in 1893". *The Quarterly Journal of Economics* (1894)

WHY BANKS FAIL

Overend, Gurney and Company (1866) – Sowerbutts, R., Schneebalg, M. and Hubert, F. "The demise of Overend Gurney". *The Bank of England Quarterly Bulletin Q2* (2016); Taylor, B. "Overend, Gurney & Co.: An Inspiration to Karl Marx and Bear Stearns". Global Financial Data (2015)

US bank failures (1921-2023); depositors lost over $1.3 billion (1930-1933); over 2,900 banks and thrifts failed, assets of over $2.2 trillion (1980-1995) – Desilver, D. "Most U.S. bank failures have come in a few big waves". Pew Research Centre (2023)

Price of oil quadrupled (1973-1974) – Corbett, M. "Oil Shock of 1973-74". Federal Reserve History (2013)

UK Secondary Banking Crisis (1974); the Bank of England bailed out/assisted 60 banks, losing £100 million – Reid, M. *The Secondary Banking Crisis, 1973-75: Its Causes and Course*. Macmillan (2003)

Savings and Loan Crisis – Robinson, K. "Savings and Loan Crisis". Federal Reserve History (2013); "An Examination of the Banking Crises of the 1980s and Early 1990s". Federal Deposit Insurance Corporation (2023)

Shōwa Financial Crisis (1927-1928); 265 bank failures – Shizume, M. "The Japanese Economy during the Interwar Period: Instability in the Financial System and the Impact of the World Depression". *Bank of Japan Review* (2009)

1997 Asian financial crisis – Kanaya, A. and Woo, D. "The Japanese Banking Crisis of the 1990s: Sources and Lessons". International Monetary Fund Working Paper (2000); Fujii, M. and Kawai, M. "Lessons from Japan's Banking Crisis". Asian Development Bank Institute Working Paper (2010)

Banco Español de Crédito (1994) – Fuller, T. "'Preemptive Action' Puts Central Bank in Control: Malaysia Takes Over MBf Finance". *The New York Times* (1999)

Malaysia's MBf Finance Berhad (1997-1999) – Pura, R. "MBf Finance Cedes Management After Holders Fail on Rescue Plan". *The Wall Street Journal* (1999)

Nationwide banking crises (1990s) – Drees, B. and Pazarbasioglu, C. *The Nordic Banking Crises: Pitfalls in Financial Liberalization*. International Monetary Fund (1998); García-Herrero, A. "Banking Crises in Latin America in the 1990s". International Monetary Fund (1997); Owen, D. and Robinson, D. *Russia Rebounds*. International Monetary Fund (2003)

Argentinian banking crisis (2001) – Kiguel, M. "Argentina's 2001 Economic and Financial Crisis: Lessons for Europe". In *Think Tank 20: Beyond Macroeconomic Policy Coordination Discussions in the G-20*. Brookings Institution (2011)

Myanmar banking crisis (2003) – Turnell, S. "Myanmar's Banking Crisis". *ASEAN Economic Bulletin* (2003)

Washington Mutual (1889-2008); largest US bank failure to date; $309 billion in assets; $16.7 billion withdrawn by customers over nine days; sold to JPMorgan Chase & Co for $1.9 billion. – Bella, T. "Even after Silicon Valley Bank's collapse, WaMu's is still the biggest". *The Washington Post* (2023)

10.6% of the world's top 1,000 banks failed/bailed out during 2007/08 Global Financial Crisis – Monocle Research Team. "The Art of Failure: Predicting Financial Distress Pre-Crisis". *Monocle Quarterly Journal* (2016)

NOTES

Credit Suisse (2023) – Walker, O. and Morris, S. "Credit Suisse: the rise and fall of the bank that built modern Switzerland". *Financial Times* (2023)

Prior to 2023, the three largest failures in the US after Washington Mutual were IndyMac Bank (2008), Colonial Bank (2009) and First Republic Bank-Dallas (1998) – Goldberg, M. "The 7 largest bank failures in US history". Bankrate (2023) Note: This list only includes banks that failed and not those that were provided federal assistance.

PART II
A SHORT HISTORY OF MONEY: 1

Cowrie shells (1200BC) – "Cowrie Shells and Trade Power". Smithsonian National Museum of African American History and Culture; "Money Cowries". MetCon website (2023)

Early coinage (6th century onwards); 12 pennies = 1 shilling, 20 shillings = 1 pound – Mundell, R. "The Birth of Coinage". Columbia University Working Paper (2002); Feliu, G. "Money and Currency". In Naismith, R. (ed). *Money and Coinage in the Middle Ages.* Brill (2018)

Bitcoin price (under \$5,500 in March 2020, almost \$65,000 in October 2021) – Coinmarketcap.com

Over 20,000 cryptocurrencies (2023) – "The Ultimate Guide To Crypto Portfolio Management". Coinmarketcap.com (22,932 cryptocurrencies in June 2023)

Euro used by twenty countries – "Countries using the euro". European Union

China paper money (7th century) – "Chinese Paper Currency". American Numismatic Association

Stockholms Banco (1657-1668); copper coin debasement (1660) – "First banknotes in Europe". Sveriges Riksbank; Högberg, S. "Sweden's first banknotes". *Scandinavian Economic History Review* (2011)

Bank of England banknotes (1965-1745); UK laws (1833) – "The Bank of England note – a short history". The Bank of England (1969)

Federal Reserve (1913) – Wheelock, D. "The History of the Federal Reserve". Federal Reserve History (2021)

Gold standard (1871) – Scammell, W. "The Working of the Gold Standard". *Bulletin of Economic Research* (1965)

JOHN LAW AND THE BANQUE GÉNÉRALE

King Louis XIV and Philippe II of Orléans – "Death of Louis XIV, 1715". Château de Versailles website (2023); "Absolutism in Early Modern France". University of Washington (2023)

A value in livres could be converted to its equivalent in dollars in 1999 by halving it, then multiplying by twelve. According to this formula, three billion livres is equivalent to \$18 billion in 1999, which is \$33 billion in 2023 – Sandrock, J. E. "John Law's Banque Royale and the Mississippi Bubble". *International Bank Note Society* (2011); Gleeson, J. "Millionaire: The Philanderer, Gambler, and Duelist Who Invented Modern Finance". *The New York Times* (2000)

John Law; Banque Générale and Banque Royale; first fully fledged European fiat currency; specie held in reserve equivalent to 50% of paper money in circulation; money supply; Law's purchase of tax collection rights and mints – Thiers, A. *The Mississippi Bubble: A Memoir of John Law.* WA Townsend (1859); Keyes, S. "John Law: the gambler who broke France". *Money Week* (2012); Velde, F. R. "Government Equity and Money: John Law's System in

215

WHY BANKS FAIL

France". Federal Reserve Bank of Chicago (2014); Narron, J. and Skeie, D. "Crisis Chronicles: The Mississippi Bubble of 1720 and the European Debt Crisis". Federal Reserve Bank of New York (2014); Velde, F. R. "John Law's System". *The American Economic Review* (2007); Martin, F. "John Law, the gambler who revolutionised French finance". *The Financial Times* (2018); Chancellor, E. "Chancellor: Lessons from the Mississippi Bubble". *Reuters* (2016)

The Mississippi Company; Law appointed Controller General and Superintendent General of Finance; collapse and bank run – Norman, J. "John Law pioneered ideas about banking and monetary policy that are important to this day". *The Spectator* (2018); Moen, J. "John Law and the Mississippi Bubble: 1718-1720". *Mississippi History Now* (2001); Sandrock, J. E. "John Law's Banque Royale and the Mississippi Bubble". *International Bank Note Society* (2011); "John Law". Encyclopedia.com (2018); "Mississippi Bubble". *Encyclopedia Britannica* (2020); Murphy, A. "Two Bubbles and a Plague". Center for the Study of Economic Liberty (2023)

Federal Reserve money supply – Buckham, D., Wilkinson, R. and Straeuli, C. *The End of Money: The Great Erosion of Trust in Banking, China's Minsky Moment and the Fallacy of Cryptocurrency.* Mercury (2021)

Equity in Mississippi Company becomes a monetary standard – Garber, P.M. "Famous First Bubbles". *Journal of Economic Perspectives* (1990)

Saudi National Bank announcement – Meredith, S. *et al.* "Credit Suisse shares tank after Saudi backer rules out further assistance". *CNBC* (2023)

A SHORT HISTORY OF MONEY: 2

Gold standard (1900); David Hume; suspension of gold standard (1914) – Cooper, R. "The Gold Standard: Historical Facts and Future Prospects". Brookings.edu; Wennerlind, C. "David Hume's Monetary Theory Revisited: Was He Really a Quantity Theorist and an Inflationist?". *Journal of Political Economy* (2005)

Dollar-gold convertibility suspended (1933) – Richardson, G., Komai, A. and Gou, M. "Roosevelt's Gold Program". Federal Reserve History (2013)

Bretton Woods System (1944-1971) – Buckham, D., Wilkinson, R. and Straeuli, C. *The End of Money: The Great Erosion of Trust in Banking, China's Minsky Moment and the Fallacy of Cryptocurrency.* Mercury (2021)

US inflation: below 2% (1960s), 6% (1970), 15% (1980) – Bryan, M. "The Great Inflation". Federal Reserve History (2013)

US balance of trade: surpluses (1870-1970), deficit (1970-) – Reinbold, N. and Wen, Y. "How Industrialization Shaped America's Trade Balance". The Federal Reserve Bank of St Louis (2020)

"We must create [...]" (Richard Nixon, 15 August 1971) – Nixon, R. "Address to the Nation Outlining a New Economic Policy: 'The Challenge of Peace'". (1971)

Nixon Shock; 90-day freeze on prices and wages, 10% tariff – Ghizoni, S. "Nixon Ends Convertibility of U.S. Dollars to Gold and Announces Wage/Price Controls". Federal Reserve History (2013); "Nixon and the End of the Bretton Woods System, 1971-1973". US Department of State Office of the Historian

Smithsonian Agreement (1971-1973) – "Nixon and the End of the Bretton Woods System, 1971-1973". US Department of State Office of the Historian

NOTES

THE FUNDAMENTALS OF BANKING

Leverage ratios; Fed's balance sheet: $800 billion-$4.5 trillion (2008-2014) – Buckham, D., Wilkinson, R. and Straeuli, C. *The End of Money: The Great Erosion of Trust in Banking, China's Minsky Moment and the Fallacy of Cryptocurrency*. Mercury (2021)

Credit Suisse: $119 billion withdrawn Q4 2022 – Daga, A. "What happened at Credit Suisse and how did it reach crisis point?". *Reuters* (2023)

Ammar Al Khudairy interview; SNB 9.9% stake – El-Din, Y. and Halftermeyer, M. "Credit Suisse Reels After Top Shareholder Rules Out Raising Stake". *Bloomberg* (2023)

Credit Suisse share price dropped 24% – Meredith, S., Smith, E. and Ward-Glenton, H. "Credit Suisse shares tank after Saudi backer rules out further assistance". *CNBC* (2023)

$54 billion liquidity backstop – Morris, S., Fontanella-Khan, J. and Massoudi, A. "How the Swiss 'trinity' forced UBS to save Credit Suisse". *Financial Times* (2023)

PART III
MARKET CONDUCT

"Today we take an essential step […]" (George W Bush, 26 October 2001) – "Remarks on Signing the USA Patriot Act of 2001". The American Presidency Project

US Patriot Act; Congress 357-66 (23 October), Senate 98-1 (25 October) – Wyden, R. "Law and Policy Efforts to balance Security, Privacy and Civil Liberties in Post-9/11 America". Stanford Law School (2006); Lindt, D. "Everyone's heard of the Patriot Act. Here's what it actually does". *Vox* (2015)

Feingold's objection – Feingold, R. "Why I Opposed the Patriot Act". *The Nation* (2021)

9/11 attacks (3,000 killed, 6,000 injured); 9/11 Commission report (2004): "the principal architect […]"; attacks cost $500,000, $300,000 passing through US bank accounts; "Neither the hijackers […]"; put-to-call ratios: American Airlines 6:1, United Airlines 25:1 – Buckham, D., Wilkinson, R. and Straeuli, C. *The End of Money: The Great Erosion of Trust in Banking, China's Minsky Moment and the Fallacy of Cryptocurrency*. Mercury (2021)

"By concealing US clients' […]" (Bradley Birkenfeld); DOJ cases against fourteen Swiss banks – Ingram, D. "Swiss banker in U.S. tax case says he was told, 'Don't get caught'". *Reuters* (2014); Mathiason, N. "Tax scandal leaves Swiss giant reeling". *The Guardian* (2008)

UBS charges (2001-2008); 52,000 clients, $20 billion in assets – Fletcher, P. and Jucca, L. "UBS, U.S. settle tax evasion case". *Reuters* (2009)

Birkenfeld conviction; forty months in a federal penitentiary (2010); $104 million reward (2012) – Temple-West, P. and Browning, L. "Whistleblower in UBS tax case gets record $104 million". *Reuters* (2012); "Former UBS Banker Sentenced to 40 Months for Aiding Billionaire Americans Evade Taxes". US Department of Justice Office of Public Affairs (2009)

UBS $780 million fine – Browning, L. "Settlement Reached in UBS Tax Case". *The New York Times* (2009)

Swiss bank secrecy; French advertisement (1910); "enables us to manage […]"; collective assets held by Swiss banks amounted to 26% of those held by French banks (1913), 73% (1929); 1934 Swiss Federal Act on Banks and Savings Banks; Swiss banks and Nazis – Makortoff, K. "How Swiss banking secrecy enabled an unequal global financial system". *The Guardian* (2022); Dorsey, A. "Shh---It's a Secret! The Evolution of the Swiss Banking System & International

217

WHY BANKS FAIL

Tax Implications". *International Program Papers* (2021); Guex, S. "The Origins of the Swiss Banking Secrecy Law and its Repercussions for Swiss Federal Policy". University of Basel Library (2017); Jones, S. "Credit Suisse linked to list of Nazi émigré accounts in Argentina". *Financial Times* (2020)

US and Switzerland tax-sharing agreements (1973-2009) – Temple-West, P. "UPDATE 2- Switzerland, U.S. sign pact on fighting tax evasion". *Reuters* (2013)

Swiss banks held $2.2 trillion/one-third of all global cross-border assets (2008) – Drawbaugh, K. "U.S. Senate panel to question Swiss banker, secrecy". *Reuters* (2009)

Names provided by UBS: initially 250, ultimately 4,500 (2009); "affirmative acts of fraud […]" – Bachmann, H. "Can Swiss Banks Thrive After the UBS-U.S. Deal?". *Time* (2009); Drawbaugh, K. and Vicini, J. "U.S. seeks more UBS account records in tax battle". *Reuters* (2009)

LGT Bank – Browning, L. "Banking Scandal Unfolds Like a Thriller". *The New York Times* (2008)

US losing $100 billion in tax revenue annually (2008) – Fletcher, P. "IRS: new UBS-style foreign bank prosecution 'shortly'". *Reuters* (2010); "Tax Havens: International Tax Avoidance and Evasion". Congressional Research (2022)

FATCA; 30% withholding tax – Foreign Account Tax Compliance Act. IRS; Song, J. "The End of Secret Swiss Accounts?: The Impact of the U.S. Foreign Account Tax Compliance Act (FATCA) on Switzerland's Status as a Haven for Offshore Accounts". *North Western Journal of International Law & Business* (2015); Mombelli, A. "Swiss banks to tell all under FATCA". Swissinfo.ch

"The American authorities […]" (Michel Dérobert) – Browning, L. "Names Deal Cracks Swiss Bank Secrecy". *The New York Times* (2009)

Wegelin (1741-2013); tax evasion totalling at least $1.2 billion (2013); $57.8 million fine – Raymond, N. and Browning, L. "Swiss bank Wegelin to close after guilty plea". *Reuters* (2013)

Switzerland-US non-prosecution agreement (2013); "enable every Swiss bank […]" – "US DOJ Statement on Non-prosecution Agreements for Swiss Banks". *Bloomberg* (2013)

"the US is simply too big […]" (Zeno Staub) – "U.S. wealth market still attractive for Swiss banks-Vontobel CEO". *Reuters* (2013)

26 FATCA intergovernmental agreements (2014) – "FATCA Agreements in Substance will be Considered in Effect". Orbitax

FATCA compliance (2023); 113 countries – "Foreign Account Tax Compliance Act". US Department of the Treasury

Standard for Automatic Exchange of Financial Information in Tax Matters; initially 38 OECD members, 114 jurisdictions compliant in 2023, nine committed to 2026 deadline – "Automatic Exchange of Information". OECD; "Automatic Exchange of Information (AEOI): Status of Commitments". OECD

Twin Peaks (1995) – Taylor, M. *"Twin Peaks": A Regulatory Structure for the New Century.* Centre for the Study of Financial Innovation (1995)

CREDIT SUISSE

Lara Banev – "Kidnapped daughter of Bulgarian money-laundering convict returned". *The Sofia Globe* (2013); "Bulgarian 'Kingpin's' Daughter Abducted to 'Keep Him Silent'". Novinite.com (2013)

NOTES

Evelin Banev – "Bulgaria: 'Cocaine King' Appears in Court, Dispels Rumors He Fled Justice". Organized Crime and Corruption Reporting Project (2015); Nebehay, S. "Ex-Credit Suisse banker says took lead from bosses in Bulgarian cocaine-cash case". *Reuters* (2022); "King of Bulgarian cocaine: Credit Suisse is condemned but Swiss justice lacks bite". *Public Eye* (2022)

Credit Suisse and Bulgarian drug traffickers (2004-2008); SFr21 million (roughly $22 million) fine – "Credit Suisse found guilty over Bulgarian drug money failings". *Financial Times* (2022); Ewing, J. "Credit Suisse is fined for helping a Bulgarian drug ring launder money, a court said". *The New York Times* (2022)

Suisse Secrets; 30,000 clients – "What is Suisse Secrets? Everything You Need to Know About the Swiss Banking Leak". Organized Crime and Corruption Reporting Project (2022); "Swiss banks accused of hiding data behind secrecy laws". Swissinfo.ch (2023); "Swiss banking secrecy law clashes with freedom of speech". Swissinfo.ch (2022)

Switzerland's FATF review (2016); "the generally good quality"; Federal Act on Combating Money Laundering and Terrorist Financing in the Financial Sector amendments (2021, came into effect 2023) – "Integrity of the financial centre". Swiss State Secretariat for International Finance; "Anti-money laundering – Switzerland only acts under pressure". *Public Eye*; "In brief: banking regulatory framework in Switzerland". Lenz & Staehelin (2023); Hofmann, A. "Bank Secrecy Laws (Switzerland)". Thomson Reuters Practical Law (2022)

Conspiring to help Americans file false tax returns (2014) – "Credit Suisse Pleads Guilty to Conspiracy to Aid and Assist U.S. Taxpayers in Filing False Returns". US Department of Justice Office of Public Affairs (2014)

$5.3 billion fine, DOJ (2017) – "Credit Suisse Agrees to Pay $5.28 Billion in Connection with its Sale of Residential Mortgage-Backed Securities". US Department of Justice Office of Public Affairs (2017)

Espionage scandal (2019); seven executives (2016-2019); Gottstein replaced Thiam (February 2020) – O'Donnell, J. and Revill, J. "Spies and lies: regulators round on Credit Suisse". *Reuters* (2021); Tsang, A. "Spying Scandal at Credit Suisse Leads to Top Executive's Resignation". *The New York Times* (2019)

Patrice Lescaudron (2021) – Jones, S. "Credit Suisse turned blind eye as top banker stole from billionaire clients". *Financial Times* (2021)

Credit Suisse history (1856-2023); Greensill Capital (2021): 1,000 Credit Suisse clients, $10 billion loss; Archegos Capital (2021): $5.5 billion loss; $1.3 billion in loans to Mozambique (2012-2016): $475 million paid to US and UK authorities, loss of project cost $400 per citizen, equivalent to the country's GDP in 2016 – Walker, O. and Morris, S. "Credit Suisse: the rise and fall of the bank that built modern Switzerland". *Financial Times* (2023)

"seriously breached […]" (FINMA) – "Credit Suisse slammed for 'serious breaches' in Greensill debacle". Swissinfo.ch (2023)

"fundamental failure of management […]"; "lackadaisical attitude towards risk" – Walker, O. "Credit Suisse prepares legal action against Archegos". *Financial Times* (2021)

October 2022 announcement: reduce costs by SFr1 billion ($1.1 billion), raise SFr4 billion ($4.3 billion) in capital to finance its restructuring; SFr2.24 billion raised in a rights offer, balance funded by Saudi National Bank (9.9%) and Qatar Investment Authority (5.6%, later 6.9%) – "Credit Suisse raises $4.3 billion capital after wild ride". *Bloomberg* (2022);

WHY BANKS FAIL

Al Sayegh, H., Hirt, O. and Mills, A. "Qatar Investment Authority raises stake in Credit Suisse to just under 7%". *Reuters* (2023)

"Markets are saying it's insolvent [...]" (Jim Lewis); Wall Street Silver, audience of over 300,000 followers – Farrell, M., Flitter, E. and Rennison, J. "How One of Switzerland's Oldest Banks Became a Meme Stock". *The New York Times* (2022)

Credit Suisse share, bond and spreads information – Walker, O. "Credit Suisse reassures investors over its financial strength". *Financial Times* (2022); Companiesmarketcap.com; Investing.com

Q4 2022, SFr111 billion ($119 billion) in customer assets withdrawn; Q4 loss of SFr1.4 billion ($1.5 billion); annual loss SFr7.3 billion ($8 billion) (2022) – Walker, O. "Credit Suisse slumps to biggest annual loss since financial crisis". *Financial Times* (2023)

Credit Suisse and UBS market capitalisation – Companiesmarketcap.com

Axel Lehmann comments (Dec 2022); Q1 2023 outflows SFr61.2 billion ($68.6 billion) – Walker, O. and Storbeck, O. "Credit Suisse chair avoids regulatory action over outflow claims". *Financial Times* (2023); Walker, O. "Credit Suisse suffered $69bn in outflows during first-quarter crisis". *Financial Times* (2023)

Credit Suisse annual report – Walker, O. "Credit Suisse shares drop as annual report delayed following SEC call". *Financial Times* (2023)

"management did not design [...]" (Credit Suisse) – Walker, O. "Credit Suisse finds 'material weaknesses' in financial reporting controls". *Financial Times* (2023)

Ammar Al Khudairy comments and resignation – El-Din, Y. and Halftermeyer, M. "Credit Suisse Reels After Top Shareholder Rules Out Raising Stake". *Bloomberg* (2023); Kerr, S. "Saudi National Bank chair resigns following Credit Suisse comments". *Financial Times* (2023)

SFr50 billion ($54 billion) liquidity backstop – Walker, O. *et al.* "Swiss central bank offers Credit Suisse liquidity backstop". *Financial Times* (2023); Morris, S., Fontanella-Khan, J. and Massoudi, A. "How the Swiss 'trinity' forced UBS to save Credit Suisse". *Financial Times* (2023)

"On Friday the liquidity outflows [...]" (Alain Berset, 19 March 2023); UBS-Credit Suisse agreement: $3.25 billion, SFr0.76 a share – Massoudi, A. *et al.* "UBS agrees $3.25bn rescue deal for rival Credit Suisse". *Financial Times* (2023)

THE SOUTH AFRICAN A2 BANKING CRISIS

"the Investec [...]" (Jeff Levenstein) – Hogg, A. "Regal Bank hits wall, clients' funds frozen". *Mail&Guardian* (2001)

Regal curatorship – Myburgh, J. "Myburgh Report on Regal Treasury Private Bank". South African Reserve Bank (2002)

Advocate John Myburgh not to be confused with Johan Myburgh, the Saambou CEO.

Regal: R1 billion in assets – Gush, H. "Bank CEO faces court action". *News24* (2002)

Exchange rates reflect the exchange rate at the time of the financial statements being discussed. "South African Rand to United States Dollar". *Yahoo Finance* (2023)

"Levenstein was [...]" (John Myburgh) – Myburgh, J. "Myburgh Report on Regal". South African Reserve Bank (2002)

Regal history; Levenstein imprisonment – Jacks, M. "Regal Bank Ex-CEO Imprisoned For Fraud". *Ventures Africa* (2013); Henderson, R. "Regal Bank fraudster Jeff Levenstein to stay

NOTES

behind bars". *TimesLive* (2015); Grobler, A. "Fraudster CEO's sentence reduced". *IOL* (2013); Theobold, S. "Regal's Levenstein getting jail for share manipulation". *Business Day* (2013)

Companies Act 61 (1973), Section 38: prohibits a company from providing financial assistance for the acquisition of shares.

"Levenstein's main motivation [...]" (John Myburgh) – Myburgh, J. "Myburgh Report on Regal". South African Reserve Bank (2002)

A2 banks – The term A2 was applied by international ratings agencies to the smaller South African banks in the early 2000s, essentially all local banks except for Absa, Nedbank, Standard Bank, FirstRand and Investec. Task Group Report. "Competition in South African Banking". National Treasury (2004)

22 of 47 banks failed or deregistered – Havemann, R. "The South African small banks' crisis of 2002/3". *Economic History of Developing Regions* (2021)

"irrational exuberance" (Alan Greenspan) – Greenspan, A. "The Challenge of Central Banking in a Democratic Society". American Enterprise Institute (1996)

Dotcom bubble – McNichol, T. "A startup's best friend? Failure". *CNN* (2007)

Nasdaq price – "Nasdaq Composite". *Yahoo Finance* (2023)

Pets.com – Tam, P. "Pets.com Will Shut Down, Citing Insufficient Funding". *The Wall Street Journal* (2000)

Fed Funds Rate – "Federal Funds Effective Rate (FEDFUNDS)". The Federal Reserve Bank of St Louis (2023)

Historical repo rate – "Repo Rate". South African Reserve Bank (2023)

"gravely concerned [...]" – Manuel, T. "New Regulations published on non-statutory deductions from Government Payroll". National Treasury (2000)

Saambou personal loan book – "Saambou Holdings Limited – Results and Declaration of Dividend". Sharenet (2001)

Saambou statement (11 October 2001) – "Saambou Expects Drop in Interim Earnings". *Mail&Guardian* (2001)

Saambou losses – Joffe, H. "SAAMBOU Set to Post Loss On Loan Slump". *Business Day* (2001)

Saambou results (October 2001) – "Saambou Holdings Limited – Results and Declaration of Dividend". Sharenet (2001)

Saambou share price – "Saambou shares plunge 18% to new year lows". *IOL* (2001)

Absa announcement – "UniFer misled board: Absa". *News24* (2002); Whitfield, B. "South Africa: Nallie Bosman: CEO, Absa". *MoneyWeb* (2002)

UniFer – "UniFer expects static earnings for year on interim surge in advances". *IOL* (2001)

"The group is solid." (Gavin Kretzschmar) – "UniFer expects static earnings for year on interim surge in advances". *IOL* (2001)

Saambou bank run; A2 failures – Havemann, R. "The South African small banks' crisis of 2002/3". *Economic History of Developing Regions* (2021); "Saambou customers cashless". *News24* (2002)

Saambou announcements – Mbuya, J. *The Rise and Fall of Saambou Bank*. Mbuya Books (2003)

Saambou alleged insider trading – "Saambou comes under insider-trading scrutiny". *IOL* (2002); "No signs of insider trading at Saambou". *News24* (2002)

"not be prudent" (Trevor Manuel) – "Statement By The Minister Of Finance On The Placement Of Saambou Bank Limited Under Curatorship". National Treasury (2002)

221

WHY BANKS FAIL

Nedbank and BOE – "Nedcor-BOE merger costs exceed target by R158m". *Mail&Guardian* (2003)
Bank failure studies – Havemann, R. "The South African small banks' crisis of 2002/3". *Economic History of Developing Regions* (2021); Monocle Research Team. "The Art of Failure: Predicting Financial Distress Pre-Crisis". *Monocle Quarterly Journal* (2016)
South Africa GDP $419 billion, Michigan GDP $480 billion (2021) – World Bank (2023)
"you can't judge […]" (Timothy Geithner) – Geithner, T. *Stress Test: Reflections on Financial Crises*. Crown (2015)

THE SOUTH AFRICAN GREYLISTING

SA greylisting – "Outcomes FATF Plenary, 22-24 February 2023". FATF (2023)
Grey and black lists – "Jurisdictions under Increased Monitoring". FATF (2023)
FATF history – "History of the FATF". FATF (2023)
"strategic deficiencies […]" – "Jurisdictions Under Increased Monitoring – 23 June 2023". FATF (2023)
G20 nations greylisted – "South Africa greylisted: What does it mean for you?". Investec (2023)
FATF funding, membership – "Annual Report 2018-2019". FATF (2023); "Financial Action Task Force 30 Years". FATF (2023)
"continuing and intensifying […]" – "FATF Statement on the Russian Federation". FATF (2023)
FATF Recommendations – "The FATF Recommendations". FATF (2023)
"The main domestic […]"; "suffered from […]" (FATF) – "Anti-money laundering and counter-terrorist financing measures South Africa Mutual Evaluation Report". FATF (2023)
Superyacht – Neate, R. "Antigua and Barbuda to auction off $81m yacht 'owned by Russian oligarch'". *The Guardian* (2023)
Mauritius greylisting – Calcutteea, S. "Mauritius Removed from the FATF Grey List". Bowmans (2023)
"General Laws (Anti-Money Laundering and Combating the Financing of Terrorism) Amendment Act 22 of 2022". South African Government (2023)
FIC – "Minister Amends The Schedules To The Financial Intelligence Centre Act". FIC (2023)
Fusion Centre – "Fusion Centre, DPSA And SASSA Make Inroads In Bringing To Book Criminal Government Employees". FIC (2023)
"Greylisting is […]" (Annabel Bishop) – "South Africa greylisted: What does it mean for you?". Investec (2023)

PART IV
BAD ACTORS AND THE PROBLEM OF HUBRIS

Kobe earthquake – "Kōbe earthquake of 1995". *Encyclopedia Britannica*
Nick Leeson; Barings collapse – Brauchli, M. *et al.* "The Crisis at Barings: Barings Ignored Early Warnings, Evidence Shows". *The Asian Wall Street Journal* (1995); Brown, S. J. and Steenbeek, O. W. "Doubling: Nick Leeson's Trading Strategy". *Pacific-Basin Finance Journal* (2001); Elle, J. "Barings Bank". *Ethical Systems* (2014); Rodrigues, J. "Barings collapse at 20: How rogue trader Nick Leeson broke the bank". *The Guardian* (2015); Kong, Y. M. and Goh, L. K. "Collapse of Barings". Singapore National Library Board (2009); Beattie, A. "How Did Nick Leeson Contribute to the Fall of Barings Bank?". *Investopedia* (2022);

NOTES

Kenton, W. "Who Is Nick Leeson?". *Investopedia* (2022); "Not Just One Man – Barings". International Financial Risk Institute (2004)

Jérôme Kerviel – Petroff, A. and Buet, P. E. "Rogue trader's fine to Societe Generale cut by 99.98%". *CNN Money* (2016); Chen, J. "Jerome Kerviel: History and Work With Derivatives". *Investopedia* (2022); Willsher, K. "French rogue trader Jérôme Kerviel freed". *The Guardian* (2014)

JPMorgan Chase & Co and Bruno Iksil – Hurtado, P. "The London Whale". *Bloomberg* (2015); Merle, R. "The 'London Whale' trader lost $6.2 billion, but he may walk off scot-free". *The Washington Post* (2017); Memmott, M. "Whale Of A Fine: JPMorgan Chase To Pay $920M In Penalties". *NPR* (2013); Stewart, J. B. "Convictions Prove Elusive in 'London Whale' Trading Case". *The New York Times* (2015); Stempel, J. "U.S. to drop criminal charges in 'London Whale' case". *Reuters* (2017)

Tom Hayes; LIBOR influenced $350 trillion worth of loans and securities – Ridley, K. "Ex-trader Hayes jailed for 14 years by London court for Libor rigging". *Reuters* (2015); Snider, C. A. and Youle, T. "Does the LIBOR Reflect Banks' Borrowing Costs?". Social Science Research Network (2010)

Robert Citron/Merrill Lynch – Martin, D. "Robert Citron, Culprit in California Fraud, Dies at 87", *The New York Times* (2013); Wayne, L. and Pollack, A. "The Master of Orange County; A Merrill Lynch Broker Survives Municipal Bankruptcy". *The New York Times* (1998); Henderson, N. and Fromson, B. D. "Merrill Lynch: The Broker Behind Orange County". *The Washington Post* (1994); Sterngold, J. "Ex-Official Pleads Guilty in Orange County's Fall". *The New York Times* (1995); Sforza, T. "Robert Citron was a hard-to-hate villain in O.C.'s bankruptcy". *The Orange County Register* (2013); Wagner, M. G. and Maharaj, D. "Citron's Friends Urge Judge to be Lenient". *Los Angeles Times* (1996)

Procter & Gamble/Bankers Trust information – Hays, L. "Bankers Trust Ends Dispute With P&G". *The Wall Street Journal* (1996); Hansell, S. "Bankers Trust Settles Suit With P.&G.". *The New York Times* (1996); Holland, K. and Himelstein, L. "The Bankers Trust Tapes". *Bloomberg* (1996); Weiser, B. "Bankers Trust Admits Diverting Unclaimed Money". *The New York Times* (1999); "BT fined $63.5 million". *CNN Money* (1999); O'Brien, T. O. "The Deep Slush at Bankers Trust". *The New York Times* (1999)

LTCM – McCauley, M. *et al.* "Russia". *Encyclopedia Britannica* (2023); Chiodo, A. J. and Owyang, M. T. "A Case Study of a Currency Crisis: The Russian Default of 1998". The Federal Reserve Bank of St Louis (2002); Yang, S. "The Epic Story Of How A 'Genius' Hedge Fund Almost Caused A Global Financial Meltdown". *Business Insider* (2014)

LTCM lost $553 million – Ferguson, N. *The Ascent of Money: A Financial History of the World*. Penguin (2007)

Lehman Brothers/Dick Fuld – Plumb, C. and Wilchins, D. "Lehman CEO Fuld's hubris contributed to meltdown". *Reuters* (2008); Backhouse, F. *et al.* "Bankruptcy of Lehman Brothers". *Encyclopedia Britannica* (2023); Becker, B. and White, B. "Lehman Managers Portrayed as Irresponsible". *The New York Times* (2008)

Lehman Brothers debt: $613 billion total debt, $155 billion in bond debt, assets worth $639 billion; total debt $129 billion larger than assets – Sorkin, A. R. "Lehman's Big Bankruptcy Filing". *The New York Times* (2008)

223

WHY BANKS FAIL

Milton Friedman – Friedman, M. "A Friedman doctrine – The Social Responsibility of Business Is to Increase Its Profits". *The New York Times* (1970)

THE CREATION OF THE FEDERAL RESERVE

American War of Independence (1775-1783); James Armistead Lafayette (1781); Battle of Yorktown (19 October 1781) – Zegart, A. "George Washington Was a Master of Deception". *The Atlantic* (2018); "A New Nation's First Spies". Intel.gov; Harty, B. "George Washington: Spymaster and General Who Saved the American Revolution". School of Advanced Military Studies (2012)

First Bank of the United States (1791-1811) – Hill, A. "The First Bank of the United States". Federal Reserve History (2015)

US coinage and banknotes; 7,000 banknotes in circulation – "History of United States Currency". Mycreditunion.gov

War of 1812; US exports $61 million-$7 million, imports $53 million-$13 million (1811-1814); "A national bank would […]" (Alexander Dallas); Second Bank (1817-1834); Andrew Jackson (1828) – "The Second Bank of the United States". Federal Reserve Bank of Philadelphia (2021); Hill, A. "The Second Bank of the United States". Federal Reserve History (2015)

"unauthorised by the Constitution […]" (Andrew Jackson) – Zuchora-Walske, C. *Andrew Jackson's Presidency*. Lerner (2017)

Panic of 1907; Federal Reserve Act (1913) – Bruner, R. and Carr, S. *The Financial Panic of 1907: Lessons Learned from the Market's Perfect Storm*. John Wiley & Sons (2007); Moen, J. R. and Tallman, E. W. "The Panic of 1907". Federal Reserve History (2015); Moen, J. R. and Tallman, E. W. "The Panic of 1907: The Role of Trust Companies". *The Journal of Economic History* (1992)

CRYPTOCURRENCIES AND THE PROBLEM OF VARIETY

"Economists are, at this moment […]" (Friedrich Hayek) – "Friedrich von Hayek Prize Lecture". The Nobel Prize (1974)

US, UK and Europe inflation – Macrotrends.com

"The inferior quality money […]" (Friedrich Hayek) – Hayek, F. *Denationalisation of Money: The Argument Refined: An Analysis of the Theory and Practice of Concurrent Currencies*. The Institute of Economic Affairs (1978); *Denationalisation of Money*. The Institute of Economic Affairs (1976)

"I don't believe […]" (Friedrich Hayek) – "An Interview with F. A. Hayek". *LibertyInOurTime* (1984)

Cryptocurrency/blockchain details and criticisms; money supply – New Scientist. *The End of Money: The Story of Bitcoin, Cryptocurrencies and the Blockchain Revolution*. Hachette UK (2017); Singh, S. *The Code Book: The Secret History of Codes and Code-Breaking*. HarperCollins (1999); Tapscott, A. and Tapscott, D. *Blockchain Revolution: How the Technology Behind Bitcoin Is Changing Money, Business, and the World*. Penguin (2016); Vigna, P. and Casey, M. *The Age of Cryptocurrency: How Bitcoin and Digital Money are Challenging the Global Economic Order*. Macmillan (2016); Haar, R. "What is Bitcoin?". *Time* (2021)

Cryptocurrency market capitalisation: $3 trillion (2022), around $1 trillion (2023) – Coinmarketcap.com

390 quintillion answers/second (in January 2023) – Blockchain.com
Note: A quintillion is 10 raised to the power of 18 (a one followed by eighteen zeros), or one million multiplied by one trillion

NOTES

4,000 cryptocurrencies/market capitalisation of $700 billion (2021); 9,000/$3 trillion (2022); over 20,000/$1 trillion (2023) – Coinmarketcap.com; Statista.com

"Will Smith Inu", $3 million in trading before collapsing; "Current 'meme' coins [...]" (Billy Markus) – Verma, P. "Will Smith's slap became crypto. Inside the wild world of memecoins". *The Washington Post* (2022)

Dogecoin price: increased 600% (2013-2021), failed to break $1 mark per unit – Statista.com; Coinbase.com

DOOMSDAY STRESS-TESTING

Stress test scenario and results (2023) – "Dodd-Frank Act Stress Test Publications". Federal Reserve (2023); "2023 Federal Reserve Stress Test Results". Federal Reserve (2023); "Federal Reserve Board releases results of annual bank stress test". Federal Reserve (2023)

"Today's results confirm [...]", "strong and resilient" (Michael Barr) – "Federal Reserve Board releases results of annual bank stress test". Federal Reserve (2023)

"doomsday economic scenario" – Franklin, J. "Largest US banks boost dividends after passing stress tests". *Financial Times* (2023)

Trump rollback – Enrich, D. "Back-to-Back Bank Collapses Came After Deregulatory Push". *The New York Times* (2023)

"severe global recession" – "Dodd-Frank Act Stress Test Publications". Federal Reserve (2023)

Bay Area – "Tracking the San Francisco Bay Area's Pandemic Recovery". Bay Area Council Economic Institute (2023)

Unrealised losses – Gandel, S. "Bank of America nurses $100bn paper loss after big bet in bond market". *Financial Times* (2023)

"We do not [...]" (CFA Institute) – Peters, S. "The SVB Collapse". CFA Institute (2023)

"In the stress [...]" (Thomas Hogan) – Estrada, S. "How the Fed's stress tests failed to stop a banking crisis". *Fortune* (2023)

"After years [...]" (Marco Nicolai) – Walker, O. "UK banks lead global rivals in passing on interest rate benefits to savers." *Financial Times* (2023)

PART V
THE POWER OF THE DOLLAR

COP 26 – "COP26: Thousands march for Glasgow's biggest protest". *BBC* (2021)

$8.5 billion – McKenzie, D. "US, UK and EU will help fund South Africa's coal phaseout". *CNN* (2021)

"This game-changing [...]" (Boris Johnson) – "France, Germany, UK, US and EU launch ground-breaking International Just Energy Transition Partnership with South Africa". European Commission (2021)

"By assisting [...]" (Joe Biden) – "Remarks by President Biden in Meeting on the Build Back Better World Initiative". White House (2023)

"At present [...] (Cyril Ramaphosa) – Khoza, A. "Ramaphosa appeals for improved lender policies for energy transition plans". *TimesLive* (2022)

$100 billion by 2020 – "Climate Finance and the USD 100 Billion Goal". OECD (2023)

WHY BANKS FAIL

"As the post-cold [...]" (Alec Russell) – Russell, A. "The à la carte world: our new geopolitical order". *Financial Times* (2023)

"the end of history"; "What we may be witnessing [...]"; "that is, the end-point [...] (Francis Fukuyama) – Fukuyama, F. "The End of History?". *The National Interest* (1989)

Bretton Woods – Buckham, D., Wilkinson, R. and Straeuli, C. *The End of Money: The Great Erosion of Trust in Banking, China's Minsky Moment and the Fallacy of Cryptocurrency.* Mercury (2021)

US GDP (1971) – World Bank (2023)

USSR GDP (1971) – Mathisen, R. "Mapped: The World's Largest Economies, Sized by GDP (1970-2020)". Visual Capitalist (2022)

Central banks' foreign reserves – "Currency Composition of Official Foreign Exchange Reserves (COFER)". IMF (2023)

Forex market data – Drehmann, M. "The global foreign exchange market in a higher-volatility environment". *BIS Quarterly Review* (2022)

US and allies freeze $300 billion – "The Impact of Sanctions and Export Controls on the Russian Federation". US State Department (2022)

"The unprecedented [...]" (Janet Yellen) – "Treasury Prohibits Transactions with Central Bank of Russia and Imposes Sanctions on Key Sources of Russia's Wealth". US Department of the Treasury (2022)

"As a result [...] (Joe Biden) – Biden, J. Twitter (2022)

Dollar to rouble rate – "United States Dollar to Russian Ruble". *Yahoo Finance* (2023)

CBR foreign reserves – "The Central Bank of Russia shifts its reserves away from the dollar". *The Economist* (2019)

Russia trade surplus – "Russia is on track for a record trade surplus". *The Economist* (2022)

Germany and Russian oil – Oltermann, P. "How reliant is Germany – and the rest of Europe – on Russian gas?". *The Guardian* (2022)

China, India, Turkey and Bulgaria buy more Russian energy – Lin, A. "China imports record volumes of Russian oil in first half of 2023". *Financial Times* (2023); Menon, S. "Ukraine crisis: Who is buying Russian oil and gas?". *BBC* (2023)

BRICS AMBITIONS, DE-DOLLARISATION AND SOUTH AFRICA'S PLACE IN THE GLOBAL ORDER

Jim O'Neill originally coined the term "BRIC" in 2001, before the inclusion of South Africa.

"Over the next [...] – O'Neill, J. "Building Better Global Economic BRICs". Goldman Sachs (2001)

BRICS population and GDP (2022) – "Size, population, GDP: The BRICS nations in numbers". *France24* (2023); World Bank (2023)

Global GDP (2022) – World Bank (2023)

"The BRICS' weaknesses [...]" (Alan Beattie) – Beattie, A. "The Brics don't stack up as a committee to run the world". *Financial Times* (2023)

"never achieved anything [...]" (Jim O'Neill) – Alim, A. "Brics creator slams 'ridiculous' idea for common currency". *Financial Times* (2023)

"is scepticism [...]" (Tim Cocks) – Cocks, T. "BRICS nations to meet in South Africa seeking to blunt Western dominance". *Reuters* (2023)

226

NOTES

Putin/Sergei Lavrov common currency – McNamara, P. "Why a Brics currency is a flawed idea". *Financial Times* (2023)

"I am in favour [...]" (Luiz Inácio Lula da Silva) – "Brazil's Lula supports trading currency for BRICS countries". *Reuters* (2023)

"flawed idea" (Paul McNamara) – McNamara, P. "Why a Brics currency is a flawed idea". *Financial Times* (2023)

"ridiculous" (Jim O'Neill) – Alim, A. "Brics creator slams 'ridiculous' idea for common currency". *Financial Times* (2023)

"mobilise financial support" – Summit for a New Global Financing Pact (2023)

"There have been [...]" (Cyril Ramaphosa) – "President Ramaphosa's remarks at Closing Ceremony of the New Global Financing Pact Summit in France". *YouTube* (2023)

"Some people [...]" (Luiz Inácio Lula da Silva) – "Speech by President Luiz Inácio Lula da Silva during the Summit for a New Global Financial Pact in France". Government of Brazil (2023)

Dilma Rousseff impeachment – Watts, J. "Dilma Rousseff impeachment: what you need to know – the Guardian briefing". *The Guardian* (2016)

NDB details – New Development Bank (2023)

"Local currencies [...]" (Dilma Rousseff) – Stott, M. "Brics bank strives to reduce reliance on the dollar". *Financial Times* (2023)

BRICS invites new members – Du Plessis, C. "BRICS welcomes new members in push to reshuffle world order". *Reuters* (2023); Imray, G. "Iran and Saudi Arabia are among 6 nations set to join China and Russia in the BRICS economic bloc". *Associated Press* (2023)

If all the aspiring countries were to join BRICS, the group would represent up to 45% of global GDP – Russell, A. "The à la carte world: our new geopolitical order". *Financial Times* (2023)

"An article written by [...]" – Jinping, X. "Sailing the giant ship of China-SA". *The Star* (2023)

Iqbal Survé – Mahlaka, R. "PIC pushes Iqbal Survé into a corner as more of his entities, including Independent Media, are dragged to court". *Daily Maverick* (2023)

"For its efforts [...]" (Cyril Ramaphosa) – "CR On Why SA Supports Expansion of BRICS". *The Star* (2023)

"CMG launches Classics Quoted by Xi Jinping (Season 2) in Africa". *The Star* (2023)

CONCLUSION

Deep sophistication of US markets – Mooney, A. "Janet Yellen defends dollar as Brics nations debate reserve status". *Financial Times* (2023)

Fed's money printing and increases in interest rates – Campos, R. "Frontier countries to suffer most if Fed rate gets to 6% – analysts". *Reuters* (2023); Buckham, D., Wilkinson, R. and Straeuli, C. *The End of Money: The Great Erosion of Trust in Banking, China's Minsky Moment and the Fallacy of Cryptocurrency*. Mercury (2021)

Sackler settlement; US opioid crisis – "Understanding the Opioid Overdose Epidemic". Centers for Disease Control and Prevention (2023); Hoffman, J. and Van Sickle, A. "Supreme Court Pauses Opioid Settlement with Sacklers Pending Review". *The New York Times* (2023); Wall, M. "The Sackler family will still be rich after the opioid epidemic payout". *The Irish Times* (2023)

Volodymyr Zelensky UN comments – Hatuqa, D. *et al*. "Russia-Ukraine war updates: Zelenskyy says 'UN ineffective'". *Al Jazeera* (2023)

"Neither global co-operation [...]" (Martin Wolf) – Wolf, M. "The G7 must accept that it cannot run the world". *Financial Times* (2023)

BIBLIOGRAPHY

In the course of researching and writing this book, we made use of a large number of books and websites. Below is a select collection of resources that we believe have had an impact on the text. A more extensive recommended reading list, organised by subject matter, can be found in *Unequal: How Extreme Inequality Is Damaging Democracy and What We Can Do About It* (2023), written by David Buckham, Robyn Wilkinson and Christiaan Straeuli.

Acemoglu, D. and Robinson, J. *The Narrow Corridor: States, Societies, and the Fate of Liberty.* Penguin (2019)

Ahamed, L. *Lords of Finance: The Bankers Who Broke the World.* Penguin (2009)

Allison, J. A. *The Financial Crisis and The Free Market Cure: Why Pure Capitalism Is the World Economy's Only Hope.* McGraw-Hill Education (2018)

Bernanke, B. *The Courage to Act.* WW Norton & Company (2017)

Bernstein, P. *The Power of Gold: The History of an Obsession.* John Wiley & Sons (2000)

Blinder, A. *After the Music Stopped: The Financial Crisis, the Response, and the Work Ahead.* Penguin (2013)

Booth, D. *Fed Up: An Insider's Take on Why the Federal Reserve Is Bad for America.* Penguin (2017)

Bruner, R. and Carr, S. *The Financial Panic of 1907: Lessons Learned from the Market's Perfect Storm.* John Wiley & Sons (2007)

Buckham, D., Wilkinson, R. and Straeuli, C. *The End of Money: The Great Erosion of Trust in Banking, China's Minsky Moment and the Fallacy of Cryptocurrency.* Mercury (2021); *The Age of Menace: Capitalism, Inequality and the Battle for Dignity.* Mercury (2022); *Unequal: How Extreme Inequality Is Damaging Democracy and What We Can Do About It.* Ad Lib (2023)

Burke, E. *Thoughts on the Cause of the Present Discontents.* Good Press (2020) (originally published in 1770)

Burrough, B. and Helyar, J. *Barbarians at the Gate: The Fall of RJR Nabisco.* HarperCollins (2009)

Chomsky, N. *Chomsky on Anarchism.* AK Press (2005); *Global Discontents.* Penguin (2018); *Who Rules the World?* Hamish Hamilton (2016)

Collier, P. *The Bottom Billion: Why the Poorest Countries Are Failing and What Can Be Done About It.* Oxford University Press (2007); *The Future of Capitalism.* Allen Lane (2018)

De Roover, R. *The Rise and Decline of the Medici Bank.* Borodino Books (1963)

Dostoevsky, F. *Crime and Punishment.* (1866)

WHY BANKS FAIL

Drees, B. and Pazarbasioglu, C. *The Nordic Banking Crisis: Pitfalls in Financial Liberalization.* IMF (1998)

Eco, U. *How to Spot a Fascist.* Harvill Secker (2020)

Ferguson, N. *The Ascent of Money: A Financial History of the World.* Penguin (2007)

Friedman, M. and Schwartz, A. J. *A Monetary History of the United States, 1867-1960.* Princeton University Press (1963)

Friedman, M. *Capitalism and Freedom.* University of Chicago Press (2020) (originally published in 1962); *A Theory of the Consumption Function.* Princeton University Press (2018) (originally published in 1957)

Fukuyama, F. *The End of History and the Last Man.* Free Press (1992); *The Origins of Political Order: From Prehuman Times to the French Revolution.* Farrar, Straus and Giroux (2011)

Gardener, E. *The Story of Florence.* JM Dent & Co (2011)

Geithner, T. *Stress Test: Reflections on Financial Crises.* Crown (2015)

Goetzmann, W. *Money Changes Everything: How Finance Made Civilization Possible.* Princeton University Press (2017)

Hayek, F. *Denationalisation of Money.* The Institute of Economic Affairs (1976); *Denationalisation of Money: The Argument Refined: An Analysis of the Theory and Practice of Concurrent Currencies.* The Institute of Economic Affairs (1978)

Kahneman, D. *et al. Choices, Values, and Frames.* Cambridge University Press (2000)

Krugman, P. *et al. International Finance: Theory and Policy.* Pearson (2017)

Lamoreaux, N. and Shapiro, I. *The Bretton Woods Agreements.* Yale University Press (2019)

LeBor, A. *Tower of Basel: The Shadowy History of the Secret Bank That Runs the World.* PublicAffairs (2013)

Leeson, N. and Whitley, E. *Rogue Trader: How I Brought Down Barings Bank and Shook the Financial World.* Little, Brown & Co (1996)

Leonard, M. *The Age of Unpeace: How Globalisation Sows the Seeds of Conflict.* Bantam Press (2021)

Lewis, M. *The Big Short: Inside the Doomsday Machine.* WW Norton & Company (2010); *Liar's Poker.* WW Norton & Company (2010)

Lowenstein, R. *America's Bank: The Epic Struggle to Create the Federal Reserve.* Penguin (2015); *When Genius Failed: The Rise and Fall of Long-Term Capital Management.* Random House (2000)

Mallaby, S. *The Man Who Knew: The Life and Times of Alan Greenspan.* Penguin (2016)

Moyo, D. *Winner Take All: China's Race for Resources and What It Means for the World.* Basic Books (2012)

Naismith, R. (ed). *Money and Coinage in the Middle Ages.* Brill (2018)

New Scientist. *The End of Money: The Story of Bitcoin, Cryptocurrencies, and the Blockchain Revolution.* Hachette UK (2017)

Owen, D. and Robinson, D. *Russia Rebounds.* IMF (2003)

Paine, T. *Rights of Man.* Broadview Press (2011) (originally published in 1791)

Partnoy, F. *Infectious Greed: How Deceit and Risk Corrupted the Financial Markets.* Holt McDougal (2003)

Paulson, H. *Dealing with China: An Insider Unmasks the New Economic Superpower.* Twelve (2015); *On the Brink: Inside the Race to Stop the Collapse of the Global Financial System.* Business Plus (2010)

BIBLIOGRAPHY

Piketty, T. *A Brief History of Equality*. Harvard University Press (2022); *Capital and Ideology*. Harvard University Press (2019); *Capital in the Twenty-First Century*. Harvard University Press (2013)

Rachman, G. *The Age of the Strongman: How the Cult of the Leader Threatens Democracy Around the World*. Other Press (2022)

Reid, M. *The Secondary Banking Crisis, 1973-75: Its Causes and Course*. Macmillan (2003)

Schumpeter, J. *The Theory of Economic Development: An Inquiry into Profits, Capital, Credit, Interest and the Business Cycle*. Harvard University Press (1934) (originally published in 1911)

Shakespeare, W. *The Merchant of Venice*. (1598)

Sorkin, A. *Too Big to Fail*. Viking Press (2009)

Standing, G. *The Corruption of Capitalism: Why Rentiers Thrive and Work Does Not Pay*. Biteback Publishing (2021)

Stiglitz, J. *Freefall: America, Free Markets, and the Sinking of the World Economy*. Penguin (2010)

Thiers, A. *The Mississippi Bubble: A Memoir of John Law*. WA Townsend (1859)

Tooze, A. *Crashed: How a Decade of Financial Crises Changed the World*. Viking (2018)

Waterstone, M. and Chomsky, N. *Consequences of Capitalism: Manufacturing Discontent and Resistance*. Haymarket Books (2020)

Wolf, M. *The Shifts and the Shocks: What We've Learned – and Have Still to Learn – from the Financial Crisis*. Penguin (2014); *The Crisis of Democratic Capitalism*. Penguin (2023)

Yergin, D. *Russia 2010, and What It Means for the World*. Vintage (1995); *Shattered Peace: The Origins of the Cold War and the National Security State*. Houghton Mifflin (1977)

Zegart, A. *Spying Blind: The CIA, the FBI, and the Origins of 9/11*. Princeton University Press (2009)

Zuchora-Walske, C. *Andrew Jackson's Presidency*. Lerner (2017)

ACKNOWLEDGEMENTS

I wish to acknowledge the enormous effort to produce *Why Banks Fail* from Chris, Robyn and Kristin de Decker. I would also like to thank Steven Mitchell for his insights and encouragement. It is a special privilege to work with Tim Richman from Burnet Media, who put his heart and soul into this book. I would also like to acknowledge the daily effort that is made by everyone at Monocle, who make projects like this possible.

INDEX

9/11 Commission, 79
9/11 terrorist attacks, 16, 79, 80, 81, 108, 119, 197
2007/08 Global Financial Crisis, 8, 10, 14, 15, 20-2, 24-6, 34, 37, 42, 57, 61, 62, 64, 65, 68, 86, 90, 95, 100, 115-7, 134, 149, 153, 162, 164, 166, 191, 192, 194, 200

A

A2 Banking Crisis, 13, 15, 42, 104, 106, 114-6, 191
Accounting Connections, 9
Africa, 45, 98, 177, 184
African Bank, 15
Aldrich, Nelson, 147, 148
Aldrich-Vreeland Act, 147
Al Khudairy, Ammar, 66, 101
Al-Qaeda, 80
Amazon, 22
America, 16, 36, 72, 73, 77, 137, 138, 143, 146, 177
American, 38, 71, 74, 77, 78, 82, 85-8, 93, 95, 136, 137, 139, 149, 163, 164, 174, 177, 193, 194
American Airlines, 78, 80
American Civil War, 147, 160
American War of Independence, 136

Amsterdam, 36
Andrew, Abram Piatt, 147
Antigua, 122
Anti-money laundering (AML), 120, 121, 124
Apple, 22
Archegos Capital, 97
Argentina, 41, 118, 119, 188
Argyll, 53
Asia/Pacific Group on Money Laundering (APG), 121
Asia Wealth Bank, 42
Australia, 177
Automatic Exchange of Information, 81

B

Banco Español de Crédito, 41
Banev, Evelin "Brendo", 91, 92
Banev, Lara, 91
Bank Bill of 1791, 138
Bankers Trust, 41, 132, 133
Bank of America (BofA), 170, 172
Bank of England (BoE), 40, 44, 50, 51, 137
Bank of the United States, 138, 140
Bank Secrecy Act, 84
Banque de France, 74
Banque Générale, 6, 52, 54, 55, 57

Banque Royale, 36, 51, 55, 56, 58, 102
Barings Bank, 41, 128
Barr, Michael, 166
Basel, 16
Basel Accords, 65
Basel Committee on Banking Supervision (BCBS), 65
Basel III, 67
Battle of Yorktown, 137
Bautista, Marilyn, 8
Bear Stearns, 42
Beattie, Alan, 184
Beck, Daniel, 9
Becker, Gregory, 8, 9, 19, 21, 23, 24
Beeld, 104
Belgium, 74, 75
Belt and Road Initiative, 177
Berlin Wall, 13, 177
Bernanke, Ben, 117, 127
Berset, Alain, 102
Biden, Joe, 175, 181
Biggerstaff, Bill, 19
Birkenfeld, Bradley, 81, 82
Bishop, Annabel, 126
Bitcoin, 46, 153, 154, 156, 159
Black Death, 32
Board of Executors (BOE), 13, 113, 114
Botticelli, 28

233

WHY BANKS FAIL

Brait Bank, 114
Brazil, 183, 185-8
Bretton Woods System, 39, 43, 72, 75, 179, 198
BRICS, 183-8, 195-7, 202
Bruges, 29, 33
Brunelleschi, Filippo, 28
Bulgaria, 42, 91, 92, 182
Burkina Faso, 126
Bush, George W, 77, 78
Byzantine-Ottoman War of 1453, 32

C

Cadiz, 113
California, 9, 10, 24, 131
Canada, 20, 42
Cape Town, 13
Caribbean, 82
Cayman Islands, 20, 118
Celebrity Apprentice Ireland, 130
Celebrity Big Brother, 130
Central Bank of Russia (CBR), 180, 181, 226
CET1 ratio, 65, 67
Chicago, 37
Chicago School of Economics, 135
China, 20, 42, 46, 48, 174, 177, 182-4, 186-9, 196, 202
China Media Group, 189
Chinese, 174, 188, 189
Chinese renminbi, 187
Chinese yuan, 181
CIA, 80
Citigroup, 131, 170
Citron, Robert, 131, 132
Clinton, Henry, 136
Cocks, Tim, 185
Coinage Act of 1792, 138
Cold War, 2, 177, 178

Colonial Bank, 42
Commercial real estate (CRE), 167, 168
Compagnie de la Louisiane, 55
Companies and Intellectual Property Commission, 125
Company of Louisiana and the West, 55
Congressional Budget Office, 21
Copenhagen, 176
Corp Capital, 114
Counter-proliferation financing (CPF), 120, 124
Counter-terrorist financing (CTF), 120, 124
Countrywide Financial, 42
Covid-19, 20, 21, 25, 39, 65, 154, 192
Credit Suisse, 10, 16, 34, 42, 58, 66, 91-3, 95-103, 157, 191, 200
Crime and Punishment, 31

D

Dallas, Alexander, 140
dal Poggetto, Paolo, 27
Da Silva, Luiz Inacio Lula, 185-7
Davison, Henry, 147
Declaration of Independence, 137
Delaware, 20
Della Robbia, Luca, 28
Democratic Republic of Congo (DRC), 118
Denmark, 14, 176
Department of Justice (DOJ), 82, 85, 87, 95
Dérobert, Michel, 87
Dick Fuld, 134

Dick, Philip K, 56
Dodd-Frank Wall Street Reform and Consumer Protection Act, 16, 21
Dogecoin, 159
Donatello, 28
Dow Jones, 163
Dutch War, 53

E

Eastern and Southern Africa Anti-Money Laundering Group, 121
Economic Growth, Regulatory Relief, and Consumer Protection Act, 21
Ecuador, 41
Edinburgh, 53
Edward, Charles, 110
Edward Snowden, 79
Egypt, 176, 188
England, 35-7, 40, 44, 50, 51, 89, 137, 143
Ethereum, 154
Ethiopia, 188
Europe, 10, 16, 28, 31, 32, 35, 46-8, 51, 54, 56, 65, 71-3, 91, 103, 147, 150, 151, 168, 169, 178, 181
European, 16, 34, 36, 48, 49, 83, 85, 133, 147, 185, 198, 199
European Commission, 120
European Community, 75
European Union (EU), 175, 176

F

Foreign Account Tax Compliance Act (FATCA), 81, 86-9, 95
FATF-style regional bodies (FSRBs), 121

INDEX

FBI, 80

Federal Act on Banks and Savings Banks, 83

Federal Deposit Insurance Corporation (FDIC), 9, 23, 24

Federal Reserve, 20-2, 25, 38, 44, 51, 57, 64, 72, 106, 107, 117, 127, 131, 136, 148, 149, 162, 163, 165, 172, 192, 194, 198

Federal Reserve Board of Governors, 25, 44

Feingold, Russell, 77, 79

Financial Action Task Force (FATF), 94, 118-126

Financial Action Task Force of Latin America, 121

Financial Intelligence Centre (FIC), 125

Financial Times, 166, 177, 184, 185, 202

Finland, 41, 205, 206

First Bank, 138, 141

FirstCorp, 13, 113

First Republic Bank, 24, 26, 42, 191

First Republic Bank-Dallas, 42

Florence, 27-9, 32-4, 47

Founders Fund, 23

Founding Fathers, 137

France, 36, 48, 51-9, 74, 75, 83, 180, 202

Frankfurt, 130

Free Banking Era, 143

Friedman, Milton, 135

The Intellectuals and Socialism (1949), 76

The Road to Serfdom (1944), 190

Fukuyama, Francis, 178

Fuld, Dick, 134, 135

G

G7, 11, 119, 176, 177, 183, 186, 195

G10, 74

G20, 88, 118

Gauteng, 106

Geithner, Timothy, 117

General Laws (Anti-Money Laundering and Combating the Financing of Terrorism) Amendment Act (SA), 124

Geneva, 29, 81, 87

Genoa, 36, 47

Germany, 36, 74, 75, 80, 84, 85, 180, 181

GFG Alliance, 97

Gilded Age, 37

Glasgow, 175, 176

Global Financial Crisis, 8, 10, 14, 15, 20-2, 24-6, 34, 37, 42, 57, 61, 62, 64, 65, 68, 86, 90, 95, 100, 115-7, 134, 149, 153, 162, 164, 166, 191, 192, 194, 200

Goldman Sachs, 196

Gottstein, Thomas, 96, 98

Great Britain, 139

Great Depression, 38, 71, 149

Greece, 46

Greensill Capital, 96

Greenspan, Alan, 106, 108, 127

Groupe d'action financière (GAFI), 119

Guernsey, 82

Guryev, Andrey, 123

H

Haiti, 118

Hamburg, 36

Hamilton, Alexander, 137-9

Hanoi, 177

Hanshin, 128

Hawaii, 8, 9

Hayes, Tom, 131, 135

Heinze, Fritz, 143

Hiring Incentives to Restore Employment Act (US), 86

Hitler, Adolf, 84

Hogan, Thomas, 172

Hong Kong, 14

Hume, David, 70

Hundred Years' War, 35

Hungary, 177

I

Iceland, 14

Iksil, Bruno, 131, 135

Illinois, 37

India, 20, 182, 183, 188

Industrial Revolution, 36, 73, 191

IndyMac Bank, 42

ING, 130

Internal Revenue Service (IRS), 82, 85, 86, 88

International Monetary Fund (IMF), 121, 178, 187, 195

Investec, 104, 126

Iran, 119, 124, 188

Israel, 20

Italy, 29, 33, 42, 75, 91

Ivanishvili, Bidzina, 96

J

Jackson, Andrew, 142

Jackson, Michael, 177

235

WHY BANKS FAIL

Japan, 40, 41, 73, 128, 129, 169, 178, 180
Jefferson, Thomas, 137, 139, 165
Jekyll Island, 147
Jinping, Xi, 174, 188, 189
Johannesburg, 13, 186, 188, 189
Johannesburg Stock Exchange (JSE), 105, 110
Johnson, Boris, 175
JPMorgan Chase & Co, 24, 131, 170

K

Kerviel, Jerome, 130
Keynes, John Maynard, 72
Khan, Iqbal, 95
King Edward III, 35
King Louis XIV, 52-5
Knickerbocker Trust, 144
Kobe, 128, 129
Körner, Ulrich, 98
Kretzschmar, Gavin, 111

L

Lafayette, James Armistead, 136
Lahaina, 8
Latin America, 177, 178
Law, John, 51-9
Leeson, Nick, 41, 128-30, 135
Lehman Brothers, 14, 37, 42, 64, 113, 134
Lehman "Minibonds", 14
Lehmann, Axel, 99, 100
Lescaudron, Patrice, 96
Levenstein, Jeff, 104-6
Lewis, Jim, 99
LGT, 85
Liechtenstein, 85

London, 14, 29-31, 36, 37, 41, 53, 96, 128
London Interbank Offered Rate (LIBOR), 131
London Whale, 131
Long-Term Capital Management (LTCM), 41, 133, 134
Louisiana, 55, 145
Louis XV, 52, 53
Luxembourg, 14, 82

M

Malaysia, 14, 41
Malkin, Vitaly, 96
Maryland, 37
Maui, 8
Mauritius, 124
MBf Finance Berhad, 41
Medearis, Robert, 19
Medici, 27-9, 31-4, 48
Medici Chapels/Cappelle Medicee, 27, 28
Mercantile Bank (South Africa), 16
Meriwether, John, 133
Merrill Lynch, 42, 131, 132
Merton, Robert, 133
Michelangelo, 27, 28, 33
Michelozzo di Bartolomeo, 28
Microsoft, 22
Middle East, 39, 121, 182
Middle East and North Africa Financial Action Task Force, 121
Minnesota, 37
Mishkin, Frederic, 44
Mississippi, 56-9
Mississippi Company, 56–9
Mohammed, Khalid Sheikh, 80
Monocle Solutions, 13
Morgan, JP, 145, 146

Morgan Stanley, 172
Morse, Charles, 143
Mozambique, 98, 118
Mullins, David, 133
Mutual Evaluation, 121-3
Myanmar, 42, 124
Myburgh, Johan, 110

N

Nasdaq, 19, 106, 107, 163
National City Bank, 147
National Commission on Terrorist Attacks upon the United States (9/11 Commission), 79
National Monetary Commission, 147
National Security Agency (NSA), 79
Nazi, 84, 93
Nedbank, 114
Netherlands, 42, 74, 75
New Development Bank (NDB), 187
New Global Financing Pact, 186
New York, 24, 37, 74, 78, 136, 137, 140, 144-6, 202
New York Clearing House Association, 143, 144
New York Panic of 1792, 36
New York Stock Exchange, 145
Nigeria, 118
Nikkei, 129, 130
Nine Years' War, 50, 53
Nixon, Richard, 74, 179
Nixon Shock, 39, 74, 160, 198
Nobel Prize, 133, 135
Northern Rock, 61, 115
North Korea, 119, 124, 197
Norway, 41

236

INDEX

O

Obama, Barack, 21, 86, 174
O'Neill, Jim, 183-5
OPEC oil crisis, 39, 75
Orange County, 131, 132
Organisation for Economic
Co-operation and
Development (OECD),
89, 119
Orwell, George, 56
Osaka Securities Exchange,
129
Overend, Gurney and
Company, 37

P

Pakistan, 182
Palais Royal, 59
Palmstruch, Johan, 48-50
Pampoulova-Bergomi,
Elena, 92
Panama, 82, 201
Panama Papers, 201
Panic of 1792, 36
Panic of 1796, 36
Panic of 1907, 38, 143,
146, 149
Paris, 36, 53-5, 74, 119,
177, 186
Patriot Software, 9, 10
Pennsylvania, 37, 78
Persia, 46
Peru, 41
Pets.com, 107
Philadelphia, 140
Philippe II, Duke of Orléans,
52-5, 59
Procter & Gamble (P&G), 132
PSG Investment Bank, 13, 113
Public Investment Fund
(PIC), 189
Putin, Vladimir, 180, 181, 185

Q

Qatar Investment Authority,
98

R

Ramaphosa, Cyril, 176, 186,
188, 189
Raskolnikov, Rodion, 31
Regal Bank, 104-6
Regal Holdings, 104, 105
Regency Council, 53
Renaissance, 6, 27, 191
Repo 105, 134
Reuters, 185
Riksens Ständers Bank, 48
Rippling, 9
Rock, Chris 159
Roosevelt, Theodore, 145
Rousseff, Dilma, 187
Russell, Alec, 177
Russia, 41, 88, 120, 180-5,
195, 202
Russian, 22, 96, 133, 181,
182
Russian Federation, 120
Russian oligarch, 96, 123

S

Saambou Bank, 109
Sackler family, 201
San Francisco, 8, 143
Santa Clara, 9
Saudi Arabia, 188
Saudi National Bank (SNB),
58, 66, 98, 101
Scandinavia, 36
Scholes, Myron, 133
Schweizerische Kreditanstalt,
102
Scotland, 175
SECIB, 114

Second Bank, 140-2
Securities and Exchange
Commission, 100
Shanghai, 187
Sharm El-Sheikh, 176
Shelton, Arthur, 147
Signature Bank, 16, 24, 26,
42, 101, 191
Silicon Valley Bancshares, 19
Silicon Valley Bank (SVB),
6, 8-10, 16, 19-26, 34,
42, 68, 101, 116, 166,
170, 171, 191
Singapore, 14, 41, 82, 128,
130
Singapore International
Monetary Exchange, 129
Smithsonian Agreement,
74, 75
Smith, Will, 159
Snowden, Edward, 79
Société Générale, 130, 131
Sofia, 91
South Africa, 3, 4, 7, 13-5,
17, 106, 108, 113-5,
118-26, 175-7, 183, 184,
186-91, 196, 202, 203
South African, 13, 14,
104, 108-11, 113,
114, 118, 197
South African Companies
Act of 1973, 105
South African Public
Investment Fund, 189
South African Reserve Bank
(SARB), 108, 113,
114, 162
South African Small Banks
Crisis, 106
South America, 91, 177
Southeast Asia, 41
South Sudan, 118, 126
Soviet Union, 133

237

S&P 500, 19
Spain, 41, 185
Stamenson, Michael, 131, 132
Stamp, Josiah, 44
Standard Bank, 114
Standard for Automatic Exchange of Financial Information in Tax Matters, 89
Staub, Zeno, 88
Stockholms Banco, 36, 48-50, 102
St Petersburg, 36
Stress Test: Reflections on Financial Crises (2014), 117
Suisse Secrets, 92, 93, 98
Surowiecki, James, 18
Survé, Iqbal, 189
SVB Capital, 19
SVB Financial Group (SVBFG), 19-21
SVB Securities, 19
Sweden, 36, 41, 42, 48, 49, 75
Swiss Federal Act on Banks and Savings Banks, 83, 84
Swiss Federal Tax Administration, 88
Swiss Financial Market Supervisory Authority (FINMA), 95-7, 100, 101
Swiss Private Bankers Association, 87
Switzerland, 81, 83-5, 87, 88, 92-5, 102, 103
Syria, 118, 126

T

TA Bank, 113
Taylor, Michael, 89
Tesla, 22

The Banker, 15
The Merchant of Venice, 31
The Star, 188, 189
Thiam, Tidjane, 95, 96
Thiel, Peter, 23
Tokyo Stock Exchange, 129
Trump, Donald, 21, 166
Turkey, 118, 119, 182
Tuscany, 29
Twin Peaks, 89, 90
Twin Towers, 78
Twitter, 98, 116

U

UBS, 42, 67, 81, 82, 85, 93, 95, 98, 99, 102, 131
Ukraine, 22, 92, 120, 123, 168, 180, 182, 185, 195, 202
Unibank, 114
UniFer, 109, 111, 112
United Airlines, 8, 78, 80
United Arab Emirates (UAE), 80, 188
United Kingdom (UK), 14, 20, 36, 40, 42, 50, 74, 85, 97, 115, 130, 143, 150, 175, 176, 180, 184, 202
United Nations' 1944 Monetary and Financial Conference, 72
United Nations Climate Change Conference of the Parties, 175, 176
United Nations Security Council, 201
United Nations (UN), 72, 119, 121, 201, 202
United States (US), 8, 10, 11, 16, 19, 21-5, 34, 36, 38-43, 51, 56, 67, 70-89, 95, 97, 99, 101, 102, 106, 108, 113, 117, 133, 137-

40, 143, 144, 146-51, 160, 163, 165-73, 175-85, 187, 192-6, 198, 199, 201, 202
US dollar, 11, 67, 72, 73, 86, 108, 148, 178-80, 187, 192, 195, 197, 198
US Freedom Act, 79
US National Commission on Terrorist Attacks upon the United States, 79
US Patriot Act 2001 (Patriot Act), 76-9
US Senate Banking Committee, 198
USSR, 179
US Treasury, 38, 72, 146, 194, 195, 198

V

Vanderlip, Frank, 147
VBS, 16
Venezuela, 41
Venice, 31, 33, 47, 48, 59
Versailles, 52, 53
Vietnam War, 73
Virginia, 146
Volcker, Paul, 73

W

Wachovia, 42
Wall Street, 16, 21, 99, 133, 145, 146, 174
Warburg, Paul, 147
War of Devolution, 53
War of the Reunions, 53
War of the Spanish Succession, 53
Washington, 148
Washington, George, 136, 137
Washington Mutual, 24, 42
Wegelin, 87

INDEX

Wells Fargo, 19, 170, 172
West Africa, 45
White, Harry Dexter, 72
Wisconsin, 37, 77
Wolf, Martin, 202
World Bank, 178, 187, 195
World Trade Center, 78
World War I, 71, 83
World War II, 43, 72, 84,
103, 149, 178

Y

Yellen, Janet, 180, 195

Z

Zelensky, Volodymyr,
201, 202
Zonderwater Correctional
Centre, 106
Zurich, 88, 95